Plato, B. Jowett

A Selection of Passages From Plato for English Readers

Plato, B. Jowett
A Selection of Passages From Plato for English Readers
ISBN/EAN: 9783337008888
Printed in Europe, USA, Canada, Australia, Japan
Cover: Foto ©Thomas Meinert / pixelio.de

More available books at **www.hansebooks.com**

A SELECTION

OF

PASSAGES FROM PLATO

FOR ENGLISH READERS

FROM THE TRANSLATION BY

B. JOWETT, M.A.

LATE MASTER OF BALLIOL COLLEGE
AND REGIUS PROFESSOR OF GREEK IN THE UNIVERSITY OF OXFORD

EDITED WITH INTRODUCTIONS

BY

M. J. KNIGHT

VOL. II

Oxford
AT THE CLARENDON PRESS
1895

Oxford
PRINTED AT THE CLARENDON PRESS
BY HORACE HART, PRINTER TO THE UNIVERSITY

CONTENTS OF VOL. II

PAGE

THE REPUBLIC 1

BOOK I 2

The commencement of the Dialogue; Cephalus on Old
Age (327—331 B) 4

BOOK II 10

(1) The Argument of Adeimantus (362 E—367 E) . . 11
(2) The true nature of God (376 D—382 E) . . . 18

BOOK III 29

(1) Grace and Beauty in Art and Education (400 C—402 A) 30
(2) The good Physician and the good Judge (408 C—409 E) 33
(3) The true use of Music and Gymnastic (410 A—412 A) 35

BOOK IV 39

Virtue the health, Vice the disease, of the soul (443 C—444 E) 40

BOOK V 43

(1) The right treatment of enemies (469 B—471 C) . . 45
(2) The Last Wave: The Government of Philosophers (471 C—473 E) 49

BOOK VI 53

(1) The Parable of the Pilot (487 A—489 D) . . . 54
(2) The low estimation in which Philosophy is held by the World (494 A—497 A) 58

CONTENTS

	PAGE
BOOK VII	63
The Allegory of the Cave (514 A—520 E)	65
BOOK VIII	75
Democracy and the Democratic Man (555 B—562 A)	76
BOOK IX	88
(1) The Many-headed Monster (588 A—591 A)	89
(2) The City of which the Pattern is laid up in Heaven (591 A—to the end of the book)	94
BOOK X	96
The Vision of Er (614 B—to the end of the book)	98

TIMAEUS:

(1) The Tale of Solon (20 E—26 D) 108
(2) The Balance of Mind and Body (87 C—90 D) . . 118

CRITIAS, OR THE ISLAND OF ATLANTIS:

The whole 123

THE LAWS 144

BOOK I 145

(1) The true nature of Education (643 A—644 B) . . 146
(2) Man the puppet of the Gods (644 D—645 B) . . 148

BOOK II 149

The habit of drinking not to be encouraged in the State (673 D—to the end of the book) 150

BOOK III 152

The Origin of Government (676 A—679 E) . 153

BOOK IV 159

(1) The virtuous Tyrant (709 C—712 A) 160
(2) The Life of Virtue (715 E—718 A) . . . 164

CONTENTS

	PAGE
Book V	168

(1) The honour of the Soul. Precepts for a virtuous life
   (726 A—732 D) 169
(2) The best and the second-best State (739 A—741 A) . 178
(3) Riches and Godliness (742 D—744 A) 182

Book VI 185

Book VII 185

(1) The good citizen must not lead an inactive life (806 D
   —808 C) 186
(2) The Education of the Young (808 D—809 A : 810 A—
   812 A) 189

Book VIII 194

Book IX 195

Book X 195

The three classes of Unbelievers 196
(1) The universal belief of mankind in the existence of God
   is not hastily to be set aside (885 B—888 D) . . 198
(2) God is not an idle Ruler of the Universe ; but orders all,
   even the smallest things, for our good (899 D—905 D) 203
(3) God cannot be propitiated by the gifts of the wicked
   (905 D—907 D) 211

Book XI 214

(1) The evils of retail trade, and the cure of them (918 A—
   919 C) 215
(2) The honour of Parents (930 E—932 A) . . . 218

Book XII 220

(1) The good State in its intercourse with the world
   (949 E—951 C) 221
(2) The Burial of the Dead (958 C—960 A) . . . 225

Index 229

SELECTIONS FROM PLATO

THE REPUBLIC

THE principal object of the Republic is the construction of an ideal state, in which, to use Plato's own significant language, 'philosophers are kings, or the kings and princes of this world have the power and spirit of philosophy, and political greatness and wisdom meet in one' (v. 473); but there is, moreover, a secondary thread of connexion running through the whole—the enquiry into the nature of Justice and the happiness of the just man.

Plato must have had at least one predecessor in his task; for Aristotle has given us (Pol. ii. 8) an interesting account of Hippodamus of Miletus (c. 444 B.C.), who was, he says, 'the first person, not a statesman, to make enquiries about the Perfect State.' Hippodamus is called by some authorities a Pythagorean; and probably the impulse to such studies came from that school, both to him and to Plato. Pythagoras and his disciples, we are told, held the government in Crotona and other cities of Magna Graecia during a considerable time; and even after they were driven from power, it is natural to think that the later philosophers of the Pythagorean school continued to include political science among the subjects with which they occupied themselves.

We can scarcely doubt, however, that Plato's thoughts were also drawn in the same direction by the events of the period in which his life was cast. He was born about the time of Pericles' death (B.C. 429), and lived to see the rise of the Macedonian power under Philip, dying in the year of the capture of Olynthus (B.C. 348). He had therefore grown up to manhood during the Peloponnesian War (B.C. 431-404), and had witnessed both the incapacity of the Athenian democracy to maintain the greatness of the city, and the cruelty and lawlessness of the oligarchical faction in the days of the Thirty Tyrants, among whom were his own kinsmen, Critias and Char-

VOL. II.

mides[1]. The death of Socrates, too, must have left an indelible impression upon him, and strengthened his dislike and distrust of the democracy. All these events had occurred (we must suppose) long before the composition of the Republic, in its present form at least; for the maturity of style, the power of thought, and the advanced character of the philosophy, as well as several other reasons, all lead us to believe that the dialogue was written by Plato in the latter half of his life[2].

Such experiences may well have made Plato—Idealist and Mystic as he was by natural temperament—despair of the world, and turn for consolation to dreams and fancies of a better future : and it was his own case which he had before his mind when he wrote the famous and pathetic words:—'The philosopher is like one who in the storm of dust and sleet which the driving wind hurries along, retires under the shelter of a wall; and seeing the rest of mankind full of wickedness, he is content, if only he can live his own life and be pure from evil and unrighteousness, and depart in peace and good will, with bright hopes' (vi. 496 D).

The characters of the Republic are few. Besides Socrates, there take part in the dialogue, Cephalus of Clazomenae, an aged and wealthy man; Polemarchus, his son; Thrasymachus, a blustering Sophist of the type of Euthydemus and Dionysodorus; Cleitophon, his disciple; Glaucon and Adeimantus, the brothers of Plato. The two last, after the end of the First Book, carry on the entire argument with Socrates.

BOOK I.

THE First Book differs in several respects from the remainder of the work. It is a whole and complete in itself, although no positive result is attained by the discussion ; and in its gracefulness, simplicity, and humour, it has much in common with some of the presumably earlier Dialogues, such as the Protagoras. There is nothing impossible in the supposition that Plato may have made a previous composition the starting-point of a greater undertaking, or rather

---

[1] Cp. the 'Life of Plato' at the commencement of Volume I.
[2] There is nothing in the Republic which definitely fixes the date of its composition. But in one passage (i. 336 A) Ismenias the Theban is alluded to as perhaps the author of the maxim that 'justice = doing good to friends and harm to enemies.' This must have been written after the death of Ismenias, who was killed B.C. 382.

that the long meditated treatise grew and expanded as his thoughts slowly matured; for works of art have a life and character of their own, and are not always tractable under their creator's hands. If however, the Republic was composed at a single time and by one effort, the First Book was probably intended by Plato to smooth and prepare the way before he undertook the more difficult task in which he was about to engage.

The Dialogue opens at the house of Cephalus in the Peiraeus.— Socrates enquires whether Cephalus thinks that old age is an evil? 'Not to the just man,' is the answer. But have not the rich an advantage in this respect? 'Yes: they are not obliged to deceive or defraud their fellow citizens.' Is justice, then, merely to speak the truth and to pay your debts?

Here Cephalus is called away, and leaves the argument to his son, Polemarchus. Socrates proceeds to show that the definition is insufficient; we are not always required to pay what we owe— e.g. to a madman; to an enemy we return evil for evil. The meaning must be that justice gives that which is due—good to the good, evil to the evil. Still this is unsatisfactory: in the arts the skilled person gives what is required; and justice is only useful where they are useless – for instance, in keeping money. And if the just man is good at keeping money, will he not be good at stealing it?... Again, we speak of friends and enemies: do we intend the 'seeming,' or the 'real,' friend or enemy? Suppose we say that 'justice does good to our friends when they are good, and harm to our enemies when they are evil'? Yet how can justice harm any one?

Thrasymachus now rudely breaks in, declaring that 'Justice is the interest of the stronger or ruler.' But may not rulers fall into error, and command that which is not to their own interest? Thrasymachus rejoins that the ruler, if he errs, ceases to be a ruler. Every art, however, aims first at the good of its subjects, and only accidentally at the good of the artist. And on the same principle, the true ruler regards the interests of his subjects, and not of himself, as his chief concern.

Thrasymachus, in order to cover his defeat, makes a speech setting forth the advantages of injustice, and then rises to go, but is detained by the company. Socrates argues that rulers are not moved by the love of office, or why are they paid? Next, he points out that the just man aims at moderation, not at excess; whereas the unjust desires to obtain more than his share. Injustice is suicidal: even the bad must be in some measure just towards one another. Again, justice and happiness coincide:—all things have an end, and a virtue or excellence by which they attain their end. The virtue of the soul is justice, the end happiness.

The commencement of the Dialogue; Cephalus on Old Age.

THE beautiful picture of old age which Plato draws in the First Book of the Republic serves to introduce the chief topic of the whole discourse—the question, What is the nature of Justice? Plato loves to reach his goal by winding and circuitous paths: and here with rare artistic skill he enlists the reader's sympathy at the very commencement of the work, and carries him by gradual stages to the more abstruse parts of the enquiry. Cephalus represents an 'old-fashioned' type:—the easy, complacent, honest man, who has been favoured by fortune during a long life, and who looks forward to death without apprehension in the consciousness that his days have been well spent. He belongs to the time before the Sophists, and seems to have had no philosophical training. He is, therefore, after the key-note of the work has been struck, withdrawn by Plato from discussions in which he could not naturally have borne a part, as Cicero remarks, on account of his age. The argument is then carried on by Polemarchus, his son, to the end of the First Book, when he, too, yields place to Glaucon and Adeimantus, the young Athenians, who are 'fitted by nature and education to take part at once both in politics and philosophy' (Tim. 19 E).

Steph. 327
I WENT down yesterday to the Piraeus with Glaucon the son of Ariston, that I might offer up my prayers to the goddess[1]; and also because I wanted to see in what manner they would celebrate the festival, which was a new thing. I was delighted with the procession of the inhabitants; but that of the Thracians was equally, if not more, beautiful. When we had finished our prayers and viewed the spectacle, we turned in the direction of the city; and at that instant Polemarchus the son of Cephalus chanced to catch sight of us from a distance as we were starting on our way home, and told his servant to run and bid us wait for him. The servant took hold of me by the cloak behind, and said: Polemarchus desires you to wait.

[1] Bendis, the Thracian Artemis.

I turned round, and asked him where his master was.

There he is, said the youth, coming after you, if you will only wait.

Certainly we will, said Glaucon; and in a few minutes Polemarchus appeared, and with him Adeimantus, Glaucon's brother, Niceratus the son of Nicias, and several others who had been at the procession.

Polemarchus said to me: I perceive, Socrates, that you and your companion are already on your way to the city.

You are not far wrong, I said.

But do you see, he rejoined, how many we are?

Of course.

And are you stronger than all these? for if not, you will have to remain where you are.

May there not be the alternative, I said, that we may persuade you to let us go?

But can you persuade us, if we refuse to listen to you? he said.

Certainly not, replied Glaucon.

Then we are not going to listen; of that you may be assured.

Adeimantus added: Has no one told you of the 328 torch-race on horseback in honour of the goddess which will take place in the evening?

With horses! I replied: That is a novelty. Will horsemen carry torches and pass them one to another during the race?

Yes, said Polemarchus, and not only so, but a festival will be celebrated at night, which you certainly ought to see. Let us rise soon after supper and see this festival; there will be a gathering of young men, and we will have a good talk. Stay then, and do not be perverse.

Glaucon said: I suppose, since you insist, that we must.

Very good, I replied.

Accordingly we went with Polemarchus to his house; and there we found his brothers Lysias and Euthydemus, and with them Thrasymachus the Chalcedonian, Charmantides the Paeanian, and Cleitophon the son of Aristonymus. There too was Cephalus the father of Polemarchus, whom I had not seen for a long time, and I thought him very much aged. He was seated on a cushioned chair, and had a garland on his head, for he had been sacrificing in the court; and there were some other chairs in the room arranged in a semicircle, upon which we sat down by him. He saluted me eagerly, and then he said:—

You don't come to see me, Socrates, as often as you ought: If I were still able to go and see you I would not ask you to come to me. But at my age I can hardly get to the city, and therefore you should come oftener to the Piraeus. For let me tell you, that the more the pleasures of the body fade away, the greater to me is the pleasure and charm of conversation. Do not then deny my request, but make our house your resort and keep company with these young men; we are old friends, and you will be quite at home with us.

I replied: There is nothing which for my part I like better, Cephalus, than conversing with aged men; for I regard them as travellers who have gone a journey which I too may have to go, and of whom I ought to enquire, whether the way is smooth and easy, or rugged and difficult. And this is a question which I should like to ask of you who have arrived at that time which the poets call the 'threshold of old age,'—Is life harder towards the end, or what report do you give of it?

I will tell you, Socrates, he said, what my own feeling

is. Men of my age flock together; we are birds of a feather, as the old proverb says; and at our meetings the tale of my acquaintance commonly is—I cannot eat, I cannot drink; the pleasures of youth and love are fled away: there was a good time once, but now that is gone, and life is no longer life. Some complain of the slights which are put upon them by relations, and they will tell you sadly of how many evils their old age is the cause. But to me, Socrates, these complainers seem to blame that which is not really in fault. For if old age were the cause, I too being old, and every other old man, would have felt as they do. But this is not my own experience, nor that of others whom I have known. How well I remember the aged poet Sophocles, when in answer to the question, How does love suit with age, Sophocles,—are you still the man you were? Peace, he replied; most gladly have I escaped the thing of which you speak; I feel as if I had escaped from a mad and furious master.

His words have often occurred to my mind since, and they seem as good to me now as at the time when he uttered them. For certainly old age has a great sense of calm and freedom; when the passions relax their hold, then, as Sophocles says, we are freed from the grasp not of one mad master only, but of many. The truth is, Socrates, that these regrets, and also the complaints about relations, are to be attributed to the same cause, which is not old age, but men's characters and tempers; for he who is of a calm and happy nature will hardly feel the pressure of age, but to him who is of an opposite disposition youth and age are equally a burden.

I listened in admiration, and wanting to draw him out, that he might go on—Yes, Cephalus, I said; but I rather suspect that people in general are not convinced by you when you speak thus; they think that old age sits lightly upon you, not because of your happy disposition, but because you are rich, and wealth is well known to be a great comforter.

You are right, he replied; they are not convinced: and there is something in what they say; not, however, so much as they imagine. I might answer them as Themistocles answered the Seriphian who was abusing him and saying that he was famous, not for his own merits but because he was an Athenian: 'If you had been a native of my country or I of yours, neither of us would have been famous.' And to those who are not rich and are impatient of old age, the same reply may be made; for to the good poor man old age cannot be a light burden, nor can a bad rich man ever have peace with himself.

May I ask, Cephalus, whether your fortune was for the most part inherited or acquired by you?

Acquired! Socrates; do you want to know how much I acquired? In the art of making money I have been midway between my father and grandfather: for my grandfather, whose name I bear, doubled and trebled the value of his patrimony, that which he inherited being much what I possess now; but my father Lysanias reduced the property below what it is at present: and I shall be satisfied if I leave to these my sons not less but a little more than I received.

That was why I asked you the question, I replied, because I see that you are indifferent about money, which is a characteristic rather of those who have inherited their fortunes than of those who have acquired them; the makers of fortunes have a second love of money as a creation of their own, resembling the affection of authors for their own poems, or of parents for their children, besides that natural love of it for the sake of use and profit which is common to them and all men. And hence they are very bad company, for they can talk about nothing but the praises of wealth.

That is true, he said.

Yes, that is very true, but may I ask another question? —What do you consider to be the greatest blessing which you have reaped from your wealth?

One, he said, of which I could not expect easily to convince others. For let me tell you, Socrates, that when a man thinks himself to be near death, fears and cares enter into his mind which he never had before; the tales of a world below and the punishment which is exacted there of deeds done here were once a laughing matter to him, but now he is tormented with the thought that they may be true: either from the weakness of age, or because he is now drawing nearer to that other place, he has a clearer view of these things; suspicions and alarms crowd thickly upon him, and he begins to reflect and consider what wrongs he has done to others. And when he finds that the sum of his transgressions is great he will many a time like a child start up in his sleep for fear, and he is filled with dark forebodings. But to him who is conscious of no sin, sweet hope, as Pindar charmingly says, is the kind nurse of his age:

'Hope,' he says, 'cherishes the soul of him who lives in justice and holiness, and is the nurse of his age and the companion of his journey;—hope which is mightiest to sway the restless soul of man.'

How admirable are his words! And the great blessing of riches, I do not say to every man, but to a good man, is, that he has had no occasion to deceive or to defraud others, either intentionally or unintentionally; and when he departs to the world below he is not in any apprehension about offerings due to the gods or debts which he owes to men. Now to this peace of mind the possession of wealth greatly contributes; and therefore I say, that, setting one thing against another, of the many advantages which wealth has to give, to a man of sense this is in my opinion the greatest.

BOOK II.

GLAUCON and Adeimantus now intervene.—Glaucon has observed that men commonly believe Justice to be a convention or an agreement made by the weak against the strong: they regard it, not as a good in itself, but only as necessary on account of its result; no one (they think) would be just, if he could sin and escape punishment. ... Let us imagine two cases :—(1) the man who is utterly unjust, and yet prospers in his ungodliness; (2) the perfectly just man who suffers every possible evil. Which of these is the happier?

Adeimantus carries the argument a stage further:—Mankind, he observes, either practise justice, because the poets and other teachers declare that the just man will have many blessings both in this world and in the next; or else they abandon themselves to injustice, believing that they can easily make atonement for their sins by sacrifices and offerings to the gods. Can Socrates show that justice is a good in itself, and should be pursued without regard to consequences?

Socrates suggests in reply that, since justice is the same in the individual and in the State, it will be better 'to take the large letters first,' i. e. to consider first the nature of justice in the greater example, the State, and afterwards proceed to the individual.

The State is created to supply the necessities of life,—food, dwelling, clothing, &c.; and there are corresponding classes of citizens,—husbandmen, builders, weavers, shoemakers, smiths, merchants, retailers, labourers; for everything is better done, if there is a division of labour. These will form the primitive state, in which men will pass their days in innocent enjoyments; their habits will be healthy, and their diet simple. 'But you are making a city of pigs!' exclaims Glaucon. 'Something more civilized is required.' Then our State will have to enlarge her borders, and will become involved in disputes with her neighbours. We shall want soldiers, men whose sole business will be war. They must be fierce to their enemies, and gentle to their friends, like well-trained dogs.

Such natures need careful training; and of education there are two kinds, (1) music [i. e. general culture] for the soul; (2) gymnastic for the body.—Education begins in childhood, and therefore we must first ask, 'What tales and stories are children to learn?' The immoral legends of Homer and Hesiod are utterly unfit for them. They must be brought up in nobler conceptions of God. We can allow nothing to be taught, which violates the two grand principles of religion:—(1) God is good and the Author of good; (2) He is true and unchanging. Falsehood is abhorrent to His Nature, and unnecessary to Him.

1. The Argument of Adeimantus.

In the arguments which Plato puts in the mouth of Glaucon and Adeimantus, he may be said to foreshadow in some measure the course of the discussion; and more especially to pave the way for the criticism of the poets and their final expulsion from the ideal commonwealth. The poets had been the teachers of Hellas; and Cephalus and Polemarchus, who reflect the older type of cultivation, have drawn their definitions and illustrations of justice from Homer and Pindar. And now Adeimantus shows that the poets are greatly to blame for the low conceptions of morality which prevail among mankind. Socrates cannot, therefore, proceed with his task until he has examined the teaching of the poets about 'the ways of God to man,' their stories of the loves and sins and sorrows of the gods, and their description of the world below.

Plato wishes to supply a better motive to religion than these appeals to the weakness and timidity of men, who seem, like children, to need alternate bribes and threats of chastisement to keep them in the path of right doing. He also finds an opportunity to satirize the credulity and superstition of the human race, and their proneness to consider the punctual fulfilment of ceremonial obligations a sufficient atonement for the remissness of their moral life. He is speaking of Athens four centuries before Christ, but his words are applicable to every age and country, and convey a lesson which is by no means superfluous, even in our own days.

Adeimantus. But let me add something more: There is another side to Glaucon's argument about the praise and censure of justice and injustice, which is equally required in order to bring out what I believe to be his meaning. Parents and tutors are always telling their sons and their wards that they are to be just; but why? not for the sake of justice, but for the sake

Steph.
362
E

363

of character and reputation; in the hope of obtaining for him who is reputed just some of those offices, marriages, and the like which Glaucon has enumerated among the advantages accruing to the unjust from the reputation of justice. More, however, is made of appearances by this class of persons than by the others; for they throw in the good opinion of the gods, and will tell you of a shower of benefits which the heavens, as they say, rain upon the pious; and this accords with the testimony of the noble Hesiod and Homer, the first of whom says, that the gods make the oaks of the just—

' To bear acorns at their summit, and bees in the middle;
And the sheep are bowed down with the weight of their fleeces [1],'

and many other blessings of a like kind are provided for them. And Homer has a very similar strain; for he speaks of one whose fame is—

' As the fame of some blameless king who, like a god,
Maintains justice; to whom the black earth brings forth
Wheat and barley, whose trees are bowed with fruit,
And his sheep never fail to bear, and the sea gives him fish [2].'

Still grander are the gifts of heaven which Musaeus and his son[3] vouchsafe to the just; they take them down into the world below, where they have the saints lying on couches at a feast, everlastingly drunk, crowned with garlands; their idea seems to be that an immortality of drunkenness is the highest meed of virtue. Some extend their rewards yet further; the posterity, as they say, of the faithful and just shall survive to the third and fourth generation. This is the style in which they praise justice. But about the wicked there

---

[1] Hesiod, Works and Days, 230.   [2] Homer, Od. xix. 109.
[3] Eumolpus.

is another strain; they bury them in a slough in Hades, and make them carry water in a sieve; also while they are yet living they bring them to infamy, and inflict upon them the punishments which Glaucon described as the portion of the just who are reputed to be unjust; nothing else does their invention supply. Such is their manner of praising the one and censuring the other.

Once more, Socrates, I will ask you to consider another way of speaking about justice and injustice, which is not confined to the poets, but is found in prose writers. The universal voice of mankind is always declaring that justice and virtue are honourable, but grievous and toilsome; and that the pleasures of vice and injustice are easy of attainment, and are only censured by law and opinion. They say also that honesty is for the most part less profitable than dishonesty; and they are quite ready to call wicked men happy, and to honour them both in public and private when they are rich or in any other way influential, while they despise and overlook those who may be weak and poor, even though acknowledging them to be better than the others.

But most extraordinary of all is their mode of speaking about virtue and the gods: they say that the gods apportion calamity and misery to many good men, and good and happiness to the wicked. And mendicant prophets go to rich men's doors and persuade them that they have a power committed to them by the gods of making an atonement for a man's own or his ancestor's sins by sacrifices or charms, with rejoicings and feasts; and they promise to harm an enemy, whether just or unjust, at a small cost; with magic arts and incantations binding heaven, as they say, to execute their will. And the poets are the authorities to whom they appeal, now smoothing the path of vice with the words of Hesiod:—

'Vice may be had in abundance without trouble; the way is smooth and her dwelling-place is near. But before virtue the gods have set toil [1],'

and a tedious and uphill road: then citing Homer as a witness that the gods may be influenced by men; for he also says:—

'The gods, too, may be turned from their purpose; and men pray to them and avert their wrath by sacrifices and soothing entreaties, and by libations and the odour of fat, when they have sinned and transgressed [2].'

And they produce a host of books written by Musaeus and Orpheus, who were children of the Moon and the Muses—that is what they say—according to which they perform their ritual, and persuade not only individuals, but whole cities, that expiations and atonements for sin may be made by sacrifices and amusements which fill a vacant hour, and are equally at the service of the living and the dead; the latter sort they call mysteries, and they redeem us from the pains of hell, but if we neglect them no one knows what awaits us.

He proceeded: And now when the young hear all this said about virtue and vice, and the way in which gods and men regard them, how are their minds likely to be affected, my dear Socrates,—those of them, I mean, who are quickwitted, and, like bees on the wing, light on every flower, and from all that they hear are prone to draw conclusions as to what manner of persons they should be and in what way they should walk if they would make the best of life? Probably the youth will say to himself in the words of Pindar—

'Can I by justice or by crooked ways of deceit ascend a loftier tower which may be a fortress to me all my days?'

---

[1] Hesiod, Works and Days, 287.   [2] Homer, Iliad, ix. 493.

For what men say is that, if I am really just and am not also thought just, profit there is none, but the pain and loss on the other hand are unmistakeable. But if, though unjust, I acquire the reputation of justice, a heavenly life is promised to me. Since then, as philosophers prove, appearance tyrannizes over truth and is lord of happiness, to appearance I must devote myself. I will describe around me a picture and shadow of virtue to be the vestibule and exterior of my house; behind I will trail the subtle and crafty fox, as Archilochus, greatest of sages, recommends. But I hear some one exclaiming that the concealment of wickedness is often difficult; to which I answer, Nothing great is easy. Nevertheless, the argument indicates this, if we would be happy, to be the path along which we should proceed. With a view to concealment we will establish secret brotherhoods and political clubs. And there are professors of rhetoric who teach the art of persuading courts and assemblies; and so, partly by persuasion and partly by force, I shall make unlawful gains and not be punished.

Still I hear a voice saying that the gods cannot be deceived, neither can they be compelled. But what if there are no gods? or, suppose them to have no care of human things—why in either case should we mind about concealment? And even if there are gods, and they do care about us, yet we know of them only from tradition and the genealogies of the poets; and these are the very persons who say that they may be influenced and turned by 'sacrifices and soothing entreaties and by offerings.'

Let us be consistent then, and believe both or neither. If the poets speak truly, why then we had better be unjust, and offer of the fruits of injustice; for if we are just, although we may escape the vengeance of heaven, we shall lose the gains of injustice; but, if we are unjust, we shall keep the gains, and by our sinning and praying, and praying and sinning, the gods will be propitiated, and we shall not be punished. 'But there is a world below in which either we or our posterity will suffer for our unjust deeds.' Yes, my friend, will be the reflection, but there are mysteries and atoning deities, and these have great power. That is what mighty cities declare; and the children of the gods, who were their poets and prophets, bear a like testimony.

On what principle, then, shall we any longer choose justice rather than the worst injustice? when, if we only unite the latter with a deceitful regard to appearances, we shall fare to our mind both with gods and men, in life and after death, as the most numerous and the highest authorities tell us. Knowing all this, Socrates, how can a man who has any superiority of mind or person or rank or wealth, be willing to honour justice; or indeed to refrain from laughing when he hears justice praised? And even if there should be some one who is able to disprove the truth of my words, and who is satisfied that justice is best, still he is not angry with the unjust, but is very ready to forgive them, because he also knows that men are not just of their own free will; unless, peradventure, there be some one whom the divinity within him may have inspired with a hatred of injustice, or who has attained knowledge of the truth—but no other man. He only blames injustice who, owing to cowardice or age or some weakness, has not the power of being unjust. And this is proved by the fact that when he obtains the power, he immediately becomes unjust as far as he can be.

The cause of all this, Socrates, was indicated by us

at the beginning of the argument, when my brother and I told you how astonished we were to find that of all the professing panegyrists of justice—beginning with the ancient heroes of whom any memorial has been preserved to us, and ending with the men of our own time—no one has ever blamed injustice or praised justice except with a view to the glories, honours, and benefits which flow from them. No one has ever adequately described either in verse or prose the true essential nature of either of them abiding in the soul, and invisible to any human or divine eye; or shown that of all the things of a man's soul which he has within him, justice is the greatest good, and injustice the greatest evil. Had this been the universal strain, 367 had you sought to persuade us of this from our youth upwards, we should not have been on the watch to keep one another from doing wrong, but every one would have been his own watchman, because afraid, if he did wrong, of harbouring in himself the greatest of evils.

I dare say that Thrasymachus and others would seriously hold the language which I have been merely repeating, and words even stronger than these about justice and injustice, grossly, as I conceive, perverting their true nature. But I speak in this vehement manner, as I must frankly confess to you, because I want to hear from you the opposite side; and I would ask you to show not only the superiority which justice has over injustice, but what effect they have on the possessor of them which makes the one to be a good and the other an evil to him. And please, as Glaucon requested of you, to exclude reputations; for unless you take away from each of them his true reputation and add on the false, we shall say that you do not praise justice, but the appearance of it; we shall think that you are only exhorting us to keep injustice dark, and that you really agree with Thrasymachus in thinking that justice is another's good and the interest of the stronger, and that injustice is a man's own profit and interest, though injurious to the weaker. Now as you have admitted that justice is one of that highest class of goods which are desired indeed for their results, but in a far greater degree for their own sakes—like sight or hearing or knowledge or health, or any other real and natural and not merely conventional good— I would ask you in your praise of justice to regard one point only: I mean the essential good and evil which justice and injustice work in the possessors of them.

Let others praise justice and censure injustice, magnifying the rewards and honours of the one and abusing the other; that is a manner of arguing which, coming from them, I am ready to tolerate, but from you who have spent your whole life in the consideration of this question, unless I hear the contrary from your own lips, I expect something better. And therefore, I say, not only prove to us that justice is better than injustice, but show what they either of them do to the possessor of them, which makes the one to be a good and the other an evil, whether seen or unseen by gods and men.

2. The true nature of God.

The religious ideas which are formulated by Plato are of the simplest kind, and may be summed up under two heads: 'God is good,' and, 'He is unchanging and true.' The Unity of the Divine Being is not directly affirmed, and hardly any distinction is drawn between 'God' and 'the gods.' In this, as in so many other respects, Plato shows himself a true Hellene; for Monotheism in the strict sense came at a later date from the Semitic races of the East, and was first worked into the fabric of Hellenic thought in the schools of Alexandria. Neither does he discuss the question of the existence of God, although he has just told us by the mouth of Adeimantus that the young men of his day treated the whole subject in a very light and indifferent way. Towards the close of his life we shall find him in the Laws arguing almost passionately against the unbelievers, and threatening them with dire punishments if they persist in their errors.

... There is also a further question raised by Plato, which is of great interest to ourselves,—Whether the young should be educated by means of ancient stories and tales which are not in agreement with our own standard of morality? We should be inclined to concur with him in the main, but hardly to go to the same lengths. Children, according to our experience, have an instinctive faculty of separating the bad from the good in such legends. They are still living in the age of imagination, like the primitive races of mankind, who were 'nearer to the gods than ourselves;' and as they grow older, they suffer these 'childish things' to pass insensibly from their minds.

Socrates. Come then, and let us pass a leisure hour in story-telling, and our story shall be the education of our heroes.

Adeimantus. By all means.

And what shall be their education? Can we find a better than the traditional sort?—and this has two divisions, gymnastic for the body, and music for the soul.

True.

Shall we begin education with music, and go on to gymnastic afterwards?

By all means.

And when you speak of music, do you include literature or not?

I do.

And literature may be either true or false?

Yes.

And the young should be trained in both kinds, and we begin with the false?

I do not understand your meaning, he said.

You know, I said, that we begin by telling children stories which, though not wholly destitute of truth, are in the main fictitious; and these stories are told them when they are not of an age to learn gymnastics.

Very true.

That was my meaning when I said that we must teach music before gymnastics.

Quite right, he said.

You know also that the beginning is the most important part of any work, especially in the case of a young and tender thing; for that is the time at which the character is being formed and the desired impression is more readily taken.

Quite true.

And shall we just carelessly allow children to hear any casual tales which may be devised by casual persons, and to receive into their minds ideas for the most part the very opposite of those which we should wish them to have when they are grown up?

We cannot.

Then the first thing will be to establish a censorship of the writers of fiction, and let the censors receive any tale of fiction which is good, and reject the bad; and we will desire mothers and nurses to tell their children the authorised ones only. Let them fashion the mind with such tales, even more fondly than they mould the body with their hands; but most of those which are now in use must be discarded.

Of what tales are you speaking? he said.

You may find a model of the lesser in the greater, I said; for they are necessarily of the same type, and there is the same spirit in both of them.

Very likely, he replied; but I do not as yet know what you would term the greater.

Those, I said, which are narrated by Homer and Hesiod, and the rest of the poets, who have ever been the great story-tellers of mankind.

But which stories do you mean, he said; and what fault do you find with them?

THE IMMORALITIES OF MYTHOLOGY

A fault which is most serious, I said; the fault of telling a lie, and, what is more, a bad lie.

But when is this fault committed? Whenever an erroneous representation is made of the nature of gods and heroes,—as when a painter paints a portrait not having the shadow of a likeness to the original.

Yes, he said, that sort of thing is certainly very blameable; but what are the stories which you mean?

First of all, I said, there was that greatest of all lies in high places, which the poet told about Uranus, and which was a bad lie too,—I mean what Hesiod says that Uranus did, and how Cronos retaliated on him[1]. The doings of Cronos, and the sufferings which in turn 378 his son inflicted upon him, even if they were true, ought certainly not to be lightly told to young and thoughtless persons; if possible, they had better be buried in silence. But if there is an absolute necessity for their mention, a chosen few might hear them in a mystery, and they should sacrifice not a common [Eleusinian] pig, but some huge and unprocurable victim; and then the number of the hearers will be very few indeed.

Why, yes, said he, those stories are extremely objectionable.

Yes, Adeimantus, they are stories not to be repeated in our State; the young man should not be told that in committing the worst of crimes he is far from doing anything outrageous; and that even if he chastises his father when he does wrong, in whatever manner, he will only be following the example of the first and greatest among the gods.

I entirely agree with you, he said; in my opinion those stories are quite unfit to be repeated.

Neither, if we mean our future guardians to regard

[1] Hesiod, Theogony, 154, 459.

the habit of quarrelling among themselves as of all things the basest, should any word be said to them of the wars in heaven, and of the plots and fightings of the gods against one another, for they are not true. No, we shall never mention the battles of the giants, or let them be embroidered on garments; and we shall be silent about the innumerable other quarrels of gods and heroes with their friends and relatives. If they would only believe us we would tell them that quarrelling is unholy, and that never up to this time has there been any quarrel between citizens; that is what old men and old women should begin by telling children; and when they grow up, the poets also should be told to compose for them in a similar spirit[1]. But the narrative of Hephaestus binding Herè his mother, or how on another occasion Zeus sent him flying for taking her part when she was being beaten, and all the battles of the gods in Homer —these tales must not be admitted into our State, whether they are supposed to have an allegorical meaning or not. For a young person cannot judge what is allegorical and what is literal; anything that he receives into his mind at that age is likely to become indelible and unalterable; and therefore it is most important that the tales which the young first hear should be models of virtuous thoughts.

There you are right, he replied; but if any one asks where are such models to be found and of what tales are you speaking—how shall we answer him?

I said to him, You and I, Adeimantus, at this moment are not poets, but founders of a State: now the founders of a State ought to know the general forms in which poets should cast their tales, and the limits which must be observed by them, but to make the tales is not their business.

---

[1] Placing the comma after γραυσί, and not after γιγνομένοις.

Very true, he said; but what are these forms of theology which you mean?

Something of this kind, I replied:—God is always to be represented as he truly is, whatever be the sort of poetry, epic, lyric or tragic, in which the representation is given.

Right.

And is he not truly good? and must he not be represented as such?

Certainly.

And no good thing is hurtful?

No, indeed.

And that which is not hurtful hurts not?

Certainly not.

And that which hurts not does no evil?

No.

And can that which does no evil be a cause of evil?

Impossible.

And the good is advantageous?

Yes.

And therefore the cause of well-being?

Yes.

It follows therefore that the good is not the cause of all things, but of the good only?

Assuredly.

Then God, if he be good, is not the author of all things, as the many assert, but he is the cause of a few things only, and not of most things that occur to men. For few are the goods of human life, and many are the evils, and the good is to be attributed to God alone; of the evils the causes are to be sought elsewhere, and not in him.

That appears to me to be most true, he said.

Then we must not listen to Homer or to any other poet who is guilty of the folly of saying that two casks

'Lie at the threshold of Zeus, full of lots, one of good, the other of evil lots[1],'

and that he to whom Zeus gives a mixture of the two

'Sometimes meets with evil fortune, at other times with good;'

but that he to whom is given the cup of unmingled ill,

'Him wild hunger drives o'er the beauteous earth.'

And again—

'Zeus, who is the dispenser of good and evil to us.'

And if any one asserts that the violation of oaths and treaties, which was really the work of Pandarus[2], was brought about by Athenè and Zeus, or that the strife and contention of the gods was instigated by Themis and Zeus[3], he shall not have our approval; neither will we allow our young men to hear the words of Aeschylus, that

'God plants guilt among men when he desires utterly to destroy a house.'

And if a poet writes of the sufferings of Niobe—the subject of the tragedy in which these iambic verses occur—or of the house of Pelops, or of the Trojan war or on any similar theme, either we must not permit him to say that these are the works of God, or if they are of God, he must devise some explanation of them such as we are seeking: he must say that God did what was just and right, and they were the better for being punished; but that those who are punished are miserable, and that God is the author of their misery—the poet is not to be permitted to say; though he may say that the wicked are miserable because they require to be punished, and are benefited by receiving punishment from God; but that God being good is the author of

[1] Iliad xxiv. 527.   [2] Ib. ii. 69.   [3] Ib. xx.

evil to any one is to be strenuously denied, and not to be said or sung or heard in verse or prose by any one whether old or young in any well-ordered commonwealth. Such a fiction is suicidal, ruinous, impious.

I agree with you, he replied, and am ready to give my assent to the law.

Let this then be one of our rules and principles concerning the gods, to which our poets and reciters will be expected to conform,—that God is not the author of all things, but of good only.

That will do, he said.

And what do you think of a second principle? Shall I ask you whether God is a magician, and of a nature to appear insidiously now in one shape, and now in another—sometimes himself changing and passing into many forms, sometimes deceiving us with the semblance of such transformations; or is he one and the same, immutably fixed in his own proper image?

I cannot answer you, he said, without more thought.

Well, I said; but if we suppose a change in anything, that change must be effected either by the thing itself, or by some other thing?

Most certainly.

And things which are at their best are also least liable to be altered or discomposed; for example, when healthiest and strongest, the human frame is least liable to be affected by meats and drinks, and the plant which is in the fullest vigour also suffers least from winds or the heat of the sun or any similar causes.

Of course.

And will not the bravest and wisest soul be least 381 confused or deranged by any external influence?

True.

And the same principle, as I should suppose, applies to all composite things—furniture, houses, garments:

when good and well made, they are least altered by time and circumstances.

Very true.

Then everything which is good, whether made by art or nature, or both, is least liable to suffer change from without?

True.

But surely God and the things of God are in every way perfect?

Of course they are.

Then he can hardly be compelled by external influence to take many shapes?

He cannot.

But may he not change and transform himself?

Clearly, he said, that must be the case if he is changed at all.

And will he then change himself for the better and fairer, or for the worse and more unsightly?

If he change at all he can only change for the worse, for we cannot suppose him to be deficient either in virtue or beauty.

Very true, Adeimantus; but then, would any one, whether God or man, desire to make himself worse?

Impossible.

Then it is impossible that God should ever be willing to change; being, as is supposed, the fairest and best that is conceivable, every God remains absolutely and for ever in his own form.

That necessarily follows, he said, in my judgment.

Then, I said, my dear friend, let none of the poets tell us that

'The gods, taking the disguise of strangers from other lands, walk up and down cities in all sorts of forms[1];'

and let no one slander Proteus and Thetis, neither let

[1] Hom Od. xvii. 485.

any one, either in tragedy or in any other kind of poetry, introduce Herè disguised in the likeness of a priestess asking an alms

'For the life-giving daughters of Inachus the river of Argos;'

—let us have no more lies of that sort. Neither must we have mothers under the influence of the poets scaring their children with a bad version of these myths— telling how certain gods, as they say, 'Go about by night in the likeness of so many strangers and in divers forms;' but let them take heed lest they make cowards of their children, and at the same time speak blasphemy against the gods.

Heaven forbid, he said.

But although the gods are themselves unchangeable, still by witchcraft and deception they may make us think that they appear in various forms?

Perhaps, he replied.

Well, but can you imagine that God will be willing to lie, whether in word or deed, or to put forth a phantom of himself?

I cannot say, he replied.

Do you not know, I said, that the true lie, if such an expression may be allowed, is hated of gods and men?

What do you mean? he said.

I mean that no one is willingly deceived in that which is the truest and highest part of himself, or about the truest and highest matters; there, above all, he is most afraid of a lie having possession of him.

Still, he said, I do not comprehend you.

The reason is, I replied, that you attribute some profound meaning to my words; but I am only saying that deception, or being deceived or uninformed about the highest realities in the highest part of themselves, which is the soul, and in that part of them to have and to hold the lie, is what mankind least like;—that, I say, is what they utterly detest.

There is nothing more hateful to them.

And, as I was just now remarking, the ignorance in the soul of him who is deceived may be called the true lie; for the lie in words is only a kind of imitation and shadowy image of a previous affection of the soul, not pure unadulterated falsehood. Am I not right?

Perfectly right.

The true lie is hated not only by the gods, but also by men?

Yes.

Whereas the lie in words is in certain cases useful and not hateful; in dealing with enemies—that would be an instance; or again, when those whom we call our friends in a fit of madness or illusion are going to do some harm, then it is useful and is a sort of medicine or preventive; also in the tales of mythology, of which we were just now speaking—because we do not know the truth about ancient times, we make falsehood as much like truth as we can, and so turn it to account.

Very true, he said.

But can any of these reasons apply to God? Can we suppose that he is ignorant of antiquity, and therefore has recourse to invention?

That would be ridiculous, he said.

Then the lying poet has no place in our idea of God?

I should say not.

Or perhaps he may tell a lie because he is afraid of enemies?

That is inconceivable.

But he may have friends who are senseless or mad?

But no mad or senseless person can be a friend of God.

Then no motive can be imagined why God should lie?
None whatever.
Then the superhuman and divine is absolutely incapable of falsehood?
Yes.
Then is God perfectly simple and true both in word and deed[1]; he changes not; he deceives not, either by sign or word, by dream or waking vision.
Your thoughts, he said, are the reflection of my own.

BOOK III.

In the Third Book Plato pursues the subject of education. . . .

We must carry out the censorship of the poets which we have begun. Their descriptions of Hades are objectionable, because they will breed in our guardians the fear of death. The pictures of gods lamenting and heroes weeping cannot be tolerated. Excessive laughter is wrong, and we cannot allow Homer to speak of the 'inextinguishable laughter' which once arose in Olympus. We must strike out, too, all the verses which praise wine and festal joys, or teach the arts of falsehood, or relate the amours of Zeus and other deities, or the faults and vices of Achilles and Theseus. Neither can the poets be permitted to persuade their youthful auditors that the unjust lead a happy life.

Next, we have to speak of the styles of poetry: Tragedy and Comedy are wholly imitative: Epic poetry combines imitation and description. Which kind should we prefer? Imitation is unsuited to our guardians: one man cannot play many parts well, and the good will only imitate noble characters and acts. Poets and musicians love imitation, but we hold fast to the simpler style, and the pantomimic artist will—with due courtesy—be banished from our State. With him will go the effeminate harmonies and the flute and the more complex musical instruments. The rhythm will follow the words, and the words depend on the temper of the soul.

The other arts must also be purged. Our youth must see and hear only what is gracious and beautiful; and for this purpose musical training is invaluable. The spirit of harmony will affect both mind and body, and teach even love to be temperate.

---

[1] Omitting κατὰ φαντασίας.

After music comes gymnastic, by which we mean a simpler art than the discipline of the athlete. A plain diet will make our guardians good and hardy soldiers, and enable them to dispense with physic; like artisans, they will have no time to waste in nursing their constitutions. Asclepius, that true statesman, would not treat men with sickly frames, because he thought them a burden to the State.

Here Glaucon interrupts with the question,—'Must not the good physician have had personal experience of disease, and the good judge be himself acquainted with evil?' There is a difference, Socrates replies. The physician is the better for having suffered illness, but the judge should be free from wickedness, and must gain his knowledge of crime by long observation.

Socrates resumes the argument: Both music and gymnastic are intended to benefit the mind. The athlete requires culture, the musician bodily training and exercise. Body and soul must make a living harmony in our guardians.

Lastly, who will be the rulers of the State? They will be selected from the younger guardians, or auxiliaries, and be tried by various tests to prove whether they can resist the attacks of pleasure and pain. In order to establish the new order of things we must venture on a 'noble lie.' The citizens will be told that their training and education has been a dream; and that they have really sprung full grown from the earth. God has infused in their veins various metals. The golden race will rule; the men of silver will be the auxiliaries: those who are composed of brass and iron will be husbandmen and craftsmen. The distinctions will generally be hereditary; if exceptions occur, there must be a corresponding transposition of rank. The auxiliaries will live like soldiers in a camp, having neither homes nor property of their own, and receiving their maintenance from the State. Their education will prevent them from becoming tyrants over their fellow-citizens.

1. Grace and Beauty in Art and Education.

Plato in all his remarks upon education shows himself fully conscious of the influence which good or bad surroundings have upon the character of the young. The effect of the few hours spent in the class or with the teacher is quickly lost unless instruction is seconded by suitable home-life and companionship: and we know how the traditions of any organized body, such as a school or a church, mould the minds and change the habits of those who come under their sway. Plato was probably drawn into this train of reflection by the evils which he had observed to arise from the military and gymnastic associations of the youth in Hellenic cities (cp. Laws i. 636), as well as by the instructive lesson which was to be derived from the effects of the Lycurgean discipline upon the citizens of Sparta. He is desirous, therefore, to combine the ease and cheerfulness of Athenian life with the 'good order' of Lacedaemon, and thus to mingle, if we may adopt one of his own metaphors, the strong wine of freedom with a more sober element.

Socrates. There is no difficulty in seeing that grace or the absence of grace is an effect of good or bad rhythm.

Glaucon. None at all.

And also that good and bad rhythm naturally assimilate to a good and bad style; and that harmony and discord in like manner follow style; for our principle is that rhythm and harmony are regulated by the words, and not the words by them.

Just so, he said, they should follow the words.

And will not the words and the character of the style depend on the temper of the soul?

Yes.

And everything else on the style?

Yes.

Then beauty of style and harmony and grace and good rhythm depend on simplicity,—I mean the true simplicity of a rightly and nobly ordered mind and character, not that other simplicity which is only an euphemism for folly?

Very true, he replied.

And if our youth are to do their work in life, must they not make these graces and harmonies their perpetual aim?

They must.

And surely the art of the painter and every other creative and constructive art are full of them,—weaving, embroidery, architecture, and every kind of manufacture; also nature, animal and vegetable,—in all of them there is grace or the absence of grace. And ugliness and discord and inharmonious motion are nearly allied to ill words and ill nature, as grace and harmony are the twin sisters of goodness and virtue and bear their likeness.

That is quite true, he said.

But shall our superintendence go no further, and are the poets only to be required by us to express the image of the good in their works, on pain, if they do anything else, of expulsion from our State? Or is the same control to be extended to other artists, and are they also to be prohibited from exhibiting the opposite forms of vice and intemperance and meanness and indecency in sculpture and building and the other creative arts; and is he who cannot conform to this rule of ours to be prevented from practising his art in our State, lest the taste of our citizens be corrupted by him? We would not have our guardians grow up amid images of moral deformity, as in some noxious pasture, and there browse and feed upon many a baneful herb and flower day by day, little by little, until they silently gather a festering mass of corruption in their own soul. Let our artists rather be those who are gifted to discern the true nature of the beautiful and graceful; then will our youth dwell in a land of health, amid fair sights and sounds, and receive the good in everything; and beauty, the effluence of fair works, shall flow into the eye and ear, like a health-giving breeze from a purer region, and insensibly draw the soul from earliest years into likeness and sympathy with the beauty of reason.

There can be no nobler training than that, he replied.

And therefore, I said, Glaucon, musical training is a more potent instrument than any other, because rhythm and harmony find their way into the inward places of the soul, on which they mightily fasten, imparting grace, and making the soul of him who is rightly educated graceful, or of him who is ill-educated ungraceful; and also because he who has received this true education of the inner being will most shrewdly perceive omissions or faults in art and nature, and with a true taste, while he praises and rejoices over and receives into his soul the good, and becomes noble and good, he will justly blame and hate the bad, now in the days of his youth, even before he is able to know the reason why; and when reason comes he will recognise and salute the friend with whom his education has made him long familiar.

402

2. The good Physician and the good Judge.

The question which is discussed in the following passage is both a curious and important one :—'Whether the judge should not have a personal knowledge of evil, and the physician have himself suffered from disease?'—In answer Plato draws a distinction between vice and disease, although in other places he more often dwells upon the analogy between them (Soph. 228; Laws x. 906 A).

The physician who enjoys perfect health will hardly be able to understand some forms of sickness. His mind and character will not be impaired by a personal experience of ill-health, whereas his knowledge will be widened and his powers of intuition and sympathy increased. On the other hand, the pursuit of evil injures and lowers the moral tone in a way which no after-repentance can entirely repair. Yet, as Plato wisely says, while the judge should be a good man, he should have had abundant opportunity of observing the world. He must understand the sources of crime, and be able to make allowance for the circumstances which help to develope the criminal instincts. The severity of Rhadamanthus must be tempered by pity and kindliness; but the judge must also keep his feelings under control, and not permit himself to be hurried into an untimely and ill-considered leniency.

Glaucon. All that, Socrates, is excellent; but I should like to put a question to you: Ought there not to be good physicians in a State, and are not the best those who have treated the greatest number of constitutions good and bad? and are not the best judges in like

Steph.
408
C

manner those who are acquainted with all sorts of moral natures?

Yes, I said, I too would have good judges and good physicians. But do you know whom I think good?

Will you tell me?

I will, if I can. Let me however note that in the same question you join two things which are not the same.

How so? he asked.

Why, I said, you join physicians and judges. Now the most skilful physicians are those who, from their youth upwards, have combined with the knowledge of their art the greatest experience of disease; they had better not be robust in health, and should have had all manner of diseases in their own persons. For the body, as I conceive, is not the instrument with which they cure the body; in that case we could not allow them ever to be or to have been sickly; but they cure the body with the mind, and the mind which has become and is sick can cure nothing.

That is very true, he said.

But with the judge it is otherwise; since he governs mind by mind; he ought not therefore to have been trained among vicious minds, and to have associated with them from youth upwards, and to have gone through the whole calendar of crime, only in order that he may quickly infer the crimes of others as he might their bodily diseases from his own self-consciousness: the honourable mind which is to form a healthy judgment should have had no experience or contamination of evil habits when young. And this is the reason why in youth good men often appear to be simple, and are easily practised upon by the dishonest, because they have no examples of what evil is in their own souls.

Yes, he said, they are far too apt to be deceived.

Therefore, I said, the judge should not be young;

he should have learned to know evil, not from his own soul, but from late and long observation of the nature of evil in others: knowledge should be his guide, not personal experience.

Yes, he said, that is the ideal of a judge.

Yes, I replied, and he will be a good man (which is my answer to your question); for he is good who has a good soul. But the cunning and suspicious nature of which we spoke,—he who has committed many crimes, and fancies himself to be a master in wickedness, when he is amongst his fellows, is wonderful in the precautions which he takes, because he judges of them by himself: but when he gets into the company of men of virtue, who have the experience of age, he appears to be a fool again, owing to his unseasonable suspicions; he cannot recognise an honest man, because he has no pattern of honesty in himself; at the same time, as the bad are more numerous than the good, and he meets with them oftener, he thinks himself, and is by others thought to be, rather wise than foolish.

Most true, he said.

Then the good and wise judge whom we are seeking is not this man, but the other; for vice cannot know virtue too, but a virtuous nature, educated by time, will acquire a knowledge both of virtue and vice: the virtuous, and not the vicious man has wisdom—in my opinion.

And in mine also.

3. The true use of Music and Gymnastic.

If we desire perfectly to understand the meaning of Plato and the other Greek philosophers when they treat of education, we must be careful to remember that with them 'Music' includes the whole culture of the mind, just as under Gymnastic is comprehended every form of bodily training. These were the two main divisions of Hellenic education: they stood on an equal footing, and were each pursued with the same earnestness. The Greek ideal was always 'the sound mind in the sound body;' and Plato is only carrying this conception a little further when he insists that gymnastic is 'designed to co-operate with music in the improvement of the soul.'

He wishes in fact to realize the favourite dream of educational reformers in our own day, and to make physical training, not a sport or an amusement to be pursued or neglected at will, but a regular part of the scheme of instruction. He is far removed from the asceticism of the Middle Ages, which in the effort to subdue the body too often enfeebled and degraded the mind; yet he has no wish to see his citizens become mere athletes in whom all the higher impulses of soul and mind have withered and died.

Steph.
410
A

Socrates. This is the sort of medicine, and this is the sort of law, which you will sanction in your State. They will minister to better natures, giving health both of soul and of body; but those who are diseased in their bodies they will leave to die, and the corrupt and incurable souls they will put an end to themselves.

Glaucon. That is clearly the best thing both for the patients and the State.

And thus our youth, having been educated only in that simple music which, as we said, inspires temperance, will be reluctant to go to law.

Clearly.

And the musician, who, keeping to the same track, is content to practise the simple gymnastic, will have nothing to do with medicine unless in some extreme case.

That I quite believe.

The very exercises and toils which he undergoes are intended to stimulate the spirited element of his nature, and not to increase his strength; he will not, like common athletes, use exercise and regimen to develope his muscles.

Very right, he said.

Neither are the two arts of music and gymnastic really designed, as is often supposed, the one for the training of the soul, the other for the training of the body.

THE EXCESS OF MUSIC AND GYMNASTIC

What then is the real object of them?

I believe, I said, that the teachers of both have in view chiefly the improvement of the soul.

How can that be? he asked.

Did you never observe, I said, the effect on the mind itself of exclusive devotion to gymnastic, or the opposite effect of an exclusive devotion to music?

In what way shown? he said.

The one producing a temper of hardness and ferocity, the other of softness and effeminacy, I replied.

Yes, he said, I am quite aware that the mere athlete becomes too much of a savage, and that the mere musician is melted and softened beyond what is good for him.

Yet surely, I said, this ferocity only comes from spirit, which, if rightly educated, would give courage, but, if too much intensified, is liable to become hard and brutal.

That I quite think.

On the other hand the philosopher will have the quality of gentleness. And this also, when too much indulged, will turn to softness, but, if educated rightly, will be gentle and moderate.

True.

And in our opinion the guardians ought to have both these qualities?

Assuredly.

And both should be in harmony?

Beyond question.

And the harmonious soul is both temperate and courageous?

Yes.

And the inharmonious is cowardly and boorish?

Very true.

And, when a man allows music to play upon him and

to pour into his soul through the funnel of his ears those sweet and soft and melancholy airs of which we were just now speaking, and his whole life is passed in warbling and the delights of song; in the first stage of the process the passion or spirit which is in him is tempered like iron, and made useful, instead of brittle and useless. But, if he carries on the softening and soothing process, in the next stage he begins to melt and waste, until he has wasted away his spirit and cut out the sinews of his soul; and he becomes a feeble warrior.

Very true.

If the element of spirit is naturally weak in him the change is speedily accomplished, but if he have a good deal, then the power of music weakening the spirit renders him excitable;—on the least provocation he flames up at once, and is speedily extinguished; instead of having spirit he grows irritable and passionate and is quite impracticable.

Exactly.

And so in gymnastics, if a man takes violent exercise and is a great feeder, and the reverse of a great student of music and philosophy, at first the high condition of his body fills him with pride and spirit, and he becomes twice the man that he was

Certainly.

And what happens? if he do nothing else, and holds no converse with the Muses, does not even that intelligence which there may be in him, having no taste of any sort of learning or enquiry or thought or culture, grow feeble and dull and blind, his mind never waking up or receiving nourishment, and his senses not being purged of their mists?

True, he said.

And he ends by becoming a hater of philosophy, uncivilized, never using the weapon of persuasion,—he is like a wild beast, all violence and fierceness, and knows no other way of dealing; and he lives in all ignorance and evil conditions, and has no sense of propriety and grace.

That is quite true, he said.

And as there are two principles of human nature, one 412 the spirited and the other the philosophical, some God, as I should say, has given mankind two arts answering to them (and only indirectly to the soul and body), in order that these two principles (like the strings of an instrument) may be relaxed or drawn tighter until they are duly harmonized.

That appears to be the intention.

And he who mingles music with gymnastic in the fairest proportions, and best attempers them to the soul, may be rightly called the true musician and harmonist in a far higher sense than the tuner of the strings.

You are quite right, Socrates.

BOOK IV.

ADEIMANTUS now interposes :—' But will not our citizens have a miserable life? They will be no better off than a garrison of mercenaries.' Nay, (replies Socrates), their lot may be a most happy one. The State is designed to be a whole, and each part will attain happiness in fulfilling its proper functions. Our guardians have a serious duty to perform; they are to be the saviours and protectors of the State, and not mere loungers and wine bibbers.

The question of Adeimantus introduces another topic,—the influence of Wealth and Poverty. Both are equally injurious when in excess. Riches breed luxury and indolence: poverty causes degeneration of character. ' Yet,' (persists Adeimantus), ' how could our poor city fight against a wealthy enemy?' Our soldiers are trained athletes, who can easily overpower their unskilled opponents. ' And suppose several cities unite?' All existing States are torn asunder by the endless quarrel of rich and poor, and there will be no difficulty in setting one party against the other. Mere size does not make greatness, and our State must only increase so far as is consistent with unity.

Rules of this kind are useful enough : the main point, however, is education, which proceeds with accumulating force from generation to generation. No innovation must be allowed in music and gymnastic: the youth must be trained in habits of order, lest licence, beginning in music, creep in and infect the whole of civic life. Minor details our citizens will settle for themselves ; they are friends who will have 'all things in common,'— property, wives, and children. The wise legislator will not make laws against the Hydra-headed evils of society, either in an ill-ordered or a well-ordered State : in the former they are useless ; in the latter, unnecessary. Matters of religion alone remain for regulation, and they may be left to the Oracle of Delphi.

But where amid all this is Justice ? In what part of the State or of man does she abide ? Wisdom will appear among the guardians : courage in the auxiliaries or soldiers. Temperance, or 'self-mastery,' is the harmony which exists in the individual when the desires and passions allow reason to rule ; and in the State when the many submit to the wiser few. Justice is our old principle,—that every man should do his own business. In the State the various classes must be kept separate, and no person be permitted to pursue two vocations. And so with the individual; justice exists when the three principles in the soul,—reason, passion, appetite,—retain their proper relation.

Are the three principles, however, one or distinct ? The latter, clearly ; for if we feel a desire of any object, the appetites will often say, 'Satisfy it !' while reason bids us refrain. And the third principle, passion, although the natural ally of reason against the appetites, is different from it, and is found even where reason is undeveloped or wanting, as in children and the animals.

Justice, then, alike in the State and the individual, is the harmonious association of the three principles ; whereas injustice is the rebellion of the lower principles against reason. Or, to use another metaphor, justice is the health, injustice the disease, of the soul. Virtue is one ; vice has many forms. And the forms of government correspond : there is a government of the best, i. e. monarchy or aristocracy, and four imperfect constitutions.

Virtue the health, Vice the disease, of the soul.

Plato in all his writings makes great use of the argument from analogy, which has been so valuable, if sometimes so fallacious an aid to the philosopher. And in the following passage we easily perceive that he is reasoning from bodily phenomena to states of the soul and mind, and employing both to illustrate the principles of civic life. No comparison seems more natural, even to ourselves, than that of the soul to the body ; for language, although the most pliable of things (Statesm. 277 B ; Rep. 9. 588 D), fails us when we pass from the concrete or material to the abstract or spiritual. The religious teacher cannot express his thoughts and aspirations except in terms of sense, nor can the philosopher set forth his conceptions without resorting to phraseology which has been borrowed from the external world. And this metaphorical language, if kept within bounds and not supposed to be literal truth, may really be an assistance to the mind. Plato's description of vice as a disease or corruption of the soul, embodies a noble idea, and has furnished many succeeding poets and philosophers and moralists with a suggestive and fertile theme, which they have applied in countless ways to the improvement and edification of the human race.

Socrates. Then our dream has been realized ; and the suspicion which we entertained at the beginning of our work of construction, that some divine power must have conducted us to a primary form of justice, has now been verified ?

Steph.
443
C

Glaucon. Yes, certainly.

And the division of labour which required the carpenter and the shoemaker and the rest of the citizens to be doing each his own business, and not another's, was a shadow of justice, and for that reason it was of use ?

Clearly.

But in reality justice was such as we were describing, being concerned however, not with the outward man, but with the inward, which is the true self and concernment of man : for the just man does not permit the several elements within him to interfere with one another, or any of them to do the work of others,—he sets in order his own inner life, and is his own master and his own law, and at peace with himself; and when he has bound together the three principles within him, which may be compared to the higher, lower, and middle notes of the scale, and the intermediate intervals—when he has bound all these together, and is no longer many, but has become one entirely temperate and perfectly adjusted nature, then he proceeds to act, if he has to act, whether in a matter of property, or in the treatment of the body, or in some affair of politics or private business; always thinking and calling that which preserves and co-operates with this harmonious condition, just and good action, and the knowledge which presides over it, wisdom, and that which at any time impairs this condition, he will call unjust action, and the opinion which presides over it ignorance.

You have said the exact truth, Socrates.

Very good; and if we were to affirm that we had discovered the just man and the just State, and the nature of justice in each of them, we should not be telling a falsehood?

Most certainly not.

May we say so, then?

Let us say so.

And now, I said, injustice has to be considered.

Clearly.

Must not injustice be a strife which arises among the three principles—a meddlesomeness, and interference, and rising up of a part of the soul against the whole, an assertion of unlawful authority, which is made by a rebellious subject against a true prince, of whom he is the natural vassal,—what is all this confusion and delusion but injustice, and intemperance and cowardice and ignorance, and every form of vice?

Exactly so.

And if the nature of justice and injustice be known, then the meaning of acting unjustly and being unjust, or, again, of acting justly, will also be perfectly clear?

What do you mean? he said.

Why, I said, they are like disease and health; being in the soul just what disease and health are in the body.

How so? he said.

Why, I said, that which is healthy causes health, and that which is unhealthy causes disease.

Yes.

And just actions cause justice, and unjust actions cause injustice?

That is certain.

And the creation of health is the institution of a natural order and government of one by another in the parts of the body; and the creation of disease is the production of a state of things at variance with this natural order?

True.

And is not the creation of justice the institution of a natural order and government of one by another in the parts of the soul, and the creation of injustice the production of a state of things at variance with the natural order?

Exactly so, he said.

Then virtue is the health and beauty and well-being of the soul, and vice the disease and weakness and deformity of the same?

True.

And do not good practices lead to virtue, and evil practices to vice?

Assuredly.

BOOK V.

SOCRATES is about to speak of the imperfect forms of government, when he is interrupted by the company, who desire to know more about the communism of wives and children which he intends to introduce into the State. With pretended reluctance he agrees to their request.

Women are somewhat weaker than men, not different from them; and they will want the same education in music, gymnastic, and military exercises. The wits may make sport of our proposal: the wise man regards only what is right... But have we not said that 'each should pursue the work to which he is suited'? and must we not now prove that there is no essential difference between men and women? The answer is that the difference is one of degree, not of kind; women, like men, vary in character, and some of them will be good guardians, while others have a turn for warlike pursuits. Our plan is therefore both possible and beneficial. The State will receive a double advantage, if men and women are equally well educated.

We have escaped one wave: a greater is coming. We must enact another law:—The wives and children of our guardians shall be common. Is this also possible, and would it be of use? Let us take the usefulness first... To begin with, there must be hymeneal festivals, at which the guardians will contrive by various devices to bring about the union of the better natures and to exclude the bad. They will also take care that the children are reared in common and have no knowledge of their parents. Those who are united at each festival will call all the children born within the ensuing year their offspring, and will be called parents by them; and so on. And what blessings will not flow from such a condition of things! There will be no disputes about 'mine' and 'thine.' The State will become a living being, feeling the joys and sorrows of its members throughout its whole frame. Rulers and citizens will be on terms of respect and affection, and no longer 'masters' and 'slaves.' The community will be one united family. Private interests will disappear: quarrels or lawsuits will be unknown, and there will be none of the petty meannesses and anxieties of life.

But how can this communism be carried out? In war, it will not be difficult. The children will go with their parents on military expeditions: they must learn to ride, and then they can easily escape danger. The valiant will receive rewards in life, and after death be honoured as heroes; cowards will be degraded. Warfare must be conducted in a mild and conciliatory temper. No Hellene may be made a slave: those who die in battle are not to be despoiled, nor may their arms be offered in temples. The lands of Hellenic cities are not to be ravaged.

Glaucon here intervenes:—'And still, Socrates, the question is, Whether communism is possible?' Socrates complains that Glaucon is bringing upon him the last and mightiest of the 'three waves.' Ideals cannot be altogether realized in action; yet our State might be called into existence on one condition:—*If philosophers became kings, or kings acquired the spirit of philosophy.* And who is the philosopher? He who loves all knowledge, not out of idle curiosity, but because he desires to behold truth. Knowledge, however, differs from opinion, and opinion, again, differs from ignorance. Knowledge and opinion are separate faculties of the soul: one has to do with absolute ideas; the other is concerned with the many, which it cannot resolve into one.

1. **The right treatment of enemies.**

It is not improbable that Plato, when speaking of the manner in which war ought to be waged by Hellenic States, had in his mind the calamities which had fallen upon Hellas in his lifetime. The events of the Peloponnesian War, and of the conflicts which succeeded, seem to have influenced his thoughts and reflections, much in the same way as the generation which survived the Thirty Years' War were affected by the horrors and cruelties of that terrible strife. He saw that Hellas had been enfeebled by ceaseless anarchy and discord until she was ready to become a prey to the conqueror; and he wished to introduce a milder system of warfare which would not permit Hellenic States to destroy each other in the vain pursuit of political supremacy. The only real enemy of the Hellene was the Barbarian; the Hellenes were brethren, who ought to forget their differences and unite against the common foe.

The time had not come for the higher lesson that men 'are all of one blood and race,' although the Sophists and their disciples were beginning to declare that slavery was contrary to nature, and that none were born to be slaves. The levelling influence, first of the Macedonian Monarchy, and afterwards of the Roman Empire, was needed in order to prepare the way for the wider conception of humanity which has since slowly prevailed in the world.

Socrates. Next, how shall our soldiers treat their enemies? What about this?

Glaucon. In what respect do you mean?

First of all, in regard to slavery. Do you think it right that Hellenes should enslave Hellenic States, or allow others to enslave them, if they can help? Should not their custom be to spare them, considering the danger which there is that the whole race may one day fall under the yoke of the barbarians?

To spare them is infinitely better.

Then no Hellene should be owned by them as a slave; that is a rule which they will observe and advise the other Hellenes to observe.

Certainly, he said; they will in this way be united

Steph.
469
B

against the barbarians and will keep their hands off one another.

Next as to the slain; ought the conquerors, I said, to take anything but their armour? Does not the practice of despoiling an enemy afford an excuse for not facing the battle? Cowards skulk about the dead, pretending that they are fulfilling a duty, and many an army before now has been lost from this love of plunder.

Very true.

And is there not illiberality and avarice in robbing a corpse, and also a degree of meanness and womanishness in making an enemy of the dead body when the real enemy has flown away and left only his fighting gear behind him,—is not this rather like a dog who cannot get at his assailant, quarrelling with the stones which strike him instead?

Very like a dog, he said.

Then we must abstain from spoiling the dead or hindering their burial?

Yes, he replied, we most certainly must.

Neither shall we offer up arms at the temples of the gods, least of all the arms of Hellenes, if we care to maintain good feeling with other Hellenes; and, indeed, we have reason to fear that the offering of spoils taken from kinsmen may be a pollution unless commanded by the god himself?

Very true.

Again, as to the devastation of Hellenic territory or the burning of houses, what is to be the practice?

May I have the pleasure, he said, of hearing your opinion?

Both should be forbidden, in my judgment; I would take the annual produce and no more. Shall I tell you why?

Pray do.

THE TWO KINDS OF WAR

Why, you see, there is a difference in the names 'discord' and 'war,' and I imagine that there is also a difference in their natures; the one is expressive of what is internal and domestic, the other of what is external and foreign; and the first of the two is termed discord, and only the second, war.

That is a very proper distinction, he replied.

And may I not observe with equal propriety that the Hellenic race is all united together by ties of blood and friendship, and alien and strange to the barbarians?

Very good, he said.

And therefore when Hellenes fight with barbarians and barbarians with Hellenes, they will be described by us as being at war when they fight, and by nature enemies, and this kind of antagonism should be called war; but when Hellenes fight with one another we shall say that Hellas is then in a state of disorder and discord, they being by nature friends; and such enmity is to be called discord.

I agree.

Consider then, I said, when that which we have acknowledged to be discord occurs, and a city is divided, if both parties destroy the lands and burn the houses of one another, how wicked does the strife appear! No true lover of his country would bring himself to tear in pieces his own nurse and mother: There might be reason in the conqueror depriving the conquered of their harvest, but still they would have the idea of peace in their hearts and would not mean to go on fighting for ever.

Yes, he said, that is a better temper than the other.

And will not the city, which you are founding, be an Hellenic city?

It ought to be, he replied.

Then will not the citizens be good and civilized?

Yes, very civilized.

And will they not be lovers of Hellas, and think of Hellas as their own land, and share in the common temples?

Most certainly.

And any difference which arises among them will be regarded by them as discord only—a quarrel among friends, which is not to be called a war?

Certainly not.

Then they will quarrel as those who intend some day to be reconciled?

Certainly.

They will use friendly correction, but will not enslave or destroy their opponents; they will be correctors, not enemies?

Just so.

And as they are Hellenes themselves they will not devastate Hellas, nor will they burn houses, nor ever suppose that the whole population of a city—men, women, and children—are equally their enemies, for they know that the guilt of war is always confined to a few persons and that the many are their friends. And for all these reasons they will be unwilling to waste their lands and raze their houses; their enmity to them will only last until the many innocent sufferers have compelled the guilty few to give satisfaction?

I agree, he said, that our citizens should thus deal with their Hellenic enemies; and with barbarians as the Hellenes now deal with one another.

Then let us enact this law also for our guardians:— that they are neither to devastate the lands of Hellenes nor to burn their houses.

Agreed; and we may agree also in thinking that these, like all our previous enactments, are very good.

2. The Last Wave; the Government of Philosophers.

The famous 'paradox' of Plato that 'Philosophers must be kings or kings become philosophers' is an instance of the manner in which he is wont to mingle jest with earnest especially at the turning-point of a discussion. He would have us to understand that, while perfectly serious in his main purpose, he is also aware that the communistic state is a 'counsel of perfection' to which men may look for guidance, but which they are not to expect to see realized in action. The doubtful legend of his life makes him twice or even thrice engage in the hopeless attempt to convert a tyrant such as Dionysius into a 'philosopher-king.' These stories may have arisen only from a misconception of the passages in the Republic, the Statesman, and the Laws, in which he speaks of the 'virtuous tyrant,' or the 'one best man,' who is to be lord over his fellow-citizens (Rep. vi. 502; Statesm. 301; Laws ii. 659 A; iv. 709 E).

There is no real reason to suppose that a sense of personal disappointment and failure lies behind the somewhat embittered tone in which, particularly in his later works, he treats of political subjects: although, as we have already seen, the historical events amid which he lived may well have cast a sombre shadow over his thoughts and reflections. Like many idealists, he was by no means free from a touch of pessimism; he had not the temper of the statesman, who is content to carry out his schemes or to abandon them, as circumstances may require. He preferred, in the language of the Phaedrus, 'to sow the fruitful seed of thought in the souls' of his hearers and readers, confident that it would hereafter ripen to a glorious and immortal harvest (Phaedr. 276).

Glaucon. But still I must say, Socrates, that if you are allowed to go on in this way you will entirely forget the other question which at the commencement of this discussion you thrust aside :—Is such an order of things possible, and how, if at all? For I am quite ready to acknowledge that the plan which you propose, if only feasible, would do all sorts of good to the State. I will add, what you have omitted, that your citizens will be the bravest of warriors, and will never leave their ranks, for they will all know one another, and each will call the other father, brother, son; and if you suppose the

Steph.
471
B

women to join their armies, whether in the same rank or in the rear, either as a terror to the enemy, or as auxiliaries in case of need, I know that they will then be absolutely invincible; and there are many domestic advantages which might also be mentioned and which I also fully acknowledge: but, as I admit all these advantages and as many more as you please, if only this State of yours were to come into existence, we need say no more about them; assuming then the existence of the State, let us now turn to the question of possibility and ways and means—the rest may be left.

If I loiter[1] for a moment, you instantly make a raid upon me, I said, and have no mercy; I have hardly escaped the first and second waves, and you seem not to be aware that you are now bringing upon me the third, which is the greatest and heaviest. When you have seen and heard the third wave, I think you will be more considerate and will acknowledge that some fear and hesitation was natural respecting a proposal so extraordinary as that which I have now to state and investigate.

The more appeals of this sort which you make, he said, the more determined are we that you shall tell us how such a State is possible: speak out and at once.

Let me begin by reminding you that we found our way hither in the search after justice and injustice.

True, he replied; but what of that?

I was only going to ask whether, if we have discovered them, we are to require that the just man should in nothing fail of absolute justice; or may we be satisfied with an approximation, and the attainment in him of a higher degree of justice than is to be found in other men?

---

[1] Reading στραγγευομένῳ.

The approximation will be enough.

We were enquiring into the nature of absolute justice and into the character of the perfectly just, and into injustice and the perfectly unjust, that we might have an ideal. We were to look at these in order that we might judge of our own happiness and unhappiness according to the standard which they exhibited and the degree in which we resembled them, but not with any view of showing that they could exist in fact.

True, he said.

Would a painter be any the worse because, after having delineated with consummate art an ideal of a perfectly beautiful man, he was unable to show that any such man could ever have existed?

He would be none the worse.

Well, and were we not creating an ideal of a perfect State?

To be sure.

And is our theory a worse theory because we are unable to prove the possibility of a city being ordered in the manner described?

Surely not, he replied.

That is the truth, I said. But if, at your request, I am to try and show how and under what conditions the possibility is highest, I must ask you, having this in view, to repeat your former admissions.

What admissions?

I want to know whether ideals are ever fully realized 473 in language? Does not the word express more than the fact, and must not the actual, whatever a man may think, always, in the nature of things, fall short of the truth? What do you say?

I agree.

Then you must not insist on my proving that the actual State will in every respect coincide with the ideal: if we are only able to discover how a city may be governed nearly as we proposed, you will admit that we have discovered the possibility which you demand; and will be contented. I am sure that I should be contented—will not you?

Yes, I will.

Let me next endeavour to show what is that fault in States which is the cause of their present maladministration, and what is the least change which will enable a State to pass into the truer form; and let the change, if possible, be of one thing only, or, if not, of two; at any rate, let the changes be as few and slight as possible.

Certainly, he replied.

I think, I said, that there might be a reform of the State if only one change were made, which is not a slight or easy though still a possible one.

What is it? he said.

Now then, I said, I go to meet that which I liken to the greatest of the waves; yet shall the word be spoken, even though the wave break and drown me in laughter and dishonour; and do you mark my words.

Proceed.

I said: *Until philosophers are kings, or the kings and princes of this world have the spirit and power of philosophy, and political greatness and wisdom meet in one, and those commoner natures who pursue either to the exclusion of the other are compelled to stand aside, cities will never have rest from their evils,—no, nor the human race, as I believe, —and then only will this our State have a possibility of life and behold the light of day.* Such was the thought, my dear Glaucon, which I would fain have uttered if it had not seemed too extravagant; for to be convinced that in no other State can there be happiness private or public is indeed a hard thing.

BOOK VI.

THE Sixth Book treats of the true and the false philosopher, and of the Idea of Good. . . . The true philosopher is a lover of all truth and being; he is temperate, caring only for the pleasures of the soul; he is absorbed in the contemplation of the Divine, and disregards the things of earth; he is brave, gentle, sociable, fond of learning, blessed with a good memory. To him and to his like we will entrust the government of the State. 'The argument is incontrovertible,' answers Adeimantus. 'Yet we must beg you to explain the undoubted fact that philosophers in general are either useless, or downright rogues.' Socrates replies by a parable:—

The State may be compared to a ship of which the captain is infirm and a poor navigator: the sailors, who are equally ignorant, insist on assuming the management: the pilot, the only man on board who has scientific knowledge, is laughed at and despised. The parable suffices to show why philosophers are useless :—what is the good of a pilot who is forbidden to take the helm? The corruption of philosophy is due to various causes: (1) The true philosophers are few in number: (2) their very virtues, and (3) the goods of life, distract them from philosophy: (4) the best natures when corrupted become the worst: (5) there is the evil influence of the world, which (6) crushes those whom it cannot pervert. Truly God alone can save the philosopher in the unequal contest!

The real corrupter is not the Sophist, but the world; the Sophist is merely the keeper of the beast, who panders to his wants and prejudices, and ends by growing like him. The young man of parts falls a victim to his own success, and is easily persuaded to embrace a career of ambition. And so philosophy, deserted by her rightful protectors, becomes the prey of mean and inferior natures. A few noble characters remain, whom the world cannot allure or terrify, and they retire from public life because they know that the evils of society are incurable. No ordinary constitution offers them a suitable field: in our own State, if their training is rightly ordered, they may find a home. At present philosophy is studied superficially and early in life; whereas it ought to be the pursuit of maturer years and the crown of old age. The dislike of the world is directed against the pretenders and not against the true philosophers. If these could hold rule in the State, the hostile feeling would disappear, and our ideal would be realized. The government would be given to them, and they would clear away all existing laws and institutions, setting in their place a new and better city, framed after the heavenly pattern.

Let us now assume that the world is converted to our views, and turn to another question:—What are to be the studies of our guardians? They will have to undergo a much longer and severer training than the other citizens, and therefore they must be both quick and solid. They will be taught to discern the true nature of the virtues, and to ascend from them to the Idea of the Good. This is that higher principle after which all men dimly grope, but which our guardians ought clearly to conceive and understand. The theme is too high for us: of the 'child of the Good,' however, we may speak. The 'child of the Good' is the sun, the lord of light, whom the Good created to be his image in the visible world. And as the eye beholds objects when the sun shines upon them, so the soul, which is like the eye, perceives truth when illuminated by the Idea of Good. The sun is the author of generation; and the Idea of Good is the cause of being and essence. The visible world is divided into (1) images, including (*a*) shadows, (*b*) reflections, and (2) realities: the intellectual world comprehends (1) intelligible things, the province of the arts and sciences, and (2) being or essence, the higher realm of dialectic. And there are four corresponding faculties in the soul,—reason, understanding, faith, perception of shadows.

1. The Parable of the Pilot.

In the allegory of the Pilot to whom the sailors refuse to entrust the helm, Plato expresses what he supposes to be the relation of philosophers to the world. He is setting forth in a picturesque and rather exaggerated form his favourite doctrine of the 'one best man' who ought to be made to rule, 'even against his own will.' He is misled in this, as in some other points, by the analogy of the arts, and thinks of the politician as an artist who has a monopoly in his own department. He did not realize sufficiently the play of forces which builds up a state, or understand how constitutions are not created in a day, but are the result or final product of many factors,—the beliefs, the historical traditions, the temperament of the nation. The ills of existing states seemed to him beyond remedy, unless an almost superhuman wisdom could be imparted to the rulers of mankind; his only hope was to convert men to a true appreciation of the philosopher, and to provide a thorough and systematic education for the few who were fitted by nature for so noble a vocation. These, accordingly, are the subjects to which he addresses himself in the Sixth and Seventh Books.

Steph.
487
A

Here Adeimantus interposed and said : To these statements, Socrates, no one can offer a reply ; but when you talk in this way, a strange feeling passes over the minds of your hearers : They fancy that they are led astray a little at each step in the argument, owing to their own want of skill in asking and answering questions; these littles accumulate, and at the end of the discussion they are found to have sustained a mighty overthrow and all their former notions appear to be turned upside down. And as unskilful players of draughts are at last shut up by their more skilful adversaries and have no piece to move, so they too find themselves shut up at last; for they have nothing to say in this new game of which words are the counters; and yet all the time they are in the right.

The observation is suggested to me by what is now occurring. For any one of us might say, that although in words he is not able to meet you at each step of the argument, he sees as a fact that the votaries of philosophy, when they carry on the study, not only in youth as a part of education, but as the pursuit of their maturer years, most of them become strange monsters, not to say utter rogues, and that those who may be considered the best of them are made useless to the world by the very study which you extol.

Well, and do you think that those who say so are wrong?

I cannot tell, he replied; but I should like to know what is your opinion.

Hear my answer; I am of opinion that they are quite right.

Then how can you be justified in saying that cities will not cease from evil until philosophers rule in them, when philosophers are acknowledged by us to be of no use to them?

You ask a question, I said, to which a reply can only be given in a parable.

Yes, Socrates; and that is a way of speaking to which you are not at all accustomed, I suppose.

I perceive, I said, that you are vastly amused at having plunged me into such a hopeless discussion; but now hear the parable, and then you will be still more amused at the meagreness of my imagination: for the manner in which the best men are treated in their own States is so grievous that no single thing on earth is comparable to it; and therefore, if I am to plead their cause, I must have recourse to fiction, and put together a figure made up of many things, like the fabulous unions of goats and stags which are found in pictures.

Imagine then a fleet or a ship in which there is a captain who is taller and stronger than any of the crew, but he is a little deaf and has a similar infirmity in sight, and his knowledge of navigation is not much better. The sailors are quarrelling with one another about the steering—every one is of opinion that he has a right to steer, though he has never learned the art of navigation and cannot tell who taught him or when he learned, and will further assert that it cannot be taught, and they are ready to cut in pieces any one who says the contrary. They throng about the captain, begging and praying him to commit the helm to them; and if at any time they do not prevail, but others are preferred to them, they kill the others or throw them overboard, and having first chained up the noble captain's senses with drink or some narcotic drug, they mutiny and take possession of the ship and make free with the stores; thus, eating and drinking, they proceed on their voyage in such manner as might be expected of them. Him who is their partisan and cleverly aids them in their plot for getting the ship out of the captain's hands into their own whether by force or persuasion, they compliment with the name of sailor, pilot, able seamen, and abuse the other sort of man, whom they call a good-for-nothing; but that the true pilot must pay attention to the year and seasons and sky and stars and winds, and whatever else belongs to his art, if he intends to be really qualified for the command of a ship, and that he must and will be the steerer, whether other people like or not—the possibility of this union of authority with the steerer's art has never seriously entered into their thoughts or been made part of their calling. Now in vessels which are in a state of mutiny and by 489 sailors who are mutineers, how will the true pilot be regarded? Will he not be called by them a prater, a star-gazer, a good-for-nothing?

Of course, said Adeimantus.

Then you will hardly need, I said, to hear the interpretation of the figure, which describes the true philosopher in his relation to the State; for you understand already.

Certainly.

Then suppose you now take this parable to the gentleman who is surprised at finding that philosophers have no honour in their cities; explain it to him and try to convince him that their having honour would be far more extraordinary.

I will.

Say to him, that, in deeming the best votaries of philosophy to be useless to the rest of the world, he is right; but also tell him to attribute their uselessness to the fault of those who will not use them, and not to themselves. The pilot should not humbly beg the sailors to be commanded by him—that is not the order of nature; neither are 'the wise to go to the doors of the rich'—the ingenious author of this saying told a lie—but the truth is, that, when a man is ill, whether he be rich or poor, to the physician he must go, and he who wants to be governed, to him who is able to govern. The ruler who is good for anything ought not to beg his subjects to be ruled by him; although the present governors of mankind are of a different stamp; they may be justly compared to the mutinous sailors, and the true helmsmen to those who are called by them good-for-nothings and star-gazers.

Precisely so, he said.

2. The low estimation in which Philosophy is held by the World.

Plato, after having declared that the Philosopher must bear rule in the State, undertakes to explain why as a matter of fact the students of philosophy have no honour among men. But his observations have a wider range; he is really speaking of the causes which bring about the deterioration of some of the most gifted characters. He is aware that great abilities also bring great temptations; and that the stronger natures are only with difficulty coerced into observing the laws, 'which, they think, are made by the weak majority for their own protection' (Gorg. 483, 484). He had seen many instances of young men rarely endowed by nature, such as were Charmides, Meno, Alcibiades (*cp. supra* i. 78), whose 'voyage through life' had ended in pitiable disaster and shipwreck. And he shows his usual keenness of insight, when he lays the blame of the 'corruption of youth,' not upon their teachers, the Sophists, but upon mankind in general.

We are constrained by a necessity 'worse than that of Diomede[1],' to conform to the moral standard of those with whom we associate; 'the World is too much with us,' and is an enchanter whose spells are not to be resisted. Only a few chosen spirits in each generation rebel against this degrading influence; and even they are apt to feel that the struggle is useless, and to seek some refuge where they may possess their souls in peace, unvexed by the storms of life. Yet Plato, like the Hebrew prophets, to whom in certain respects he may fitly be compared, is not content to resign himself to despair, or to acknowledge that improvement is impossible; and he cherishes to the last a dream of a better state of society, 'the City of which the pattern is laid up in Heaven,' wherein men will walk according to the laws of justice and righteousness.

---

[1] The Greek proverb is thus explained by the Scholiast. Diomede, when returning with Odysseus from the theft of the Palladium, discovered that his companion intended to kill him so as to secure the whole glory of the exploit. Whereupon he bound Odysseus and compelled him to go in front of him, until they reached the ships.

Socrates. You recognize the truth of what I have been saying? Then let me ask you to consider further whether the world will ever be induced to believe in the existence of absolute beauty rather than of the many beautiful, or of the absolute in each kind rather than of the many in each kind?

Steph.
494
A

Adeimantus. Certainly not.

Then the world cannot possibly be a philosopher?

Impossible.

And therefore philosophers must inevitably fall under the censure of the world?

They must.

And of individuals who consort with the mob and seek to please them?

That is evident.

Then, do you see any way in which the philosopher can be preserved in his calling to the end? and remember what we were saying of him, that he was to have quickness and memory and courage and magnificence—these were admitted by us to be the true philosopher's gifts.

Yes.

Will not such an one from his early childhood be in all things first among all, especially if his bodily endowments are like his mental ones?

Certainly, he said.

And his friends and fellow-citizens will want to use him as he gets older for their own purposes?

No question.

Falling at his feet, they will make requests to him and do him honour and flatter him, because they want to get into their hands now, the power which he will one day possess.

That often happens, he said.

And what will a man such as he is be likely to do

under such circumstances, especially if he be a citizen of a great city, rich and noble, and a tall proper youth? Will he not be full of boundless aspirations, and fancy himself able to manage the affairs of Hellenes and of barbarians, and having got such notions into his head will he not dilate and elevate himself in the fulness of vain pomp and senseless pride?

To be sure he will.

Now, when he is in this state of mind, if some one gently comes to him and tells him that he is a fool and must get understanding, which can only be got by slaving for it, do you think that, under such adverse circumstances, he will be easily induced to listen?

Far otherwise.

And even if there be some one who through inherent goodness or natural reasonableness has had his eyes opened a little and is humbled and taken captive by philosophy, how will his friends behave when they think that they are likely to lose the advantage which they were hoping to reap from his companionship? Will they not do and say anything to prevent him from yielding to his better nature and to render his teacher powerless, using to this end private intrigues as well as public prosecutions?

There can be no doubt of it.

And how can one who is thus circumstanced ever become a philosopher?

Impossible.

Then were we not right in saying that even the very qualities which make a man a philosopher may, if he be ill-educated, divert him from philosophy, no less than riches and their accompaniments and the other so-called goods of life?

We were quite right.

Thus, my excellent friend, is brought about all that

ruin and failure which I have been describing of the natures best adapted to the best of all pursuits; they are natures which we maintain to be rare at any time; this being the class out of which come the men who are the authors of the greatest evil to States and individuals; and also of the greatest good when the tide carries them in that direction; but a small man never was the doer of any great thing either to individuals or to States.

That is most true, he said.

And so philosophy is left desolate, with her marriage rite incomplete: for her own have fallen away and forsaken her, and while they are leading a false and unbecoming life, other unworthy persons, seeing that she has no kinsmen to be her protectors, enter in and dishonour her; and fasten upon her the reproaches which, as you say, her reprovers utter, who affirm of her votaries that some are good for nothing, and that the greater number deserve the severest punishment.

That is certainly what people say.

Yes; and what else would you expect, I said, when you think of the puny creatures who, seeing this land open to them—a land well stocked with fair names and showy titles—like prisoners running out of prison into a sanctuary, take a leap out of their trades into philosophy; those who do so being probably the cleverest hands at their own miserable crafts? For, although philosophy be in this evil case, still there remains a dignity about her which is not to be found in the arts. And many are thus attracted by her whose natures are imperfect and whose souls are maimed and disfigured by their meannesses, as their bodies are by their trades and crafts. Is not this unavoidable?

Yes.

Are they not exactly like a bald little tinker who has

just got out of durance and come into a fortune; he takes a bath and puts on a new coat, and is decked out as a bridegroom going to marry his master's daughter, who is left poor and desolate?

496 A most exact parallel.

What will be the issue of such marriages? Will they not be vile and bastard?

There can be no question of it.

And when persons who are unworthy of education approach philosophy and make an alliance with her who is in a rank above them, what sort of ideas and opinions are likely to be generated? Will they not be sophisms captivating to the ear, having nothing in them genuine, or worthy of or akin to true wisdom?

No doubt, he said.

Then Adeimantus, I said, the worthy disciples of philosophy will be but a small remnant: perchance some noble and well-educated person, detained by exile in her service, who in the absence of corrupting influences remains devoted to her; or some lofty soul born in a mean city, the politics of which he contemns and neglects; and there may be a gifted few who leave the arts, which they justly despise, and come to her;— or peradventure there are some who are restrained by our friend Theages' bridle; for everything in the life of Theages conspired to divert him from philosophy; but ill-health kept him away from politics. My own case of the internal sign is hardly worth mentioning, for rarely, if ever, has such a monitor been given to any other man. Those who belong to this small class have tasted how sweet and blessed a possession philosophy is, and have also seen enough of the madness of the multitude; and they know that no politician is honest, nor is there any champion of justice at whose side they may fight and be saved.

Such an one may be compared to a man who has fallen among wild beasts—he will not join in the wickedness of his fellows, but neither is he able singly to resist all their fierce natures, and therefore seeing that he would be of no use to the State or to his friends, and reflecting that he would have to throw away his life without doing any good either to himself or others, he holds his peace, and goes his own way. He is like one who, in the storm of dust and sleet which the driving wind hurries along, retires under the shelter of a wall; and seeing the rest of mankind full of wickedness, he is content, if only he can live his own life and be pure from evil or unrighteousness, and depart in peace and good-will, with bright hopes.

Yes, he said, and he will have done a great work before he departs.

A great work—yes; but not the greatest, unless he find a State suitable to him; for in a State which is suitable to him, he will have a larger growth and be the saviour of his country, as well as of himself.

BOOK VII.

THE Seventh Book commences with another parable:—The world is like a cave where men sit in fetters: above and behind them is a fire, and between them and the fire is a raised way with a low wall in front. Along this way men go to and fro carrying various objects, and the captives, seeing the passing shadows cast upon the opposite wall of the cave, believe that they are beholding realities and not shadows. If one of them is released from bondage and mounts up into the light, he is at first dazzled and blinded, but as soon as he grows accustomed to the brightness he sees and recognizes things in their true nature. And when, again, such an one returns to the cave, the darkness bewilders him, and he becomes a laughing-stock to his fellows, until at last he recovers his sight, and is then a better judge of the shadows than the others, because he also knows real existence. The cave is the world of sight; the light of the fire is the sun; the journey upward is the ascent of the soul to the Idea of Good. The philosopher who has reached the Beatific Vision is naturally confused when he is forced to descend into the arena of the world; yet he is to be envied, not pitied, on this account.

The argument also supplies a further lesson:—Education is not a process of putting knowledge into the soul; it is the conversion of the soul from darkness to light. Intelligence is innate, not acquired, and may receive either a bad or a good direction. And our guardians require an education which will adapt them equally to the life of speculation and the life of action. They must be willing, when their turn comes, to leave their studies and go down into the den; and they will assume office as a duty, and not because they love power.

And now, what subjects are they to be taught? The first education included Music and Gymnastic: for the second there remain, (1) Arithmetic, (2) Geometry, (3) Astronomy, (4) Harmony.— (1) Arithmetic is useful in war, and trains the mind to distinguish between the contradictory impressions of sense. It leads us from plurality to unity, and is therefore a study eminently worthy of a philosopher, so long as it is concerned with abstract numbers, and not merely with visible or tangible objects. (2) Geometry, although not without practical uses, is also chiefly to be valued because it aids in the acquisition of the higher knowledge. (3) Astronomy, like Arithmetic and Geometry, is generally pursued in a wrong spirit. The true astronomer neglects the transient phenomena of nature, and fixes his gaze upon the eternal abstractions of space and time. '(4) Harmony is the sister science of Arithmetic. And here, again, there is an error to be avoided. We must not, after the fashion of Pythagorean philosophers and musical amateurs, investigate the notes actually heard by us and omit to consider the real cause of harmony.

These studies lead up to the highest of all,—Dialectic, which is concerned with reason alone and is unaided by sense. Its true nature cannot be revealed except to the initiated who have studied the preliminary sciences, which are related to Dialectic as what we have called Understanding is to Reason or Pure Intellect. There are two divisions of the mind;—Intellect, which has to do with Being, and Opinion, which is concerned with Becoming. Intellect is divided into Science and Understanding: Opinion into Belief and Perception of Shadows.

Now Being is the realm of Dialectic; and our guardians ought to be able to understand things in their essence and comprehend the Idea of Good. They must have every excellence of body and mind, and possess every virtue. They will be occupied with the preliminary sciences in their youth; three years will be spent in gymnastic; and at twenty the best of them will commence the higher studies. At thirty there will be a further selection, and the most promising will take up philosophy for five years.

At this point caution is necessary. Young men on their first introduction to philosophy often lose their mental balance. Their case is much like that of one who supposes himself to be the son of wealthy parents: when he discovers that they are not his real father and mother, he quickly forgets his former respect for them. And so the youthful dialectician, who is taught to analyze the traditional notions of morality, ends by disbelieving in virtue altogether. We shall lessen the danger by deferring their entrance on the study until thirty, when their character will be more formed. From thirty-five to fifty they will be employed in active life. After fifty they will devote themselves chiefly to abstract speculation, but must occasionally return to politics. All that has been said applies equally to men and women.

And how can such a state be realized? Easily, we reply, if our dream of 'Philosopher-kings' were once fulfilled. They would send off the parents, take possession of the children, and train them up in the principles of the new constitution.

The Allegory of the Cave.

The quaint parable with which the Seventh Book opens is intended by Plato as a preface to the discussion which immediately follows upon the right education of the philosopher-rulers of his State. He wishes us to understand that their training should be abstract, and not directed towards practical purposes. His design is not merely to form a body of capable and intelligent officials in the modern sense of the term; he seems rather to have had in his mind what may be described as a revival of the Pythagorean brotherhoods with some additions and improvements. He desires to create a ruling caste who would have for their sole occupation the government of the commonwealth. They would be in a manner an incarnation on earth of the 'demi-gods' whom the Platonic theology interposes between the Creator and the Universe (Statesm. 271 D); their true place is in 'the heaven of ideas,' and they only leave the delights of speculation and abstract thought when the stern voice of Duty calls them to take their place at the helm of State.

This is no more than a dream to Plato himself, as he intimates to us in many passages. Nor could he fill up the outline or explain precisely the kind of knowledge which the guardians were to seek, and the possession of which was to mark them off from the rest of the community. He is convinced that there is a truth beyond sense, something which is higher than the phenomena of earth, and which cannot be understood except by the philosopher 'who has been initiated in the mysteries' (Phaedo 69). And we must confess that if such ideals are vague and indefinite, it is also certain that they have a real value, no less in philosophy than in religion, because they give unity and direction to our thoughts, and tend to raise the mind above the narrowing influence of too exclusive a devotion to any single department of knowledge.

Steph.
514
A

Socrates. And now, I said, let me show in a figure how far our nature is enlightened or unenlightened:—Behold! human beings living in an underground den, which has a mouth open toward the light and reaching all along the den; here they have been from their childhood, and have their legs and necks chained so that they cannot move, and can only see before them, being prevented by the chains from turning round their heads. Above and behind them a fire is blazing at a distance, and between the fire and the prisoners there is a raised way; and you will see, if you look, a low wall built along the way, like the screen which marionette players have in front of them, over which they show the puppets.

Glaucon. I see.

And do you see, I said, men passing along the wall carrying all sorts of vessels, and statues and figures of animals made of wood and stone and various materials, which appear over the wall? Some of them are talking, others silent.

515

You have shown me a strange image, and they are strange prisoners.

Like ourselves, I replied; and they see only their own shadows, or the shadows of one another, which the fire throws on the opposite wall of the cave?

True, he said; how could they see anything but the shadows if they were never allowed to move their heads?

And of the objects which are being carried in like manner they would only see the shadows?

Yes, he said.

And if they were able to converse with one another, would they not suppose that they were naming what was actually before them[1]?

Very true.

And suppose further that the prison had an echo which came from the other side, would they not be sure to fancy when one of the passers-by spoke that the voice which they heard came from the passing shadow?

No question, he replied.

To them, I said, the whole truth would be literally nothing but the shadows of the images.

That is certain.

And now look again, and see what will naturally follow if the prisoners are released and disabused of their error. At first, when any of them is liberated and compelled suddenly to stand up and turn his neck round and walk and look towards the light, he will suffer sharp pains; the glare will distress him, and he will be unable to see the realities of which in his former state he had seen the shadows; and then conceive some one saying to him, that what he saw before was an illusion, but that now, when he is approaching nearer to being and his eye is turned towards more real existence, he has a clearer vision,—what will be his reply? And you may further imagine that his instructor is pointing to the objects as they pass and requiring him to name them,—will he not be perplexed? Will he not fancy that the shadows which he formerly saw are truer than the objects which are now shown to him?

---

[1] Reading παρόντα.

Far truer.

And if he is compelled to look straight at the light, will he not have a pain in his eyes which will make him turn away to take refuge in the objects of vision which he can see, and which he will conceive to be in reality clearer than the things which are now being shown to him?

True, he said.

And suppose once more, that he is reluctantly dragged up a steep and rugged ascent, and held fast until he is forced into the presence of the sun himself, is he not likely to be pained and irritated? When he approaches the light his eyes will be dazzled, and he will not be able to see anything at all of what are now called realities.

Not all in a moment, he said.

He will require to grow accustomed to the sight of the upper world. And first he will see the shadows best, next the reflections of men and other objects in the water, and then the objects themselves; then he will gaze upon the light of the moon and the stars and the spangled heaven; and he will see the sky and the stars by night better than the sun or the light of the sun by day.

Certainly.

Last of all he will be able to see the sun, and not mere reflections of him in the water, but he will see him in his own proper place, and not in another; and he will contemplate him as he is.

Certainly.

He will then proceed to argue that this is he who gives the season and the years, and is the guardian of all that is in the visible world, and in a certain way the cause of all things which he and his fellows have been accustomed to behold?

Clearly, he said, he would first see the sun and then reason about him.

And when he remembered his old habitation, and the wisdom of the den and his fellow-prisoners, do you not suppose that he would felicitate himself on the change, and pity them?

Certainly, he would.

And if they were in the habit of conferring honours among themselves on those who were quickest to observe the passing shadows and to remark which of them went before, and which followed after, and which were together; and who were therefore best able to draw conclusions as to the future, do you think that he would care for such honours and glories, or envy the possessors of them? Would he not say with Homer,

'Better to be the poor servant of a poor master,'

and to endure anything, rather than think as they do and live after their manner?

Yes, he said, I think that he would rather suffer anything than entertain these false notions and live in this miserable manner.

Imagine once more, I said, such an one coming suddenly out of the sun to be replaced in his old situation; would he not be certain to have his eyes full of darkness?

To be sure, he said.

And if there were a contest, and he had to compete in measuring the shadows with the prisoners who had never moved out of the den, while his sight was still 517 weak, and before his eyes had become steady (and the time which would be needed to acquire this new habit of sight might be very considerable), would he not be ridiculous? Men would say of him that up he went and down he came without his eyes; and that it was better not even to think of ascending; and if any one tried to loose another and lead him up to the light, let them only catch the offender, and they would put him to death.

No question, he said.

This entire allegory, I said, you may now append, dear Glaucon, to the previous argument; the prison-house is the world of sight, the light of the fire is the sun, and you will not misapprehend me if you interpret the journey upwards to be the ascent of the soul into the intellectual world according to my poor belief, which, at your desire, I have expressed—whether rightly or wrongly God knows. But, whether true or false, my opinion is that in the world of knowledge the idea of good appears last of all, and is seen only with an effort; and, when seen, is also inferred to be the universal author of all things beautiful and right, parent of light and of the lord of light in this invisible world, and the immediate source of reason and truth in the intellectual; and that this is the power upon which he who would act rationally either in public or private life must have his eye fixed.

I agree, he said, as far as I am able to understand you.

Moreover, I said, you must not wonder that those who attain to this beatific vision are unwilling to descend to human affairs; for their souls are ever hastening into the upper world where they desire to dwell; which desire of theirs is very natural, if our allegory may be trusted.

Yes, very natural.

And is there anything surprising in one who passes from divine contemplations to the evil state of man, misbehaving himself in a ridiculous manner; if, while his eyes are blinking and before he has become accustomed to the surrounding darkness, he is compelled to fight in courts of law, or in other places, about the images or the shadows of images of justice, and is endeavouring to meet the conceptions of those who have never yet seen absolute justice?

Anything but surprising, he replied.

Any one who has common sense will remember that 518 the bewilderments of the eyes are of two kinds, and arise from two causes, either from coming out of the light or from going into the light, which is true of the mind's eye, quite as much as of the bodily eye; and he who remembers this when he sees any one whose vision is perplexed and weak, will not be too ready to laugh; he will first ask whether that soul of man has come out of the brighter life, and is unable to see because unaccustomed to the dark, or having turned from darkness to the day is dazzled by excess of light. And he will count the one happy in his condition and state of being, and he will pity the other; or, if he have a mind to laugh at the soul which comes from below into the light, there will be more reason in this than in the laugh which greets him who returns from above out of the light into the den.

That, he said, is a very just distinction.

But then, if I am right, certain professors of education must be wrong when they say that they can put a knowledge into the soul which was not there before, like sight into blind eyes.

They undoubtedly say this, he replied.

Whereas, our argument shows that the power and capacity of learning exists in the soul already; and that just as the eye was unable to turn from darkness to light without the whole body, so too the instrument of knowledge can only by the movement of the whole soul be turned from the world of becoming into that of being, and learn by degrees to endure the sight of being, and of the brightest and best of being, or in other words, of the good.

Very true.

And must there not be some art which will effect conversion in the easiest and quickest manner; not implanting the faculty of sight, for that exists already, but has been turned in the wrong direction, and is looking away from the truth?

Yes, he said, such an art may be presumed.

And whereas the other so-called virtues of the soul seem to be akin to bodily qualities, for even when they are not originally innate they can be implanted later by habit and exercise, the virtue of wisdom more than anything else contains a divine element which always remains, and by this conversion is rendered useful and profitable; or, on the other hand, hurtful and useless. Did you never observe the narrow intelligence flashing from the keen eye of a clever rogue—how eager he is, how clearly his paltry soul sees the way to his end; he is the reverse of blind, but his keen eye-sight is forced into the service of evil, and he is mischievous in proportion to his cleverness?

Very true, he said.

But what if there had been a circumcision of such natures in the days of their youth; and they had been severed from those sensual pleasures, such as eating and drinking, which, like leaden weights, were attached to them at their birth, and which drag them down and turn the vision of their souls upon the things that are below—if, I say, they had been released from those impediments and turned in the opposite direction, the very same faculty in them would have seen the truth as keenly as they see what their eyes are turned to now.

Very likely.

Yes, I said; and there is another thing which is likely, or rather a necessary inference from what has preceded, that neither the uneducated and uninformed of the truth, nor yet those who never make an end of their education, will be able ministers of State; not the former, because they have no single aim of duty which is the rule of all their actions, private as well as public; nor the latter, because they will not act at all except upon compulsion, fancying that they are already dwelling apart in the islands of the blest.

Very true, he replied.

Then, I said, the business of us who are the founders of the State will be to compel the best minds to attain that knowledge which we have already shown to be the greatest of all—they must continue to ascend until they arrive at the good; but when they have ascended and seen enough we must not allow them to do as they do now.

What do you mean?

I mean that they remain in the upper world: but this must not be allowed; they must be made to descend again among the prisoners in the den, and partake of their labours and honours, whether they are worth having or not.

But is not this unjust? he said; ought we to give them a worse life, when they might have a better?

You have again forgotten, my friend, I said, the intention of the legislator, who did not aim at making any one class in the State happy above the rest; the happiness was to be in the whole State, and he held the citizens together by persuasion and necessity, making them benefactors of the State, and therefore benefactors of one another; to this end he created 520 them, not to please themselves, but to be his instruments in binding up the State.

True, he said, I had forgotten.

Observe, Glaucon, that there will be no injustice in compelling our philosophers to have a care and providence of others; we shall explain to them that in other States, men of their class are not obliged to share in the toils of politics: and this is reasonable, for they grow up at their own sweet will, and the government would rather not have them. Being self-taught, they cannot be expected to show any gratitude for a culture which they have never received. But we have brought you into the world to be rulers of the hive, kings of yourselves and of the other citizens, and have educated you far better and more perfectly than they have been educated, and you are better able to share in the double duty. Wherefore each of you, when his turn comes, must go down to the general underground abode, and get the habit of seeing in the dark. When you have acquired the habit, you will see ten thousand times better than the inhabitants of the den, and you will know what the several images are, and what they represent, because you have seen the beautiful and just and good in their truth. And thus our State, which is also yours, will be a reality, and not a dream only, and will be administered in a spirit unlike that of other States, in which men fight with one another about shadows only and are distracted in the struggle for power, which in their eyes is a great good. Whereas the truth is that the State in which the rulers are most reluctant to govern is always the best and most quietly governed, and the State in which they are most eager, the worst.

Quite true, he replied.

And will our pupils, when they hear this, refuse to

take their turn at the toils of State, when they are allowed to spend the greater part of their time with one another in the heavenly light?

Impossible, he answered; for they are just men, and the commands which we impose upon them are just; there can be no doubt that every one of them will take office as a stern necessity, and not after the fashion of our present rulers of State.

BOOK VIII.

IN the Eighth Book Plato returns to the subject of which he had spoken at the end of Book IV,—the imperfect forms of government. There are four of these,—timocracy, oligarchy, democracy, tyranny; and over against each State may be set the individual who corresponds to it. The different forms have a regular order of succession: and first (1) the perfect State changes into timocracy in the following manner :—There is a mystic number which regulates births and deaths in the State, and which the guardians will one day fail to observe. The consequence will be that an inferior generation will grow up who suffer education to fall into decay. Strife will arise between the golden and silver races and those who have brass and iron in their veins. Communism will be abandoned, and the government will pass into the hands of the military class. The new rulers will be covetous of gain and lovers of power and honour.

Such is the origin of timocracy; and what manner of man is he who answers to the State? His father is an easy going person who is disgusted with politics; but the son is driven into an ambitious career by the entreaties and reproaches of the family, although, owing to his father's influence, he rests at a middle point and puts the 'spirited element' in authority over his soul.

(2) Timocracy in turn gives place to oligarchy. The love of money increases; wealth is praised and virtue cried down; the citizens become traders, and the rich monopolize office. The quarrel between rich and poor grows fiercer; the State is weakened for war by the internal dissension; poverty spreads, and 'drones' multiply in the hive, some with stings, (criminals), and some without, (paupers).

As to the oligarchical man, he is the son of the timocrat, and at first, like his father, he treads the paths of ambition. Soon he sees his father ruined by some change in affairs, and immediately he deposes ambition and enthrones the love of gain in its place. All his energies turn to money-making, although he cloaks his meanness of soul by an enforced virtue, because he dare not abandon himself to his passions.

(3) The change from oligarchy to democracy is brought about by the spendthrift class, whom the money-lenders have reduced to poverty, and who are ripe for revolution. A time of danger arrives; the poor perceive and despise the weakness of the rich; a slight spark kindles the flame of civil war; the democrats triumph, the oligarchs are slain or expelled. And so democracy is established, which is a government of uncontrolled freedom; there is no order of any kind, and everybody is good enough to be a statesman.

The democratical man is the son of a miserly father, who has taught him to restrain unnecessary desires. But the young man is drawn away by his wild associates, 'the drones,' and there is strife within him between the opposing principles. At last the evil spirits prevail and seize the citadel of his soul: the Virtues are cast out and the Vices installed in their room. Sometimes, however, in a saner interval he re-admits a part of the exiled Virtues; and henceforward he allows bad and good desires to influence him indifferently, and makes no distinction between them. He scorns advice, and regulates his life by the whim of the moment.

(4) Tyranny springs naturally out of democracy. The excessive desire of freedom begets anarchy; there is no respect for age or honour paid to parents; the slave is as good as his master; and the very animals demand their rights and liberties. Meanwhile the 'drones' grow more numerous; they prey upon the rich, and yield a share of the spoil to the people. The rich unite for protection; and the people seek a leader against them.

Revolution breaks out; the demagogue is expelled, but contrives to come back; and then he asks the people 'to give him a guard.' By degrees he becomes a full-blown tyrant, and practises all the arts of tyranny. He imposes heavy taxes; he destroys the best and noblest citizens; he forms an army of mercenaries and emancipated slaves; he gathers poets about him who sing his praises for hire; he confiscates private estates and robs the temple treasuries. Finally the people tire of him, and try to shake off his yoke. Too late they discover what a monster they have begotten and nourished. He lays his impious hands upon them, and forces them to pass into a slavery no less great than their former freedom.

Democracy and the Democratic Man.

The changes from one state to another which Plato describes in the Eighth Book, are not to be regarded as historical, nor ought they to

THE RISE OF DEMOCRACY

be treated in the dry and serious manner which Aristotle adopts in his criticism of the Republic (Pol. v. 12, § 8). Plato is giving us the reflections of a philosopher upon the course of Greek history: he is not analyzing its events in the scientific spirit of Thucydides or Polybius. And he casts the whole into the dramatic or concrete form which best suited his genius, when he sketches for us the pictures of the various individuals who represent the different principles of government. Not the least remarkable among these is the portrait of the Democratic Man. Plato was no friend to democracy in the shape which it assumed at Athens; nor could he do entire justice even to Pericles, the statesman who had been the friend and disciple of Zeno and Anaxagoras (Phaedr. 270 A), and who, as Thucydides tells us, ruled the city with uncontrolled power by his integrity and force of character (ii. 65). Neither did he remember that the faults of the Athenian people were to a large extent the typical defects of the Hellenic temperament, and could not properly be ascribed merely to political institutions.

Democracy in his eyes appeared to be the incorporation of the evil spirit of faction and strife which had brought ruin upon Hellas. The want of stability which he deplored was really inherent in the small and ill-balanced Hellenic communities, as it also was in the Italian Republics of the Middle Ages. And since he could not, like the great thinkers of Italy, turn for refuge to the Papacy or the Holy Roman Empire, he hoped by the creation of a fixed and immutable type, both in the citizen and in the State, to gain the steadiness and security which he so earnestly longed to obtain for his ideal commonwealth.

Socrates. Next comes democracy; of this the origin and nature have still to be considered by us; and then we will enquire into the ways of the democratic man, and bring him up for judgment. [Steph. 555 B]

Glaucon. That, he said, is our method.

Well, I said, and how does the change from oligarchy into democracy arise? Is it not on this wise? —The good at which such a State aims is to become as rich as possible, a desire which is insatiable?

What then?

The rulers, being aware that their power rests upon their wealth, refuse to curtail by law the extravagance of the spendthrift youth because they gain by their ruin; they take interest from them and buy up their estates and thus increase their own wealth and importance?

To be sure.

There can be no doubt that the love of wealth and the spirit of moderation cannot exist together in citizens of the same state to any considerable extent; one or the other will be disregarded.

That is tolerably clear.

And in oligarchical States, from the general spread of carelessness and extravagance, men of good family have often been reduced to beggary?

Yes, often.

And still they remain in the city; there they are, ready to sting and fully armed, and some of them owe money, some have forfeited their citizenship; a third class are in both predicaments; and they hate and conspire against those who have got their property, and against everybody else, and are eager for revolution.

That is true.

On the other hand, the men of business, stooping as they walk, and pretending not even to see those whom they have already ruined, insert their sting that is, their money—into some one else who is not on his guard against them, and recover the parent sum many times over multiplied into a family of children: and so they make drone and pauper to abound in the State.

Yes, he said, there are plenty of them—that is certain.

The evil blazes up like a fire; and they will not extinguish it, either by restricting a man's use of his own property, or by another remedy:

What other?

One which is the next best, and has the advantage of compelling the citizens to look to their characters:— Let there be a general rule that every one shall enter into voluntary contracts at his own risk, and there will be less of this scandalous money-making, and the evils of which we were speaking will be greatly lessened in the State.

Yes, they will be greatly lessened.

At present the governors, induced by the motives which I have named, treat their subjects badly; while they and their adherents, especially the young men of the governing class, are habituated to lead a life of luxury and idleness both of body and mind ; they do nothing, and are incapable of resisting either pleasure or pain.

Very true.

They themselves care only for making money, and are as indifferent as the pauper to the cultivation of virtue.

Yes, quite as indifferent.

Such is the state of affairs which prevails among them. And often rulers and their subjects may come in one another's way, whether on a journey or on some other occasion of meeting, on a pilgrimage or a march, as fellow-soldiers or fellow-sailors ; aye and they may observe the behaviour of each other in the very moment of danger—for where danger is, there is no fear that the poor will be despised by the rich—and very likely the wiry sunburnt poor man may be placed in battle at the side of a wealthy one who has never spoilt his complexion and has plenty of superfluous flesh—when he sees such an one puffing and at his wits'-end, how can he avoid drawing the conclusion that men like him are only rich because no one has the courage to despoil them ? And when they meet in private will not people be saying to one another ' Our warriors are not good for much' ?

Yes, he said, I am quite aware that this is their way of talking.

And, as in a body which is diseased the addition of

a touch from without may bring on illness, and sometimes even when there is no external provocation a commotion may arise within—in the same way wherever there is weakness in the State there is also likely to be illness, of which the occasion may be very slight, the one party introducing from without their oligarchical, the other their democratical allies, and then the State falls sick, and is at war with herself; and may be at times distracted, even when there is no external cause.

Yes, surely.

And then democracy comes into being after the poor have conquered their opponents, slaughtering some and banishing some, while to the remainder they give an equal share of freedom and power; and this is the form of government in which the magistrates are commonly elected by lot.

Yes, he said, that is the nature of democracy, whether the revolution has been effected by arms, or whether fear has caused the opposite party to withdraw.

And now what is their manner of life, and what sort of a government have they? for as the government is, such will be the man.

Clearly, he said.

In the first place, are they not free; and is not the city full of freedom and frankness—a man may say and do what he likes?

'Tis said so, he replied.

And where freedom is, the individual is clearly able to order for himself his own life as he pleases?

Clearly.

Then in this kind of State there will be the greatest variety of human natures?

There will.

This, then, seems likely to be the fairest of States, being like an embroidered robe which is spangled with every sort of flower[1]. And just as women and children think a variety of colours to be of all things most charming, so there are many men to whom this State, which is spangled with the manners and characters of mankind, will appear to be the fairest of States.

Yes.

Yes, my good Sir, and there will be no better in which to look for a government.

Why?

Because of the liberty which reigns there—they have a complete assortment of constitutions; and he who has a mind to establish a State, as we have been doing, must go to a democracy as he would to a bazaar at which they sell them, and pick out the one that suits him; then, when he has made his choice, he may found his State.

He will be sure to have patterns enough.

And there being no necessity, I said, for you to govern in this State, even if you have the capacity, or to be governed, unless you like, or to go to war when the rest go to war, or to be at peace when others are at peace, unless you are so disposed—there being no necessity also, because some law forbids you to hold office or be a dicast, that you should not hold office or be a dicast, if you have a fancy—is not this a way of life 558 which for the moment is supremely delightful?

For the moment, yes.

And is not their humanity to the condemned[2] in some cases quite charming? Have you not observed how, in a democracy, many persons, although they have been sentenced to death or exile, just stay where they are and walk about the world—the gentleman parades like a hero, and nobody sees or cares?

[1] Omitting τί μήν; ἔφη.
[2] Or, 'the philosophical temper of the condemned.'

Yes, he replied, many and many a one.

See too, I said, the forgiving spirit of democracy, and the 'don't care' about trifles, and the disregard which she shows of all the fine principles which we solemnly laid down at the foundation of the city—as when we said that, except in the case of some rarely gifted nature, there never will be a good man who has not from his childhood been used to play amid things of beauty and make of them a joy and a study—how grandly does she trample all these fine notions of ours under her feet, never giving a thought to the pursuits which make a statesman, and promoting to honour any one who professes to be the people's friend.

Yes, she is of a noble spirit.

These and other kindred characteristics are proper to democracy, which is a charming form of government, full of variety and disorder, and dispensing a sort of equality to equals and unequals alike.

We know her well.

Consider now, I said, what manner of man the individual is, or rather consider, as in the case of the State, how he comes into being.

Very good, he said.

Is not this the way—he is the son of the miserly and oligarchical father who has trained him in his own habits?

Exactly.

And, like his father, he keeps under by force the pleasures which are of the spending and not of the getting sort, being those which are called unnecessary?

Obviously.

Would you like, for the sake of clearness, to distinguish which are the necessary and which are the unnecessary pleasures?

I should.

Are not necessary pleasures those of which we cannot get rid, and of which the satisfaction is a benefit to us? And they are rightly called so, because we are framed by nature to desire both what is beneficial and what is necessary, and cannot help it.

True. 559

We are not wrong therefore in calling them necessary?

We are not.

And the desires of which a man may get rid, if he takes pains from his youth upwards—of which the presence, moreover, does no good, and in some cases the reverse of good—shall we not be right in saying that all these are unnecessary?

Yes, certainly.

Suppose we select an example of either kind, in order that we may have a general notion of them?

Very good

Will not the desire of eating, that is, of simple food and condiments, in so far as they are required for health and strength, be of the necessary class?

That is what I should suppose.

The pleasure of eating is necessary in two ways; it does us good and it is essential to the continuance of life?

Yes.

But the condiments are only necessary in so far as they are good for health?

Certainly.

And the desire which goes beyond this, of more delicate food, or other luxuries, which might generally be got rid of, if controlled and trained in youth, and is hurtful to the body, and hurtful to the soul in the pursuit of wisdom and virtue, may be rightly called unnecessary?

Very true.

May we not say that these desires spend, and that the others make money because they conduce to production?

Certainly.

And of the pleasures of love, and all other pleasures, the same holds good?

True.

And the drone of whom we spoke was he who was surfeited in pleasures and desires of this sort, and was the slave of the unnecessary desires, whereas he who was subject to the necessary only was miserly and oligarchical?

Very true.

Again, let us see how the democratical man grows out of the oligarchical: the following, as I suspect, is commonly the process.

What is the process?

When a young man who has been brought up as we were just now describing, in a vulgar and miserly way, has tasted drones' honey and has come to associate with fierce and crafty natures who are able to provide for him all sorts of refinements and varieties of pleasure —then, as you may imagine, the change will begin of the oligarchical principle within him into the democratical?

Inevitably.

And as in the city like was helping like, and the change was effected by an alliance from without assisting one division of the citizens, so too the young man is changed by a class of desires coming from without to assist the desires within him, that which is akin and alike again helping that which is akin and alike?

Certainly.

And if there be any ally which aids the oligarchical principle within him, whether the influence of a father or of kindred, advising or rebuking him, then there arises in his soul a faction and an opposite faction, and he goes to war with himself.

It must be so.

And there are times when the democratical principle gives way to the oligarchical, and some of his desires die, and others are banished; a spirit of reverence enters into the young man's soul and order is restored.

Yes, he said, that sometimes happens.

And then, again, after the old desires have been driven out, fresh ones spring up, which are akin to them, and because he their father does not know how to educate them, wax fierce and numerous.

Yes, he said, that is apt to be the way.

They draw him to his old associates, and holding secret intercourse with them, breed and multiply in him.

Very true.

At length they seize upon the citadel of the young man's soul, which they perceive to be void of all accomplishments and fair pursuits and true words, which make their abode in the minds of men who are dear to the gods, and are their best guardians and sentinels.

None better.

False and boastful conceits and phrases mount upwards and take their place.

They are certain to do so.

And so the young man returns into the country of the lotus-eaters, and takes up his dwelling there in the face of all men; and if any help be sent by his friends to the oligarchical part of him, the aforesaid vain conceits shut the gate of the king's fastness; and they will neither allow the embassy itself to enter, nor if private advisers offer the fatherly counsel of the aged will they listen to them or receive them. There is a battle and they gain the day, and then modesty, which they call silliness, is ignominiously thrust into exile by them, and temperance, which they nickname unmanliness, is trampled in the mire and cast forth; they persuade men that moderation and orderly expenditure are vulgarity and meanness, and so, by the help of a rabble of evil appetites, they drive them beyond the border.

Yes, with a will.

And when they have emptied and swept clean the soul of him who is now in their power and who is being initiated by them in great mysteries, the next thing is to bring back to their house insolence and anarchy and waste and impudence in bright array having garlands on their heads, and a great company with them, hymning their praises and calling them by sweet names; insolence they term breeding, and anarchy liberty, and waste magnificence, and impudence courage. And so the young man passes out of his original nature, which was trained in the school of necessity, into the freedom and libertinism of useless and unnecessary pleasures.

Yes, he said, the change in him is visible enough.

After this he lives on, spending his money and labour and time on unnecessary pleasures quite as much as on necessary ones; but if he be fortunate, and is not too much disordered in his wits, when years have elapsed, and the heyday of passion is over—supposing that he then re-admits into the city some part of the exiled virtues, and does not wholly give himself up to their successors—in that case he balances his pleasures and lives in a sort of equilibrium, putting the government of himself into the hands of the one which comes first and wins the turn ; and when he has had enough of that, then into the hands of another; he despises none of them but encourages them all equally.

Very true, he said.

Neither does he receive or let pass into the fortress any true word of advice; if any one says to him that some pleasures are the satisfactions of good and noble desires, and others of evil desires, and that he ought to use and honour some and chastise and master the others —whenever this is repeated to him he shakes his head and says that they are all alike, and that one is as good as another.

Yes, he said; that is the way with him.

Yes, I said, he lives from day to day indulging the appetite of the hour; and sometimes he is lapped in drink and strains of the flute; then he becomes a water-drinker, and tries to get thin; then he takes a turn at gymnastics; sometimes idling and neglecting everything, then once more living the life of a philosopher; often he is busy with politics, and starts to his feet and says and does whatever comes into his head; and, if he is emulous of any one who is a warrior, off he is in that direction, or of men of business, once more in that. His life has neither law nor order; and this distracted existence he terms joy and bliss and freedom; and so he goes on.

Yes, he replied, he is all liberty and equality.

Yes, I said; his life is motley and manifold and an epitome of the lives of many;—he answers to the State which we described as fair and spangled. And many a man and many a woman will take him for their pattern, and many a constitution and many an example of manners is contained in him.

Just so.

Let him then be set over against democracy; he may 562 truly be called the democratic man.

BOOK IX.

The Ninth Book commences with a digression on the 'wild-beast nature' which exists to some degree in every one, and takes entire possession of the tyrant... The growth of the tyrannical man is thus related :—The democrat has a son who, like his father before him, is led astray by evil counsellors. These implant in his soul a monstrous passion, 'a drone,' which overpowers all remains of good. His wants continuing to increase, he first robs his father and mother, and then turns temple-robber or highwayman. Soon he gathers round him a band of associates, and finally he makes himself tyrant.

And how does our city which was under a king[1] compare with a city which is ruled by a tyrant? One is the best, the other the worst, of governments. For the city which is subject to a tyrant is full of wretchedness, and the tyrannical man is unhappy in scarcely less degree. But his misery culminates when he becomes a public tyrant; he resembles a slave-owner who fears that his slaves will set upon him. His life is an endless struggle; he cannot leave the city, as other men do, and see the world. His wants are insatiable; he is obliged to flatter the vilest among mankind; power corrupts him, and he grows ever worse and worse.

And what of the pleasure which just and unjust respectively enjoy? There are three kinds of pleasures corresponding to the three principles of the soul. The object of the appetitive element is gain; of 'passion,' fame; of reason, knowledge : and thus arise three classes of men,—lovers of gain, of honour, of wisdom. Each class despises the pleasures which the others seek; the philosopher alone can judge because he has tried and rejected the lower pleasures, whereas the covetous and ambitious know nothing of the higher pleasures. And the philosopher places first the love of knowledge; second, of honour; third, of gain.

Twice has the just overthrown the unjust ; now comes a third test. Which of them has pure and true pleasure? Pleasure and pain are relative, not opposed, to each other. There is in nature a gradation from the lower to the higher, and he who ascends to the middle, fancies that he has reached the top, and, if he were taken back again, would suppose that he was descending. A similar confusion exists about pleasure and pain. Further, hunger and thirst are inanitions of the body, and ignorance is an inanition of the soul; the one is satisfied by food or drink, the other by knowledge. And since the soul has more of existence and truth than the body, she has also

---

[1] i.e. the best state, in which the perfectly just man bears rule.

a truer and more real satisfaction. The vulgar herd fight for the shadows of pleasure; they go up and down between the lower and middle regions, but never ascend to the upper world. The pleasure of the tyrant is farthest from law; that of the king nearest to it. For the tyrant is the third removed from the oligarch, and has only the shadow of a shadow of pleasure. The oligarch, again, is thrice removed from the king; and thus we obtain a number, which, if we raise the power and make the plane a solid, fairly expresses the difference between the king and the tyrant in respect of pleasure ($3 \times 3 = 9 : 9^3 = 729$).

And now we may return to the assertion [of Thrasymachus] that injustice is profitable. Let us suppose a composite figure ;—a many-headed beast, a lion, and a man, combined in a single human form. The supporter of injustice fosters the beasts and weakens the man; the lover of justice unites the higher elements in resistance to the lower nature.

The allegory shows that the just man has the advantage over the unjust. He who sells his soul for gain is guilty of a worse crime than Eriphylè, who bartered her husband's life for a necklace. And we blame those who suffer the brute to predominate within them, or who pursue ignoble occupations which degrade the soul. Every one should allow the Divine to rule, or else submit to some external authority; nor do we give children freedom of control until the higher principles are established in their souls. He who is wise profits by correction : he is moderate in his pleasures and desires, and only accepts such honours as will not interfere with the pursuit of virtue. No city on earth, perhaps, is worthy of him; but there is a pattern laid up in heaven, by which he will guide his steps through life.

1. The Many-headed Monster.

'The war against ourselves which goes on within every one of us' (Laws i. 626 E) is here described by Plato in a figure. The soul is compared to a creature with many heads (the appetites), combined with a lion (passion), and a man (reason) under a human form. The unjust cherishes the monster or the lion at the expense of the man; the just makes the man and the lion allies against the monster.

The fertile fancy of Plato revels in such metaphors:—the thought which underlies them is the same, ' that the soul is next to the gods in honour, . . . and is always to be preferred to the body' (Laws v. 726, 727). They are analogous to the parables of the Gospels. Like them they present in a vivid and dramatic form the chief points of the previous discussion or discourse. They belong to an age of oral teaching, when the master walked and talked with his disciples in the groves of the Academy, or under the colonnades of the Lyceum.

They may also be regarded as a 'late-born growth' of the mythopoeic tendency which was so deeply engrained in the Hellenic character, and which made the Passions and Feelings of Man and the Powers of Nature alike into living beings. This mythical or poetical element is already superseded by the 'dry light' of science in the works of Aristotle and his school, and is ill replaced by the rhetorical airs and graces of succeeding writers.

Steph
588
A

Socrates. Well, I said, and now having arrived at this stage of the argument, we may revert to the words which brought us hither: Was not some one saying that injustice was a gain to the perfectly unjust who was reputed to be just?

Glaucon. Yes, that was said.

Now then, having determined the power and quality of justice and injustice, let us have a little conversation with him.

What shall we say to him?

Let us make an image of the soul, that he may have his own words presented before his eyes.

Of what sort?

An ideal image of the soul, like the composite creations of ancient mythology, such as the Chimera or Scylla or Cerberus, and there are many others in which two or more different natures are said to grow into one.

There are said to have been such unions.

Then do you now model the form of a multitudinous, many-headed monster, having a ring of heads of all manner of beasts, tame and wild, which he is able to generate and metamorphose at will.

You suppose marvellous powers in the artist; but, as language is more pliable than wax or any similar substance, let there be such a model as you propose.

Suppose now that you make a second form as of a lion and a third of a man, the second smaller than the first, and the third smaller than the second.

That, he said, is an easier task; and I have made them as you say.

And now join them, and let the three grow into one.

That has been accomplished.

Next fashion the outside of them into a single image, as of a man, so that he who is not able to look within, and sees only the outer hull, may believe the beast to be a single human creature.

I have done so, he said.

And now, to him who maintains that it is profitable for the human creature to be unjust, and unprofitable to be just, let us reply that, if he be right, it is profitable for this creature to feast the multitudinous monster and strengthen the lion and the lion-like qualities, but to starve and weaken the man, who is consequently liable to be dragged about at the mercy of either of the other two; and he is not to attempt to familiarize or harmonize them with one another—he ought rather to suffer them to fight and bite and devour one another.

Certainly, he said; that is what the approver of injustice says.

To him the supporter of justice makes answer that he should ever so speak and act as to give the man within him in some way or other the most complete mastery over the entire human creature. He should watch over the many-headed monster like a good husbandman, fostering and cultivating the gentle qualities, and preventing the wild ones from growing; he should be making the lion-heart his ally, and in common care of them all should be uniting the several parts with one another and with himself.

Yes, he said, that is quite what the maintainer of justice will say.

And so from every point of view, whether of pleasure, honour. or advantage, the approver of justice is right and speaks the truth, and the disapprover is wrong and false and ignorant?

Yes, from every point of view.

Come, now, and let us gently reason with the unjust, who is not intentionally in error. 'Sweet Sir,' we will say to him, 'what think you of things esteemed noble and ignoble? Is not the noble that which subjects the beast to the man, or rather to the god in man; and the ignoble that which subjects the man to the beast?' He can hardly avoid saying Yes—can he now?

Not if he has any regard for my opinion.

But, if he agree so far, we may ask him to answer another question: 'Then how would a man profit if he received gold and silver on the condition that he was to enslave the noblest part of him to the worst? Who can imagine that a man who sold his son or daughter into slavery for money, especially if he sold them into the hands of fierce and evil men, would be the gainer, however large might be the sum which he received? And will any one say that he is not a miserable caitiff who remorselessly sells his own divine being to that which is most godless and detestable? Eriphylè took the necklace as the price of her husband's life, but he is taking a bribe in order to compass a worse ruin.'

Yes, said Glaucon, far worse—I will answer for him.

Has not the intemperate been censured of old, because in him the huge multiform monster is allowed to be too much at large?

Clearly.

And men are blamed for pride and bad temper when the lion and serpent element in them disproportionately grows and gains strength?

Yes.

And luxury and softness are blamed, because they

relax and weaken this same creature, and make a coward of him?

Very true.

And is not a man reproached for flattery and meanness who subordinates the spirited animal to the unruly monster, and, for the sake of money, of which he can never have enough, habituates him in the days of his youth to be trampled in the mire, and from being a lion to become a monkey?

True, he said.

And why are mean employments and manual arts a reproach? Only because they imply a natural weakness of the higher principle; the individual is unable to control the creatures within him, but has to court them, and his great study is how to flatter them.

Such appears to be the reason.

And therefore, being desirous of placing him under a rule like that of the best, we say that he ought to be the servant of the best, in whom the Divine rules; not, as Thrasymachus supposed, to the injury of the servant, but because every one had better be ruled by divine wisdom dwelling within him; or, if this be impossible, then by an external authority, in order that we may be all, as far as possible, under the same government, friends and equals.

True, he said.

And this is clearly seen to be the intention of the law, which is the ally of the whole city; and is seen also in the authority which we exercise over children, and the refusal to let them be free until we have established in them a principle analogous to the constitution of a state, and by cultivation of this higher element have set up in their hearts a guardian and ruler like our own, and when this is done they may go their ways.

Yes, he said, the purpose of the law is manifest.

2. The City of which the Pattern is laid up in Heaven.

Plato finishes this part of the work by a new intimation that he does not expect to see his ideal state play a part in actual life. The just man, we hear with some surprise, will not be a statesman in any city which exists upon earth; he will be a citizen of another and a better country, whose laws he will observe, wherever his lot may be cast.

The commonwealth of the Republic is, therefore, not the idle fabric of a poet's dream, like the 'Cloud-Cuckoo Town' with the creation of which Aristophanes diverts himself in his comedy of the 'Birds.' The play of fancy only thinly veils the earnestness with which Plato pursues his object. He wishes to analyze the ills from which the governments of his day were suffering, and to discover a remedy for them. But he despaired of the world: the influences of evil seemed beyond the power of human nature to resist. And he would have the just man find consolation by withdrawing within himself, and seeking guidance in the contemplation of a high and lofty ideal.

Steph.
591
A

Socrates. From what point of view, then, and on what ground can we say that a man is profited by injustice or intemperance or other baseness, which will make him a worse man, even though he acquire money or power by his wickedness?

Glaucon. From no point of view at all.

What shall he profit, if his injustice be undetected and unpunished? He who is undetected only gets worse, whereas he who is detected and punished has the brutal part of his nature silenced and humanized; the gentler element in him is liberated, and his whole soul is perfected and ennobled by the acquirement of justice and temperance and wisdom, more than the body ever is by receiving gifts of beauty, strength and health, in proportion as the soul is more honourable than the body.

Certainly, he said.

To this nobler purpose the man of understanding will devote the energies of his life. And in the first place, he will honour studies which impress these qualities on his soul, and will disregard others?

Clearly, he said.

In the next place, he will regulate his bodily habit and training, and so far will he be from yielding to brutal and irrational pleasures, that he will regard even health as quite a secondary matter; his first object will be not that he may be fair or strong or well, unless he is likely thereby to gain temperance, but he will always desire so to attemper the body as to preserve the harmony of the soul?

Certainly he will, if he has true music in him.

And in the acquisition of wealth there is a principle of order and harmony which he will also observe; he will not allow himself to be dazzled by the foolish applause of the world, and heap up riches to his own infinite harm?

Certainly not, he said.

He will look at the city which is within him, and take heed that no disorder occur in it, such as might arise either from superfluity or from want; and upon this principle he will regulate his property and gain or spend according to his means.

Very true.

And, for the same reason, he will gladly accept and enjoy such honours as he deems likely to make him a better man; but those, whether private or public, which are likely to disorder his life, he will avoid?

Then, if that is his motive, he will not be a statesman.

By the dog of Egypt, he will! in the city which is his own he certainly will, though in the land of his birth perhaps not, unless he have a divine call.

I understand; you mean that he will be a ruler in the city of which we are the founders, and which exists in idea only; for I do not believe that there is such an one anywhere on earth?

In heaven, I replied, there is laid up a pattern of it,

methinks, which he who desires may behold, and beholding, may set his own house in order[1]. But whether such an one exists, or ever will exist in fact, is no matter; for he will live after the manner of that city, having nothing to do with any other.

I think so, he said.

BOOK X.

The Tenth Book begins abruptly (1) with a resumption of the attack upon the poets; (2) passes on to a demonstration of the immortality of the soul; and finally (3) shows that the just enjoy happiness in this life, and are also rewarded in a future state.

(1) Poetry is an imitative art; and in order to judge of its effects upon the feelings, we must first discuss the nature of imitation in general. Let us start from the doctrine of universals. Of a bed or a table there is (a) the idea which is created by God; (b) the realization of the idea,—the actual bed or table; (c) the counterfeit of the concrete idea drawn by the painter, who, being only an imitator, is thrice removed from truth. He deceives children and simple persons into supposing that he knows everything because he can imitate everything; and the same may be said of the poet. To what city did Homer ever give laws? Was he a famous general or the inventor of any useful art? Assuredly not, or he would not have been left to spend his days as a wandering rhapsode. The poet is, in fact, a painter, who works with words, not with colours, and, like the painter, has no real knowledge of what he imitates.

Again, there are three arts which are concerned with all things,—the arts of making, of using, of imitating. The user has the knowledge given by experience; the maker trusts to the user's directions, and so he has belief; the imitator has neither knowledge nor belief. And imitation, which deals only with appearances, is the lower faculty of the soul; the higher element tests the contradictions of sense by the art of measure. In the case of poetry, the poet appeals to feeling and sentiment, bidding us yield to sorrow instead of seeking a cure for our griefs. He prefers to imitate the unstable and passionate temperament; the gravity and calmness of the good man has no charm to him.

---

[1] Or, 'take up his abode there.'

BOOK X

And there is a still heavier count in the indictment against him :—
We feel a natural sympathy with the misfortunes of a stage hero,
and we forget that we are insensibly weakening our own powers
of resistance to calamity; or we laugh at the unseemly jests of the
comedian, and too late find ourselves playing the comic poet at
home. The encomiasts of Homer may truly declare that he is the
greatest of poets; but he and his kin cannot be suffered in a well-
regulated commonwealth which sets reason above pleasure. Yet,
lest the Muse accuse us of harshness, let us assure her, that, although
we remember the immemorial quarrel between poetry and philosophy, we will receive her into the state, if her admirers can prove
that poetry is profitable as well as pleasant to mankind. Otherwise
we must turn a deaf ear to her enchantments, and manfully adhere
to the cause of truth.

(2) For what gain have we, if in the pursuit of power or riches
or under the influence of poetry, we neglect virtue and justice, above
all when we consider that the rewards of righteousness extend
beyond the brief span of human life to the whole of existence?
'What do you mean?' says Glaucon. Are you unaware that the
soul is immortal? 'Certainly, I am.' Come, then, and let us try
to prove that lofty theme. There is in everything a good and an
evil; the good preserves, the evil destroys; and that which is not
destroyed by its own inherent evil, cannot be destroyed by anything
else. The evil of the soul is injustice, which, we know, has not
the power of destroying her, and still less can she be harmed by
any physical evil. Thus we reach the conclusion that the soul is
immortal and indestructible; and therefore also the number of the
souls can neither increase nor diminish. But if we would see the
soul in her true nature, we must contemplate her with the eye of
reason, and reflect what she would become if she were stripped
of the ills which disfigure her while she remains in communion
with the body, and free to seek her kindred in the Eternal and
Divine.

(3) We have proved that justice is the good of the soul as she
truly is, and now we are in a position to return to our old argument,
and to affirm that justice has the goods both of this life and of that
which is to come. The just man is the friend of the Gods, who
will always have a care of him; whereas the unjust is like a runner,
who, after making a great display at first, comes in limping at the
end, disgraced and dishonoured. There is a story which will confirm
our words.—Er, the son of Armenius, was supposed to have been
slain in battle. He was already laid on the pyre when he returned
to his senses and related a vision which he had beheld. He had
seen, he said, the Judgment of Souls, their wanderings in Hades,

their choice of another existence and return to the world of light. And all his tale went to show that righteousness was the safeguard and preserver of the soul, and that the Gods love and reward virtue.

The Vision of Er.

None of the many stories with which Plato delights us is related with more grace and beauty than the myth which so fitly closes the Republic. The ideas which he wishes to convey are in the main those with which we have become acquainted in the myths of the Phaedo and the Gorgias (*cp.* vol. i. pp 151, 171). They may be conveniently summed up as follows:—The soul is immortal, and after she has been released by death has to give account of her deeds while in the body. The righteous go to the Isles of the Blest, the wicked depart into Tartarus. The happiness of the righteous is not eternal, and still less is the misery of the wicked everlasting (except in the case of a few great criminals); for the punishments of God are not vindictive, but are intended to correct and improve the offender. When a certain period has elapsed the souls of the good and of the bad meet together, in order to choose a new existence, either in the shape of a man or an animal. The responsibility is our own, and the choice once made is immutable.

Plato does not intend us to receive his words with implicit credence, or to form a system of dogma out of them. He is well aware, as he frequently intimates to us, that no man can expect to attain absolute truth about things of the highest import. But the moral of the tale remains, and can never lose its force by time or change of circumstance, that we must hold fast to virtue, both in this life and after death.

Steph.
614
B

WELL, I said, I will tell you a tale; not one of the tales which Odysseus tells to the hero Alcinous, yet this too is a tale of a hero, Er the son of Armenius, a Pamphylian by birth. He was slain in battle, and ten days afterwards, when the bodies of the dead were taken up already in a state of corruption, his body was found unaffected by decay, and carried away home to be buried. And on the twelfth day, as he was lying on the funeral pile, he returned to life and told them what he had seen in the other world.

He said that when his soul left the body he went on a journey with a great company, and that they came to a mysterious place at which there were two openings in the earth ; they were near together, and over against them were two other openings in the heaven above. In the intermediate space there were judges seated, who commanded the just, after they had given judgment on them and had bound their sentences in front of them, to ascend by the heavenly way on the right hand ; and in like manner the unjust were bidden by them to descend by the lower way on the left hand ; these also bore the symbols of their deeds, but fastened on their backs. He drew near, and they told him that he was to be the messenger who would carry the report of the other world to men, and they bade him hear and see all that was to be heard and seen in that place.

Then he beheld and saw on one side the souls departing at either opening of heaven and earth when sentence had been given on them ; and at the two other openings other souls, some ascending out of the earth dusty and worn with travel, some descending out of heaven clean and bright. And arriving ever and anon they seemed to have come from a long journey, and they went forth with gladness into the meadow, where they encamped as at a festival ; and those who knew one another embraced and conversed, the souls which came from earth curiously enquiring about the things above, and the souls which came from heaven about the things beneath. And they told one another of what had happened by the way, those from below weeping and sorrowing at the remembrance of the things which they had endured and seen in their journey beneath the earth (now the journey lasted a thousand years), while those from above were describing heavenly delights and visions of inconceivable beauty.

The story, Glaucon, would take too long to tell ; but the sum was this :—He said that for every wrong which they had done to any one they suffered tenfold; or once in a hundred years—such being reckoned to be the length of man's life, and the penalty being thus paid ten times in a thousand years. If, for example, there were any who had been the cause of many deaths, or had betrayed or enslaved cities or armies, or been guilty of any other evil behaviour, for each and all of their offences they received punishment ten times over, and the rewards of beneficence and justice and holiness were in the same proportion. I need hardly repeat what he said concerning young children dying almost as soon as they were born. Of piety and impiety to gods and parents, and of murderers[1], there were retributions other and greater far which he described.

He mentioned that he was present when one of the spirits asked another, 'Where is Ardiaeus the Great?' (Now this Ardiaeus lived a thousand years before the time of Er: he had been the tyrant of some city of Pamphylia, and had murdered his aged father and his elder brother, and was said to have committed many other abominable crimes.) The answer of the other spirit was: 'He comes not hither and will never come. And this,' said he, 'was one of the dreadful sights which we ourselves witnessed. We were at the mouth of the cavern, and, having completed all our experiences, were about to reascend, when of a sudden Ardiaeus appeared and several others, most of whom were tyrants; and there were also besides the tyrants private individuals who had been great criminals: they were just, as they fancied, about to return into the upper world, but the mouth, instead of admitting them, gave a roar, whenever any of these incurable sinners or some one who had not been sufficiently punished tried to ascend; and then wild men of fiery aspect, who were standing by

[1] Reading αὐτόχειρας.

and heard the sound, seized and carried them off; and
Ardiaeus and others they bound head and foot and 616
hand, and threw them down and flayed them with
scourges, and dragged them along the road at the
side, carding them on thorns like wool, and declaring
to the passers-by what were their crimes, and that[1]
they were being taken away to be cast into hell.' And
of all the many terrors which they had endured, he
said that there was none like the terror which each of
them felt at that moment, lest they should hear the
voice; and when there was silence, one by one they
ascended with exceeding joy. These, said Er, were
the penalties and retributions, and there were blessings
as great.

Now when the spirits which were in the meadow had
tarried seven days, on the eighth they were obliged to
proceed on their journey, and, on the fourth day after,
he said that they came to a place where they could see
from above a line of light, straight as a column, extending right through the whole heaven and through
the earth, in colour resembling the rainbow, only
brighter and purer; another day's journey brought them
to the place, and there, in the midst of the light, they
saw the ends of the chains of heaven let down from
above: for this light is the belt of heaven, and holds
together the circle of the universe, like the under-
girders of a trireme. From these ends is extended
the spindle of Necessity, on which all the revolutions
turn.

The shaft and hook of this spindle are made of steel,
and the whorl is made partly of steel and also partly
of other materials. Now the whorl is in form like
the whorl used on earth; and the description of it
implied that there is one large hollow whorl which is

[1] Reading καὶ ὅτι.

quite scooped out, and into this is fitted another lesser one, and another, and another, and four others, making eight in all, like vessels which fit into one another; the whorls show their edges on the upper side, and on their lower side all together form one continuous whorl. This is pierced by the spindle, which is driven home through the centre of the eighth. The first and outermost whorl has the rim broadest, and the seven inner whorls are narrower, in the following proportions—the sixth is next to the first in size, the fourth next to the sixth; then comes the eighth; the seventh is fifth, the fifth is sixth, the third is seventh, last and eighth comes the second. The largest [or fixed stars] is spangled, and the seventh [or sun] is brightest; the eighth [or moon] coloured by the reflected light of the seventh; the second and fifth [Saturn and Mercury] are in colour like one another, and yellower than the preceding; the third [Venus] has the whitest light; the fourth [Mars] is reddish; the sixth [Jupiter] is in whiteness second.

Now the whole spindle has the same motion; but, as the whole revolves in one direction, the seven inner circles move slowly in the other, and of these the swiftest is the eighth; next in swiftness are the seventh, sixth, and fifth, which move together; third in swiftness appeared to move according to the law of this reversed motion the fourth; the third appeared fourth and the second fifth. The spindle turns on the knees of Necessity; and on the upper surface of each circle is a siren, who goes round with them, hymning a single tone or note. The eight together form one harmony; and round about, at equal intervals, there is another band, three in number, each sitting upon her throne: these are the Fates, daughters of Necessity, who are clothed in white robes and have chaplets upon their heads, Lachesis and Clotho and Atropos, who accompany with their voices the harmony of the sirens—Lachesis singing of the past, Clotho of the present, Atropos of the future; Clotho from time to time assisting with a touch of her right hand the revolution of the outer circle of the whorl or spindle, and Atropos with her left hand touching and guiding the inner ones, and Lachesis laying hold of either in turn, first with one hand and then with the other.

When Er and the spirits arrived, their duty was to go at once to Lachesis; but first of all there came a prophet who arranged them in order; then he took from the knees of Lachesis lots and samples of lives, and having mounted a high pulpit, spoke as follows: 'Hear the word of Lachesis, the daughter of Necessity. Mortal souls, behold a new cycle of life and mortality. Your genius will not be allotted to you, but you will choose your genius; and let him who draws the first lot have the first choice, and the life which he chooses shall be his destiny. Virtue is free, and as a man honours or dishonours her he will have more or less of her; the responsibility is with the chooser—God is justified.'

When the Interpreter had thus spoken he scattered lots indifferently among them all, and each of them took up the lot which fell near him, all but Er himself (he was not allowed), and each as he took his lot perceived 618 the number which he had obtained. Then the Interpreter placed on the ground before them the samples of lives; and there were many more lives than the souls present, and they were of all sorts. There were lives of every animal and of man in every condition. And there were tyrannies among them, some lasting out the tyrant's life, others which broke off in the middle and came to an end in poverty and exile and beggary; and there were lives of famous men, some who were famous for their form and beauty as well as for their strength and success in games, or again, for their birth and the qualities of their ancestors; and some who were the reverse of famous for the opposite qualities. And of women likewise; there was not, however, any definite character in them, because the soul, when choosing a new life, must of necessity become different. But there was every other quality, and they all mingled with one another, and also with elements of wealth and poverty, and disease and health; and there were mean states also.

And here, my dear Glaucon, is the supreme peril of our human state; and therefore the utmost care should be taken. Let each one of us leave every other kind of knowledge and seek and follow one thing only, if peradventure he may be able to learn and may find some one who will make him able to learn and discern between good and evil, and so to choose always and everywhere the better life as he has opportunity. He should consider the bearing of all these things which have been mentioned severally and collectively upon virtue; he should know what the effect of beauty is when combined with poverty or wealth in a particular soul, and what are the good and evil consequences of noble and humble birth, of private and public station, of strength and weakness, of cleverness and dullness, and of all the natural and acquired gifts of the soul, and the operation of them when conjoined; he will then look at the nature of the soul, and from the consideration of all these qualities he will be able to determine which is the better and which is the worse; and so he will choose, giving the name of evil to the life which will make his soul more unjust, and good to the life which will make his soul more just; all else he will disregard. For we have seen and know that this is the best choice both in life and after death.

A man must take with him into the world below an 619
adamantine faith in truth and right, that there too he
may be undazzled by the desire of wealth or the other
allurements of evil, lest, coming upon tyrannies and
similar villanies, he do irremediable wrongs to others
and suffer yet worse himself; but let him know how
to choose the mean and avoid the extremes on either
side, as far as possible, not only in this life but in
all that which is to come. For this is the way of
happiness.

And according to the report of the messenger from
the other world this was what the prophet said at
the time: 'Even for the last comer, if he chooses
wisely and will live diligently, there is appointed a
happy and not undesirable existence. Let not him
who chooses first be careless, and let not the last
despair.' And when he had spoken, he who had the
first choice came forward and in a moment chose the
greatest tyranny; his mind having been darkened by
folly and sensuality, he had not thought out the whole
matter before he chose, and did not at first sight
perceive that he was fated, among other evils, to devour
his own children. But when he had time to reflect,
and saw what was in the lot, he began to beat his
breast and lament over his choice, forgetting the pro-
clamation of the prophet; for, instead of throwing
the blame of his misfortune on himself, he accused
chance and the gods, and everything rather than
himself.

Now he was one of those who came from heaven,
and in a former life had dwelt in a well-ordered State,
but his virtue was a matter of habit only, and he had
no philosophy. And it was true of others who were
similarly overtaken, that the greater number of them
came from heaven and therefore they had never been

schooled by trial, whereas the pilgrims who came from earth, having themselves suffered and seen others suffer, were not in a hurry to choose. And owing to this inexperience of theirs, and also because the lot was a chance, many of the souls exchanged a good destiny for an evil or an evil for a good. For if a man had always on his arrival in this world dedicated himself from the first to sound philosophy, and had been moderately fortunate in the number of the lot, he might, as the messenger reported, be happy here, and also his journey to another life and return to this, instead of being rough and underground, would be smooth and heavenly.

Most curious, he said, was the spectacle—sad and laughable and strange; for the choice of the souls was in most cases based on their experience of a previous life. There he saw the soul which had once been Orpheus choosing the life of a swan out of enmity to the race of women, hating to be born of a woman because they had been his murderers; he beheld also the soul of Thamyras choosing the life of a nightingale; birds, on the other hand, like the swan and other musicians, wanting to be men. The soul which obtained the twentieth[1] lot chose the life of a lion, and this was the soul of Ajax the son of Telamon, who would not be a man, remembering the injustice which was done him in the judgment about the arms. The next was Agamemnon, who took the life of an eagle, because, like Ajax, he hated human nature by reason of his sufferings. About the middle came the lot of Atalanta; she, seeing the great fame of an athlete, was unable to resist the temptation: and after her there followed the soul of Epeus the son of Panopeus passing into the nature of a woman cunning in the arts; and

[1] Reading εἰκοστήν.

far away among the last who chose, the soul of the
jester Thersites was putting on the form of a monkey.
There came also the soul of Odysseus having yet
to make a choice, and his lot happened to be the last
of them all. Now the recollection of former toils had
disenchanted him of ambition, and he went about for
a considerable time in search of the life of a private
man who had no cares; he had some difficulty in
finding this, which was lying about and had been
neglected by everybody else; and when he saw it,
he said that he would have done the same had his lot
been first instead of last, and that he was delighted
to have it. And not only did men pass into animals,
but I must also mention that there were animals tame
and wild who changed into one another and into corresponding human natures—the good into the gentle
and the evil into the savage, in all sorts of com-
binations.

All the souls had now chosen their lives, and they
went in the order of their choice to Lachesis, who sent
with them the genius whom they had severally chosen,
to be the guardian of their lives and the fulfiller of the
choice: this genius led the souls first to Clotho, and
drew them within the revolution of the spindle impelled
by her hand, thus ratifying the destiny of each; and
then, when they were fastened to this, carried them
to Atropos, who spun the threads and made them
irreversible, whence without turning round they passed 621
beneath the throne of Necessity; and when they had
all passed, they marched on in a scorching heat to the
plain of Forgetfulness, which was a barren waste
destitute of trees and verdure; and then towards
evening they encamped by the river of Unmindfulness,
whose water no vessel can hold; of this they were
all obliged to drink a certain quantity, and those who

were not saved by wisdom drank more than was necessary; and each one as he drank forgot all things. Now after they had gone to rest, about the middle of the night there was a thunderstorm and earthquake, and then in an instant they were driven upwards in all manner of ways to their birth, like stars shooting. He himself was hindered from drinking the water. But in what manner or by what means he returned to the body he could not say; only, in the morning, awaking suddenly, he found himself lying on the pyre.

And thus, Glaucon, the tale has been saved and has not perished, and will save us if we are obedient to the word spoken; and we shall pass safely over the river of Forgetfulness and our soul will not be defiled. Wherefore my counsel is, that we hold fast ever to the heavenly way and follow after justice and virtue always, considering that the soul is immortal and able to endure every sort of good and every sort of evil. Thus shall we live dear to one another and to the gods, both while remaining here and when, like conquerors in the games who go round to gather gifts, we receive our reward. And it shall be well with us both in this life and in the pilgrimage of a thousand years which we have been describing.

TIMAEUS.

1. The Tale of Solon.

The Timaeus is connected by Plato himself with the Republic and the Critias. Socrates is supposed to have recounted on the following day the conversation recorded in the Republic to a circle of friends who have promised to deliver in turn a discourse upon some philosophical topic. The persons named are Timaeus, a citizen of Locri in Italy, Hermocrates, probably the famous Syracusan general, and Critias, the Athenian, who has previously appeared in the Charmides and Protagoras. A fifth member of the group, whose name is not mentioned, is said to have been absent through illness.

We hear nothing of any other auditors, and we miss the dramatic or artistic setting which enhances the effect of the earlier Platonic writings. In these respects the Timaeus seems akin to the Sophist and the Statesman, which it also resembles in the circumstance that Socrates is no longer the chief speaker, but a stranger who has come on a visit to Athens. Here Timaeus is the protagonist, no doubt because, as a native of Southern Italy, he could fitly expound a theory of the Cosmos which was to a considerable extent based upon Pythagorean ideas. His task is to explain how the world came into being, and how man and the animals were created. Before, however, Timaeus commences his speech, Critias relates in outline a story which he proposes to take for his theme on the morrow.

This is the famous legend of Atlantis, the great island which once existed in the Atlantic and afterwards sank beneath the waves. The tale has exercised a curious power of attraction over the imagination, which has lasted almost to our own time: the site of Atlantis has been gravely debated by learned writers, and has formed the subject of many treatises. Yet the story is probably only the birth of Plato's prolific fancy, or rests at most upon a vague tradition of a land beyond the Atlantic which had reached Athens from the Western Mediterranean. For it is not unreasonable to suppose that the nations who lived upon the verge of the great ocean may have dreamed of a 'New World' on the other side, which their fancy would paint in bright and alluring colours as the seat of an ancient and primitive civilization. And it is even possible that the adventurous Phoenicians may have gained a knowledge of one or more of the Atlantic islands which would gradually come to the ears of the Greek sailors and merchants.

However this may be, the object of Plato in narrating the legend is clearly enough indicated by him. He wishes to picture, as he himself says, 'the ideal state engaged in a conflict with her neighbours, and showing by her actions and the magnanimity of her words a result worthy of her training' (19 C). He invents, therefore, an imaginary Athenian commonwealth which is supposed to have existed many centuries ago, and to have waged a victorious war with the people of Atlantis. This is at the same time an allegory or another version of the unceasing struggle between the Hellenes and the Barbarian, which so greatly occupied the Greek mind; and Plato's use of the legend may be compared to the manner in which Herodotus turns the ancient myths into a prelude of the Persian War.

Atlantis is the typical Barbarian power, like Babylon or Egypt, full of luxury and vain pomp and glory; while Athens is the Hellenic state, 'endowed with slender means,' but strong in the virtue and patriotism of its citizens. The conflict is unequal; yet the issue is not doubtful. Hellenic valour and discipline prevail, as they did when the Athenians and their allies triumphed over the unwieldy hosts of Persia on the plains of Marathon, or when Xenophon led the Ten Thousand through the heart of the Persian empire to the shores of the Pontus.

Steph.
20
E.
Critias. Then listen, Socrates, to a tale which, though strange, is certainly true, having been attested by Solon, who was the wisest of the seven sages. He was a relative and a dear friend of my great-grandfather, Dropides, as he himself says in many passages of his poems; and he told the story to Critias, my grandfather, who remembered and repeated it to us. There were of old, he said, great and marvellous actions of the Athenian city, which have passed into oblivion through lapse of time and the destruction of mankind, and one in
21 particular, greater than all the rest. This we will now rehearse. It will be a fitting monument of our gratitude to you, and a hymn of praise true and worthy of the goddess, on this her day of festival.

Socrates. Very good. And what is this ancient famous action of the Athenians, [1]which Critias declared, on the authority of Solon, to be not a mere legend, but an actual fact[1]?

Crit. I will tell an old-world story which I heard from an aged man; for Critias, at the time of telling it, was, as he said, nearly ninety years of age, and I was about ten. Now the day was that day of the Apaturia which is called the Registration of Youth, at which, according to custom, our parents gave prizes for recitations, and

---

[1] Or 'which, though unrecorded in history, Critias declared, on the authority of Solon, to be an actual fact?'

the poems of several poets were recited by us boys, and many of us sang the poems of Solon, which at that time had not gone out of fashion. One of our tribe, either because he thought so or to please Critias, said that in his judgment Solon was not only the wisest of men, but also the noblest of poets. The old man, as I very well remember, brightened up at hearing this and said, smiling: Yes, Amynander, if Solon had only, like other poets, made poetry the business of his life, and had completed the tale which he brought with him from Egypt, and had not been compelled, by reason of the factions and troubles which he found stirring in his own country when he came home, to attend to other matters, in my opinion he would have been as famous as Homer or Hesiod, or any poet.

And what was the tale about, Critias? said Amynander.

About the greatest action which the Athenians ever did, and which ought to have been the most famous, but, through the lapse of time and the destruction of the actors, it has not come down to us.

Tell us, said the other, the whole story, and how and from whom Solon heard this veritable tradition.

He replied:—In the Egyptian Delta, at the head of which the river Nile divides, there is a certain district which is called the district of Sais, and the great city of the district is also called Sais, and is the city from which King Amasis came. The citizens have a deity for their foundress; she is called in the Egyptian tongue Neith, and is asserted by them to be the same whom the Hellenes call Athenè; they are great lovers of the Athenians, and say that they are in some way related to them.

To this city came Solon, and was received there with great honour; he asked the priests who were most skilful in such matters, about antiquity, and made the discovery that neither he nor any other Hellene knew anything worth mentioning about the times of old. On one occasion, wishing to draw them on to speak of antiquity, he began to tell about the most ancient things in our part of the world—about Phoroneus, who is called 'the first man,' and about Niobè; and after the Deluge, of the survival of Deucalion and Pyrrha; and he traced the genealogy of their descendants, and reckoning up the dates, tried to compute how many years ago the events of which he was speaking happened. Thereupon one of the priests, who was of a very great age, said: O Solon, Solon, you Hellenes are never anything but children, and there is not an old man among you. Solon in return asked him what he meant.

I mean to say, he replied, that in mind you are all young; there is no old opinion handed down among you by ancient tradition, nor any science which is hoary with age. And I will tell you why. There have been, and will be again, many destructions of mankind arising out of many causes; the greatest have been brought about by the agencies of fire and water, and other lesser ones by innumerable other causes. There is a story, which even you have preserved, that once upon a time Phaëthon, the son of Helios, having yoked the steeds in his father's chariot, because he was not able to drive them in the path of his father, burnt up all that was upon the earth, and was himself destroyed by a thunderbolt. Now this has the form of a myth, but really signifies a declination of the bodies moving in the heavens around the earth, and a great conflagration of things upon the earth, which recurs after long intervals; at such times those who live upon the mountains and in dry and lofty places are more liable to destruction than those who dwell by rivers or on the seashore.

And from this calamity the Nile, who is our neverfailing saviour, delivers and preserves us.

When, on the other hand, the gods purge the earth with a deluge of water, the survivors in your country are herdsmen and shepherds who dwell on the mountains, but those who, like you, live in cities are carried by the rivers into the sea. Whereas in this land, neither then nor at any other time, does the water come down from above on the fields, having always a tendency to come up from below; for which reason the traditions preserved here are the most ancient. The fact is, that wherever the extremity of winter frost or of summer sun does not prevent, mankind exist, sometimes in greater, sometimes in lesser numbers. And whatever happened either in your country or in ours, or in any other region of which we are informed—if there were any actions noble or great or in any other way remarkable, they have all been written down by us of old, and are preserved in our temples. Whereas just when you and other nations are beginning to be provided with letters and the other requisites of civilized life, after the usual interval, the stream from heaven, like a pestilence, comes pouring down, and leaves only those of you who are destitute of letters and education; and so you have to begin all over again like children, and know nothing of what happened in ancient times, either among us or among yourselves.

As for those genealogies of yours which you just now recounted to us, Solon, they are no better than the tales of children. In the first place, you remember a single deluge only, but there were many previous ones; in the next place, you do not know that there formerly dwelt in your land the fairest and noblest race of men which ever lived, and that you and your whole city are descended from a small seed or remnant of them which survived. And this was unknown to you, because, for many generations, the survivors of that destruction died, leaving no written word. For there was a time, Solon, before the great deluge of all, when the city which now is Athens was first in war and in every way the best governed of all cities, and is said to have performed the noblest deeds and to have had the fairest constitution of any of which tradition tells, under the face of heaven. Solon marvelled at his words, and earnestly requested the priests to inform him exactly and in order about these former citizens.

You are welcome to hear about them, Solon, said the priest, both for your own sake and for that of your city, and above all, for the sake of the goddess who is the common patron and parent and educator of both our cities. She founded your city a thousand years before ours[1], receiving from the Earth and Hephaestus the seed of your race, and afterwards she founded ours, of which the constitution is recorded in our sacred registers to be 8000 years old. As touching your citizens of 9000 years ago, I will briefly inform you of their laws and of their most famous action; the exact particulars of the whole we will hereafter go through at our leisure in the sacred registers themselves. If you compare these very laws with ours you will find that many of ours are the counterpart of yours as they were in the olden time. In the first place, there is the caste of priests, which is separated from all the others; next, there are the artificers, who ply their several crafts by themselves and do not intermix; and also there is the class of shepherds and of hunters[2], as well as that of

---

[1] Observe that Plato gives the same date (9000 years ago) for the foundation of Athens and for the repulse of the invasion from Atlantis. (Crit. 108 E.)

[2] Reading τὸ τῶν θηρευτῶν.

husbandmen; and you will observe, too, that the warriors in Egypt are distinct from all the other classes, and are commanded by the law to devote themselves solely to military pursuits; moreover, the weapons which they carry are shields and spears, a style of equipment which the goddess taught of Asiatics first to us, as in your part of the world first to you. Then as to wisdom, do you observe how our law from the very first made a study of the whole order of things, extending even to prophecy and medicine which gives health; out of these divine elements deriving what was needful for human life, and adding every sort of knowledge which was akin to them.

All this order and arrangement the goddess first imparted to you when establishing your city; and she chose the spot of earth in which you were born, because she saw that the happy temperament of the seasons in that land would produce the wisest of men. Wherefore the goddess, who was a lover both of war and of wisdom, selected and first of all settled that spot which was the most likely to produce men likest herself. And there you dwelt, having such laws as these and still better ones, and excelled all mankind in all virtue, as became the children and disciples of the gods.

Many great and wonderful deeds are recorded of your state in our histories. But one of them exceeds all the rest in greatness and valour. For these histories tell of a mighty power which unprovoked made an expedition against the whole of Europe and Asia, and to which your city put an end. This power came forth out of the Atlantic Ocean, for in those days the Atlantic was navigable; and there was an island situated in front of the straits which are by you called the pillars of Heracles; the island was larger than Libya and Asia put together, and was the way to other islands, and from these you might pass to the whole of the opposite continent which surrounded the true ocean; for this sea which is within the Straits of Heracles is only a harbour, having a narrow entrance, but that other is a real sea, and the surrounding land may be most truly called a boundless continent.

Now in this island of Atlantis there was a great and wonderful empire which had rule over the whole island and several others, and over parts of the continent, and, furthermore, the men of Atlantis had subjected the parts of Libya within the columns of Heracles as far as Egypt, and of Europe as far as Tyrrhenia. This vast power, gathered into one, endeavoured to subdue at a blow our country and yours and the whole of the region within the straits; and then, Solon, your country shone forth, in the excellence of her virtue and strength, among all mankind. She was pre-eminent in courage and military skill, and was the leader of the Hellenes. And when the rest fell off from her, being compelled to stand alone, after having undergone the very extremity of danger, she defeated and triumphed over the invaders, and preserved from slavery those who were not yet subjugated, and generously liberated all the rest of us who dwell within the pillars. But afterwards there occurred violent earthquakes and floods; and in a single day and night of misfortune all your warlike men in a body sank into the earth, and the island of Atlantis in like manner disappeared in the depths of the sea. For which reason the sea in those parts is impassable and impenetrable, because there is a shoal of mud in the way; and this was caused by the subsidence of the island.

I have told you briefly, Socrates, what the aged Critias heard from Solon and related to us. And when you were speaking yesterday about your city and citizens, the tale which I have just been repeating to you came into my mind, and I remarked with astonishment how, by some mysterious coincidence, you agreed in almost every particular with the narrative of Solon; but I did not like to speak at the moment. For a long time 26 had elapsed, and I had forgotten too much; I thought that I must first of all run over the narrative in my own mind, and then I would speak. And so I readily assented to your request yesterday, considering that in all such cases the chief difficulty is to find a tale suitable to our purpose, and that with such a tale we should be fairly well provided.

And therefore, as Hermocrates has told you, on my way home yesterday I at once communicated the tale to my companions as I remembered it; and after I left them, during the night by thinking I recovered nearly the whole of it. Truly, as is often said, the lessons of our childhood make a wonderful impression on our memories; for I am not sure that I could remember all the discourse of yesterday, but I should be much surprised if I forgot any of these things which I have heard very long ago. I listened at the time with childlike interest to the old man's narrative; he was very ready to teach me, and I asked him again and again to repeat his words, so that like an indelible picture they were branded into my mind. As soon as the day broke, I rehearsed them as he spoke them to my companions, that they, as well as myself, might have something to say.

And now, Socrates, to make an end of my preface, I am ready to tell you the whole tale. I will give you not only the general heads, but the particulars, as they were told to me. The city and citizens, which you yesterday described to us in fiction, we will now transfer to the world of reality. It shall be the ancient city of Athens, and we will suppose that the citizens whom you imagined, were our veritable ancestors, of whom the priest spoke; they will perfectly harmonize, and there will be no inconsistency in saying that the citizens of your republic are these ancient Athenians.

2. The Balance of Mind and Body.

The Timaeus, after the close of the Introduction, is a monologue unbroken by any of the auditors. Timaeus gives a description of the Cosmos, in which he enlarges upon the Creation of the World and of Man, the Starry System, the Four Elements, the Senses, the Nature of Disease, the Parts of the Soul, the Fate of the Soul after Death, and other kindred topics. Towards the end of his discourse he takes occasion to speak of a subject, which, although not immediately connected with the main scheme of the work, is of the highest interest and importance,—the relation of the Soul to the Body, and the influence which each of them exercises upon the other.

Plato is here enforcing from a rather different side the lesson which he has already taught us in the Republic, (iii. 410), that the cultivation of the mind and the training of the body ought to be pursued in common. He perhaps exaggerates the necessity of harmony between the soul and the bodily frame; for many instances might be quoted in which the very weaknesses and infirmities of the body seem not to have hindered, but even to have quickened and stimulated, the intellectual powers. Yet it is also hardly possible to doubt that a certain sobriety and sanity of judgment is enjoyed by the happy possessor of a healthy and robust constitution. He is freer from morbid and unwholesome thoughts, and his outlook on life is brighter and more cheerful.

In this respect Plato may have been to some extent influenced by the antipathy to deformity and suffering which forms a marked characteristic of the Hellenic temper: and the same spirit is apparently betrayed by the manner in which he speaks of the inutility of attempting to contend against disease, just as in the Republic he derides Herodicus, the 'inventor of valetudinarianism,' who taught men to protract a useless existence to extreme old age, and to spend on the care of their bodies the time which would have been better employed on the improvement of their minds (Rep. iii. 406–408).

Steph.
87
C

Timaeus. There is a corresponding enquiry concerning the mode of treatment by which the mind and the body are to be preserved, about which it is meet and right that I should say a word in turn; for it is more our duty to speak of the good than of the evil. Everything that is good is fair, and the fair is not without proportion, and the animal which is to be fair must have due proportion. Now we perceive lesser symmetries or proportions and reason about them, but of the highest and greatest we take no heed; for there is no proportion or disproportion more productive of health and disease, and virtue and vice, than that between soul and body.

This however we do not perceive, nor do we reflect that when a weak or small frame is the vehicle of a great and mighty soul, or conversely, when a little soul is encased in a large body, then the whole animal is not fair, for it lacks the most important of all symmetries; but the due proportion of mind and body is the fairest and loveliest of all sights to him who has the seeing eye. Just as a body which has a leg too long, or which is unsymmetrical in some other respect, is an unpleasant sight, and also, when doing its share of work, is much distressed and makes convulsive efforts, and often stumbles through awkwardness, and is the cause of infinite evil to its own self—in like manner we should conceive of the double nature which we call the living being; and when in this compound there is an impassioned soul more powerful than the body, that soul, I say, convulses and fills with disorders 88 the whole inner nature of man; and when eager in the pursuit of some sort of learning or study, causes wasting; or again, when teaching or disputing in private or in public, and strifes and controversies arise, inflames and dissolves the composite frame of man and introduces rheums; and the nature of this phenomenon is not understood by most professors of medicine, who ascribe it to the opposite of the real cause. And once more, when a body large and too strong for the soul is united to a small and weak intelligence, then inasmuch as there are two desires natural to man,—one of food for the sake of the body, and one of wisdom for the sake of the diviner part of us—then, I say, the motions of the stronger, getting the better and increasing their own power, but making the soul dull, and stupid, and forgetful, engender ignorance, which is the greatest of diseases.

There is one protection against both kinds of disproportion :—that we should not move the body without the soul or the soul without the body, and thus they will be on their guard against each other, and be healthy and well balanced. And therefore the mathematician or any one else whose thoughts are much absorbed in some intellectual pursuit, must allow his body also to have due exercise, and practise gymnastic; and he who is careful to fashion the body, should in turn impart to the soul its proper motions, and should cultivate music and all philosophy, if he would deserve to be called truly fair and truly good.

And the separate parts should be treated in the same manner, in imitation of the pattern of the universe; for as the body is heated and also cooled within by the elements which enter into it, and is again dried up and moistened by external things, and experiences these and the like affections from both kinds of motions, the result is that the body if given up to motion when in a state of quiescence is over-mastered and perishes; but if any one, in imitation of that which we call the foster-mother and nurse of the universe, will not allow the body ever to be inactive, but is always producing motions and agitations through its whole extent, which form the natural defence against other motions both internal and external, and by moderate exercise reduces to order according to their affinities the particles and affections which are wandering about the body, as we have already said when speaking of the universe[1], he will not allow enemy placed by the side of enemy to stir up wars and disorders in the body, but he will place friend by the side of friend, so as to create health.

Now of all motions that is the best which is produced in a thing by itself, for it is most akin to the motion of thought and of the universe; but that motion which is caused by others is not so good, and worst of all is that which moves the body, when at rest, in parts only and by some external agency. Wherefore of all modes of purifying and re-uniting the body the best is gymnastic; the next best is a surging motion, as in sailing or any other mode of conveyance which is not fatiguing; the third sort of motion may be of use in a case of extreme necessity, but in any other will be adopted by no man of sense: I mean the purgative treatment of physicians; for diseases unless they are very dangerous should not be irritated by medicines, since every form of disease is in a manner akin to the living being, whose complex frame has an appointed term of life. For not the whole race only, but each individual—barring inevitable accidents—comes into the world having a fixed span, and the triangles in us are originally framed with power to last for a certain time, beyond which no man can prolong his life. And this holds also of the constitution of diseases; if any one regardless of the appointed time tries to subdue them by medicine, he only aggravates and multiplies them. Wherefore we ought always to manage them by regimen, as far as a man can spare the time, and not provoke a disagreeable enemy by medicines.

Enough of the composite animal, and of the body

[1] *Supra*, 33 A.

which is a part of him, and of the manner in which a man may train and be trained by himself so as to live most according to reason : and we must above and before all provide that the element which is to train him shall be the fairest and best adapted to that purpose. A minute discussion of this subject would be a serious task ; but if, as before, I am to give only an outline, the subject may not unfitly be summed up as follows.

I have often remarked that there are three kinds of soul located within us, having each of them motions, and I must now repeat in the fewest words possible, that one part, if remaining inactive and ceasing from its natural motion, must necessarily become very weak, but that which is trained and exercised, very strong. Wherefore we should take care that the movements of the different parts of the soul should be in due proportion.

And we should consider that God gave the sovereign part of the human soul to be the divinity of each one, being that part which, as we say, dwells at the top of the body, and inasmuch as we are a plant not of an earthly but of a heavenly growth, raises us from earth to our kindred who are in heaven. And in this we say truly; for the divine power suspended the head and root of us from that place where the generation of the soul first began, and thus made the whole body upright. When a man is always occupied with the cravings of desire and ambition, and is eagerly striving to satisfy them, all his thoughts must be mortal, and, as far as it is possible altogether to become such, he must be mortal every whit, because he has cherished his mortal part. But he who has been earnest in the love of knowledge and of true wisdom, and has exercised his intellect more than any other part of him, must have thoughts immortal and divine, if he attain truth, and in so far as human nature is capable of sharing in immortality, he must altogether be immortal; and since he is ever cherishing the divine power, and has the divinity within him in perfect order, he will be perfectly happy.

Now there is only one way of taking care of things, and this is to give to each the food and motion which are natural to it. And the motions which are naturally akin to the divine principle within us are the thoughts and revolutions of the universe. These each man should follow, and correct the courses of the head which were corrupted at our birth, and by learning the harmonies and revolutions of the universe, should assimilate the thinking being to the thought, renewing his original nature, and having assimilated them should attain to that perfect life which the gods have set before mankind, both for the present and the future.

CRITIAS,
Or the Island of Atlantis.

THE legend of Atlantis is resumed in the Critias, but the story is abruptly broken off a short way from the commencement. Why the work was not completed by Plato, we cannot say. He may have found the task too difficult even for his artistic powers. The theme would scarcely bear elaboration, nor could the result, we may think, have been entirely satisfactory. Allegory and satire have generally been most successful in proportion to their shortness; longer writings of this class are apt to retain only a romantic or a poetical interest for the reader, while their deeper meaning is forgotten or ignored.

It is, however, possible that Plato may have been compelled by circumstances of which we are ignorant to 'leave half-told' the myth of Atlantis. We may please ourselves, if we choose, by imagining that the second or third journey which Plato is alleged to have made to Sicily was the cause of the interruption. Yet such a conjecture does not give us any real assistance, and we must be content to let the question, like so many other literary problems, remain without an answer.

Timaeus. How thankful I am, Socrates, that I have arrived at last, and, like a weary traveller after a long journey, may be at rest! And I pray the being who always was of old, and has now been by me revealed, to grant that my words may endure in so far as they have been spoken truly and acceptably to him; but if unintentionally I have said anything wrong, I pray that he will impose upon me a just retribution, and the just retribution of him who errs is that he should be set right. Wishing, then, to speak truly in future concerning the generation of the gods, I pray him to give me knowledge, which of all medicines is the most perfect and best. And now having offered my prayer I deliver up the argument to Critias, who is to speak next according to our agreement[1].

Critias. And I, Timaeus, accept the trust, and as you at first said that you were going to speak of high matters, and begged that some forbearance might be shown to you, I too ask the same or greater forbearance for what I am about to say. And although I very well know that my request may appear to be somewhat ambitious and discourteous, I must make it nevertheless. For will any man of sense deny that you have spoken well? I can only attempt to show that I ought to have more indulgence than you, because my theme is more difficult; and I shall argue that to seem to speak well of the gods to men is far easier than to speak well of men to men: for the inexperience and utter ignorance of his hearers about any subject is a great assistance to him who has to speak of it, and we know how ignorant we are concerning the gods. But I should like to make my meaning clearer, if you will follow me.

All that is said by any of us can only be imitation and representation. For if we consider the likenesses which

[1] Tim. 27 A.

painters make of bodies divine and heavenly, and the different degrees of gratification with which the eye of the spectator receives them, we shall see that we are satisfied with the artist who is able in any degree to imitate the earth and its mountains, and the rivers, and the woods, and the universe, and the things that are and move therein, and further, that knowing nothing precise about such matters, we do not examine or analyze the painting; all that is required is a sort of indistinct and deceptive mode of shadowing them forth. But when a person endeavours to paint the human form we are quick at finding out defects, and our familiar knowledge makes us severe judges of any one who does not render every point of similarity. And we may observe the same thing to happen in discourse; we are satisfied with a picture of divine and heavenly things which has very little likeness to them; but we are more precise in our criticism of mortal and human things. Wherefore if at the moment of speaking I cannot suitably express my meaning, you must excuse me, considering that to form approved likenesses of human things is the reverse of easy. This is what I want to suggest to you, and at the same time to beg, Socrates, that I may have not less, but more indulgence conceded to me in what I am about to say. Which favour, if I am right in asking, I hope that you will be ready to grant.

Socrates. Certainly, Critias, we will grant your request, and we will grant the same by anticipation to Hermocrates, as well as to you and Timaeus; for I have no doubt that when his turn comes a little while hence, he will make the same request which you have made. In order, then, that he may provide himself with a fresh beginning, and not be compelled to say the same things over again, let him understand that the indulgence is already extended by anticipation to him. And now, friend Critias, I will announce to you the judgment of the theatre. They are of opinion that the last performer was wonderfully successful, and that you will need a great deal of indulgence before you will be able to take his place.

Hermocrates. The warning, Socrates, which you have addressed to him, I must also take to myself. But remember, Critias, that faint heart never yet raised a trophy; and therefore you must go and attack the argument like a man. First invoke Apollo and the Muses, and then let us hear you sound the praises and show forth the virtues of your ancient citizens.

Crit. Friend Hermocrates, you, who are stationed last and have another in front of you, have not lost heart as yet; the gravity of the situation will soon be revealed to you; meanwhile I accept your exhortations and encouragements. But besides the gods and goddesses whom you have mentioned, I would specially invoke Mnemosynè; for all the important part of my discourse is dependent on her favour, and if I can recollect and recite enough of what was said by the priests and brought hither by Solon, I doubt not that I shall satisfy the requirements of this theatre. And now, making no more excuses, I will proceed.

Let me begin by observing first of all, that nine thousand was the sum of years which had elapsed since the war which was said to have taken place between those who dwelt outside the pillars of Heracles and all who dwelt within them; this war I am going to describe. Of the combatants on the one side, the city of Athens was reported to have been the leader and to have fought out the war; the combatants on the other side were commanded by the kings of Atlantis, which, as I was saying, was an island greater in extent than Libya and Asia, and when afterwards sunk by an earthquake, became an impassable barrier of mud to voyagers sailing from hence to any part of the ocean. The progress of the history will unfold the various nations of barbarians and families of Hellenes which then existed, as they successively appear on the scene; but I must describe first of all the Athenians of that day, and their enemies who fought with them, and then the respective powers and governments of the two kingdoms. Let us give the precedence to Athens.

In the days of old, the gods had the whole earth distributed among them by allotment[1]. There was no quarrelling; for you cannot rightly suppose that the gods did not know what was proper for each of them to have, or, knowing this, that they would seek to procure for themselves by contention that which more properly belonged to others. They all of them by just apportionment obtained what they wanted, and peopled their own districts; and when they had peopled them they tended us, their nurselings and possessions, as shepherds tend their flocks, excepting only that they did not use blows or bodily force, as shepherds do, but governed us like pilots from the stern of the vessel, which is an easy way of guiding animals, holding our souls by the rudder of persuasion according to their own pleasure ;—thus did they guide all mortal creatures.

Now different gods had their allotments in different places which they set in order. Hephaestus and Athenè, who were brother and sister, and sprang from the same father, having a common nature, and being united also in the love of philosophy and art, both obtained as their common portion this land, which was naturally adapted for wisdom and virtue; and there they implanted brave children of the soil, and put into

[1] Cp. Statesm. 271 ff.

their minds the order of government; their names are preserved, but their actions have disappeared by reason of the destruction of those who received the tradition, and the lapse of ages. For when there were any survivors, as I have already said, they were men who dwelt in the mountains; and they were ignorant of the art of writing, and had heard only the names of the chiefs of the land, but very little about their actions. The names they were willing enough to give to their children; but the virtues and the laws of their predecessors, they knew only by obscure traditions; and as they themselves and their children lacked for many generations the necessaries of life, they directed their attention to the supply of their wants, and of them they conversed, to the neglect of events that had happened in times long past; for mythology and the enquiry into antiquity are first introduced into cities when they begin to have leisure[1], and when they see that the necessaries of life have already been provided, but not before. And this is the reason why the names of the ancients have been preserved to us and not their actions. This I infer because Solon said that the priests in their narrative of that war mentioned most of the names which are recorded prior to the time of Theseus, such as Cecrops, and Erechtheus, and Erichthonius, and Erysichthon, and the names of the women in like manner. Moreover, since military pursuits were then common to men and women, the men of those days in accordance with the custom of the time set up a figure and image of the goddess in full armour, to be a testimony that all animals which associate together, male as well as female, may, if they please, practise in common the virtue which belongs to them without distinction of sex.

Now the country was inhabited in those days by

[1] Cp Arist. Metaphys. I. 1, § 16.

various classes of citizens;—there were artisans, and there were husbandmen, and there was also a warrior class originally set apart by divine men. The latter dwelt by themselves, and had all things suitable for nurture and education; neither had any of them anything of their own, but they regarded all that they had as common property; nor did they claim to receive of the other citizens anything more than their necessary food. And they practised all the pursuits which we yesterday described as those of our imaginary guardians.

Concerning the country the Egyptian priests said what is not only probable but manifestly true, that the boundaries were in those days fixed by the Isthmus, and that in the direction of the continent they extended as far as the heights of Cithaeron and Parnes; the boundary line came down in the direction of the sea, having the district of Oropus on the right, and with the river Asopus as the limit on the left. The land was the best in the world, and was therefore able in those days to support a vast army, raised from the surrounding people. Even the remnant of Attica which now exists may compare with any region in the world for the variety and excellence of its fruits and the suitableness of its pastures to every sort of animal, which proves what I am saying; but in those days the country was fair as now and yielded far more abundant produce.

How shall I establish my words? and what part of it can be truly called a remnant of the land that then was? The whole country is only a long promontory extending far into the sea away from the rest of the continent, while the surrounding basin of the sea is everywhere deep in the neighbourhood of the shore. Many great deluges have taken place during the nine thousand years, for that is the number of years which have elapsed since the time of which I am speaking; and during all

VOL. II.   K

this time and through so many changes, there has never been any considerable accumulation of the soil coming down from the mountains, as in other places, but the earth has fallen away all round and sunk out of sight.

The consequence is, that in comparison of what then was, there are remaining only the bones of the wasted body, as they may be called, as in the case of small islands, all the richer and softer parts of the soil having fallen away, and the mere skeleton of the land being left. But in the primitive state of the country, its mountains were high hills covered with soil, and the plains, as they are termed by us, of Phelleus were full of rich earth, and there was abundance of wood in the mountains. Of this last the traces still remain, for although some of the mountains now only afford sustenance to bees, not so very long ago there were still to be seen roofs of timber cut from trees growing there, which were of a size sufficient to cover the largest houses; and there were many other high trees, cultivated by man and bearing abundance of food for cattle. Moreover, the land reaped the benefit of the annual rainfall, not as now losing the water which flows off the bare earth into the sea, but, having an abundant supply in all places, and receiving it into herself and treasuring it up in the close clay soil, it let off into the hollows the streams which it absorbed from the heights, providing everywhere abundant fountains and rivers, of which there may still be observed sacred memorials in places where fountains once existed; and this proves the truth of what I am saying.

Such was the natural state of the country, which was cultivated, as we may well believe, by true husbandmen, who made husbandry their business, and were lovers of honour, and of a noble nature, and had a soil the best in the world, and abundance of water, and in the heaven above an excellently attempered climate.

Now the city in those days was arranged on this wise. In the first place the Acropolis was not as now. For the fact is that a single night of excessive rain washed away the earth and laid bare the rock; at the same time there were earthquakes, and then occurred the extraordinary inundation, which was the third before the great destruction of Deucalion. But in primitive times the hill of the Acropolis extended to the Eridanus and Ilissus, and included the Pnyx on one side, and the Lycabettus as a boundary on the opposite side to the Pnyx, and was all well covered with soil, and level at the top, except in one or two places. Outside the Acropolis and under the sides of the hill there dwelt artisans, and such of the husbandmen as were tilling the ground near; the warrior class dwelt by themselves around the temples of Athenê and Hephaestus at the summit, which moreover they had enclosed with a single fence like the garden of a single house.

On the north side they had dwellings in common and had erected halls for dining in winter, and had all the buildings which they needed for their common life, besides temples, but there was no adorning of them with gold and silver, for they made no use of these for any purpose; they took a middle course between meanness and ostentation, and built modest houses in which they and their children's children grew old, and they handed them down to others who were like themselves, always the same. But in summer-time they left their gardens and gymnasia and dining halls, and then the southern side of the hill was made use of by them for the same purpose. Where the Acropolis now is there was a fountain, which was choked by the earthquake, and has left only the few small streams which still exist in the vicinity, but in those days the fountain gave an abundant supply of water for all and of suitable temperature in summer and in winter. This is how they dwelt, being the guardians of their own citizens and the leaders of the Hellenes, who were their willing followers. And they took care to preserve the same number of men and women through all time, being so many as were required for warlike purposes, then as now,—that is to say, about twenty thousand.

Such were the ancient Athenians, and after this manner they righteously administered their own land and the rest of Hellas; they were renowned all over Europe and Asia for the beauty of their persons and for the many virtues of their souls, and of all men who lived in those days they were the most illustrious. And next, if I have not forgotten what I heard when I was a child, I will impart to you the character and origin of their adversaries. For friends should not keep their stories to themselves, but have them in common.

113 Yet, before proceeding further in the narrative, I ought to warn you, that you must not be surprised if you should perhaps hear Hellenic names given to foreigners. I will tell you the reason of this: Solon, who was intending to use the tale for his poem, enquired into the meaning of the names, and found that the early Egyptians in writing them down had translated them into their own language, and he recovered the meaning of the several names and when copying them out again translated them into our language. My great-grandfather, Dropides, had the original writing, which is still in my possession, and was carefully studied by me when I was a child. Therefore if you hear names such as are used in this country, you must not be surprised, for I have told how they came to be introduced. The tale, which was of great length, began as follows:—

THE FOUNDATION OF ATLANTIS

I have before remarked in speaking of the allotments of the gods, that they distributed the whole earth into portions differing in extent, and made for themselves temples and instituted sacrifices. And Poseidon, receiving for his lot the island of Atlantis, begat children by a mortal woman, and settled them in a part of the island, which I will describe. Looking towards the sea, but in the centre of the whole island, there was a plain which is said to have been the fairest of all plains and very fertile. Near the plain again, and also in the centre of the island at a distance of about fifty stadia, there was a mountain not very high on any side. In this mountain there dwelt one of the earth-born primeval men of that country, whose name was Evenor, and he had a wife named Leucippè, and they had an only daughter who was called Cleito. The maiden had already reached womanhood, when her father and mother died ; Poseidon fell in love with her and had intercourse with her, and breaking the ground, inclosed the hill in which she dwelt all round, making alternate zones of sea and land larger and smaller, encircling one another; there were two of land and three of water, which he turned as with a lathe, each having its circumference equidistant every way from the centre, so that no man could get to the island, for ships and voyages were not as yet. He himself, being a god, found no difficulty in making special arrangements for the centre island, bringing up two springs of water from beneath the earth, one of warm water and the other of cold, and making every variety of food to spring up abundantly from the soil.

He also begat and brought up five pairs of twin male children; and dividing the island of Atlantis into ten portions, he gave to the first-born of the eldest pair his mother's dwelling and the surrounding allotment, which was the largest and best, and made him king over the rest; the others he made princes, and gave them rule over many men, and a large territory. And he named them all; the eldest, who was the first king, he named Atlas, and after him the whole island and the ocean were called Atlantic. To his twin brother, who was born after him, and obtained as his lot the extremity of the island towards the pillars of Heracles, facing the country which is now called the region of Gades in that part of the world, he gave the name which in the Hellenic language is Eumelus, in the language of the country which is named after him, Gadeirus. Of the second pair of twins he called one Ampheres, and the other Evaemon. To the elder of the third pair of twins he gave the name Mneseus, and Autochthon to the one who followed him. Of the fourth pair of twins he called the elder Elasippus, and the younger Mestor. And of the fifth pair he gave to the elder the name of Azaes, and to the younger that of Diaprepes. All these and their descendants for many generations were the inhabitants and rulers of divers islands in the open sea; and also, as has been already said, they held sway in our direction over the country within the pillars as far as Egypt and Tyrrhenia.

Now Atlas had a numerous and honourable family, and they retained the kingdom, the eldest son handing it on to his eldest for many generations; and they had such an amount of wealth as was never before possessed by kings and potentates, and is not likely ever to be again, and they were furnished with everything which they needed, both in the city and country. For because of the greatness of their empire many things were brought to them from foreign countries, and the island itself provided most of what was required by them for the uses of life.

In the first place, they dug out of the earth whatever was to be found there, solid as well as fusile, and that which is now only a name and was then something more than a name, orichalcum, was dug out of the earth in many parts of the island, being more precious in those days than anything except gold. There was an abundance of wood for carpenter's work, and sufficient maintenance for tame and wild animals. Moreover, there were a great number of elephants in the island; for as there was provision for all other sorts of animals, both for those which live in lakes and marshes and rivers, and also for those which live in mountains and on plains, so there was for the animal which is the largest and most voracious of all.

Also whatever fragrant things there now are in the earth, whether roots, or herbage, or woods, or essences which distil from fruit and flower, grew and thrived in that land; also the fruit which admits of cultivation, both the dry sort, which is given us for nourishment, and any other which we use for food—we call them all by the common name of pulse, and the fruits having a hard rind, affording drinks and meats and ointments, and good store of chestnuts and the like, which furnish pleasure and amusement, and are fruits which spoil with keeping, and the pleasant kinds of dessert, with which we console ourselves after dinner, when we are tired of eating—all these that sacred island which then beheld the light of the sun, brought forth fair and wondrous and in infinite abundance. With such blessings the earth freely furnished them; meanwhile they went on constructing their temples and palaces and harbours and docks. And they arranged the whole country in the following manner:—

First of all they bridged over the zones of sea which surrounded the ancient metropolis, making a road to and from the royal palace. And at the very beginning they built the palace in the habitation of the god and of their ancestors, which they continued to ornament in successive generations, every king surpassing the one who went before him to the utmost of his power, until they made the building a marvel to behold for size and for beauty. And beginning from the sea they bored a canal of three hundred feet in width and one hundred feet in depth and fifty stadia in length, which they carried through to the outermost zone, making a passage from the sea up to this, which became a harbour, and leaving an opening sufficient to enable the largest vessels to find ingress. Moreover, they divided at the bridges the zones of land which parted the zones of sea, leaving room for a single trireme to pass out of one zone into another, and they covered over the channels so as to leave a way underneath for the ships; for the banks were raised considerably above the water. Now the largest of the zones into which a passage was cut from the sea was three stadia in breadth, and the zone of land which came next of equal breadth; but the next two zones, the one of water, the other of land, were two stadia, and the one which surrounded the central island was a stadium only in width. The island in which the palace was situated had a diameter of five stadia. All this including the zones and the bridge, which was the sixth part of a stadium in width, they surrounded by a stone wall on every side, placing towers and gates on the bridges where the sea passed in. The stone which was used in the work they quarried from underneath the centre island, and from underneath the zones, on the outer as well as the inner side. One kind was white, another black, and a third red, and as they quarried, they at the same time hollowed out double docks, having roofs formed out of the native rock. Some of their buildings were simple, but in others they put together different stones, varying the colour to please the eye, and to be a natural source of delight. The entire circuit of the wall, which went round the outermost zone, they covered with a coating of brass, and the circuit of the next wall they coated with tin, and the third, which encompassed the citadel, flashed with the red light of orichalcum.

The palaces in the interior of the citadel were constructed on this wise:—In the centre was a holy temple dedicated to Cleito and Poseidon, which remained inaccessible, and was surrounded by an enclosure of gold; this was the spot where the family of the ten princes first saw the light, and thither the people annually brought the fruits of the earth in their season from all the ten portions, to be an offering to each of the ten. Here was Poseidon's own temple, which was a stadium in length, and half a stadium in width, and of a proportionate height, having a strange barbaric appearance. All the outside of the temple, with the exception of the pinnacles, they covered with silver, and the pinnacles with gold. In the interior of the temple the roof was of ivory, curiously wrought everywhere with gold and silver and orichalcum; and all the other parts, the walls and pillars and floor, they coated with orichalcum. In the temple they placed statues of gold: there was the god himself standing in a chariot —the charioteer of six winged horses—and of such a size that he touched the roof of the building with his head; around him there were a hundred Nereids riding on dolphins, for such was thought to be the number of them by the men of those days. There were also in the interior of the temple other images which had been dedicated by private persons. And around the temple on the outside were placed statues of gold of all the descendants of the ten kings and of their wives, and there were many other great offerings of kings and of private persons, coming both from the city itself and from the foreign cities over which they held sway. There was an altar too, which in size and workmanship corresponded to this magnificence, and the palaces, in like manner, answered to the greatness of the kingdom and the glory of the temple.

In the next place, they had fountains, one of cold and another of hot water, in gracious plenty flowing; and they were wonderfully adapted for use by reason of the pleasantness and excellence of their waters[1]. They constructed buildings about them and planted suitable trees; also they made cisterns, some open to the heaven, others roofed over, to be used in winter as warm baths; there were the kings' baths, and the baths of private persons, which were kept apart; and there were separate baths for women, and for horses and cattle, and to each of them they gave as much adornment as was suitable. Of the water which ran off they carried some to the grove of Poseidon, where were growing all manner of trees of wonderful height and beauty, owing to the excellence of the soil, while the remainder was conveyed by aqueducts along the bridges to the outer circles; and there were many temples built and dedicated to many gods; also gardens and places of exercise, some for men, and others for horses in both of the two islands formed by the zones; and in the centre of the larger of the two there was set apart a race-course of a stadium in width, and in length allowed to extend all round the island, for horses to race in. Also there were guard-houses at intervals for the guards, the more trusted of whom were appointed to keep watch in the lesser zone, which was nearer the

[1] Reading ἑκατέρου πρὸς τὴν χρῆσιν.

Acropolis; while the most trusted of all had houses given them within the citadel, near the persons of the kings. The docks were full of triremes and naval stores, and all things were quite ready for use. Enough of the plan of the royal palace.

Leaving the palace and passing out across the three harbours, you came to a wall which began at the sea and went all round: this was everywhere distant fifty stadia from the largest zone or harbour, and enclosed the whole, the ends meeting at the mouth of the channel which led to the sea. The entire area was densely crowded with habitations; and the canal and the largest of the harbours were full of vessels and merchants coming from all parts, who, from their numbers, kept up a multitudinous sound of human voices, and din and clatter of all sorts night and day.

I have described the city and the environs of the ancient palace nearly in the words of Solon, and now I must endeavour to represent to you the nature and arrangement of the rest of the land. The whole country was said by him to be very lofty and precipitous on the side of the sea, but the country immediately about and surrounding the city was a level plain, itself surrounded by mountains which descended towards the sea; it was smooth and even, and of an oblong shape, extending in one direction three thousand stadia, but across the centre inland it was two thousand stadia. This part of the island looked towards the south, and was sheltered from the north. The surrounding mountains were celebrated for their number and size and beauty, far beyond any which still exist, having in them also many wealthy villages of country folk, and rivers, and lakes, and meadows supplying food enough for every animal, wild or tame, and much wood of various sorts, abundant for each and every kind of work.

I will now describe the plain, as it was fashioned by nature and by the labours of many generations of kings through long ages. It was for the most part rectangular and oblong, and where falling out of the straight line followed the circular ditch. The depth, and width, and length of this ditch were incredible, and gave the impression that a work of such extent, in addition to so many others, could never have been artificial. Nevertheless I must say what I was told. It was excavated to the depth of a hundred feet, and its breadth was a stadium everywhere; it was carried round the whole of the plain, and was ten thousand stadia in length. It received the streams which came down from the mountains, and winding round the plain and meeting at the city, was there let off into the sea. Further inland, likewise, straight canals of a hundred feet in width were cut from it through the plain, and again let off into the ditch leading to the sea: these canals were at intervals of a hundred stadia, and by them they brought down the wood from the mountains to the city, and conveyed the fruits of the earth in ships, cutting transverse passages from one canal into another, and to the city. Twice in the year they gathered the fruits of the earth—in winter having the benefit of the rains of heaven, and in summer the water which the land supplied by introducing streams from the canals.

119 As to the population, each of the lots in the plain had to find a leader for the men who were fit for military service, and the size of a lot was a square of ten stadia each way, and the total number of all the lots was sixty thousand. And of the inhabitants of the mountains and of the rest of the country there was also a vast multitude, which was distributed among the lots and had leaders assigned to them according to their districts and villages.

The leader was required to furnish for the war the sixth portion of a war-chariot, so as to make up a total of ten thousand chariots; also two horses and riders for them, and a pair of chariot-horses without a seat, accompanied by a horseman who could fight on foot carrying a small shield, and having a charioteer who stood behind the man-at-arms to guide the two horses; also, he was bound to furnish two heavy-armed soldiers, two archers, two slingers, three stone-shooters and three javelin-men, who were light-armed, and four sailors to make up the complement of twelve hundred ships. Such was the military order of the royal city—the order of the other nine governments varied, and it would be wearisome to recount their several differences.

As to offices and honours, the following was the arrangement from the first. Each of the ten kings in his own division and in his own city had the absolute control of the citizens, and, in most cases, of the laws, punishing and slaying whomsoever he would. Now the order of precedence among them and their mutual relations were regulated by the commands of Poseidon which the law had handed down. These were inscribed by the first kings on a pillar of orichalcum, which was situated in the middle of the island, at the temple of Poseidon, whither the kings were gathered together every fifth and every sixth year alternately, thus giving equal honour to the odd and to the even number. And when they were gathered together they consulted about their common interests, and enquired if any one had transgressed in anything, and passed judgment, and before they passed judgment they gave their pledges to one another on this wise:—There were bulls who had the range of the temple of Poseidon; and the ten kings, being left alone in the temple, after they had offered prayers to the god that they might capture the victim which was acceptable to him, hunted the bulls, without weapons, but with staves and nooses; and the bull which they caught they led up to the pillar and cut its throat over the top of it so that the blood fell upon the sacred inscription. Now on the pillar, besides the laws, there was inscribed an oath invoking mighty curses on the disobedient.

When therefore, after slaying the bull in the accustomed manner, they had burnt its limbs, they filled a bowl of wine and cast in a clot of blood for each of them; the rest of the victim they put in the fire, after having purified the column all round. Then they drew from the bowl in golden cups, and pouring a libation on the fire, they swore that they would judge according to the laws on the pillar, and would punish him who in any point had already transgressed them, and that for the future they would not, if they could help, offend against the writing on the pillar, and would neither command others, nor obey any ruler who commanded them, to act otherwise than according to the laws of their father Poseidon. This was the prayer which each of them offered up for himself and for his descendants, at the same time drinking and dedicating the cup out of which he drank in the temple of the god; and after they had supped and satisfied their needs, when darkness came on, and the fire about the sacrifice was cool, all of them put on most beautiful azure robes, and, sitting on the ground, at night, over the embers of the sacrifices by which they had sworn, and extinguishing all the fire about the temple, they received and gave judgment, if any of them had an accusation to bring against any one; and when they had given judgment, at daybreak they wrote down their sentences on a golden tablet, and dedicated it together with their robes to be a memorial.

THE DECLINE OF ATLANTIS

There were many special laws affecting the several kings inscribed about the temples, but the most important was the following: They were not to take up arms against one another, and they were all to come to the rescue if any one in any of their cities attempted to overthrow the royal house; like their ancestors, they were to deliberate in common about war and other matters, giving the supremacy to the descendants of Atlas. And the king was not to have the power of life and death over any of his kinsmen unless he had the assent of the majority of the ten.

Such was the vast power which the god settled in the lost island of Atlantis; and this he afterwards directed against our land for the following reasons, as tradition tells: For many generations, as long as the divine nature lasted in them, they were obedient to the laws, and well-affectioned towards the god, whose seed they were; for they possessed true and in every way great spirits, uniting gentleness with wisdom in the various chances of life, and in their intercourse with one another. They despised everything but virtue, caring little for their present state of life, and thinking lightly of the possession of gold and other property, which seemed only a burden to them; neither were they intoxicated by luxury; nor did wealth deprive them of their self-control; but they were sober, and saw clearly that all these goods are increased by virtue and friendship with one another, whereas by too great regard and respect for them, they are lost and friendship with them. By such reflections and by the continuance in them of a divine nature, the qualities which we have described grew and increased among them; but when the divine portion began to fade away, and became diluted too often and too much with the mortal admixture, and the human nature got the upper hand, they then, being unable to bear their fortune, behaved unseemly, and to him who had an eye to see, grew visibly debased, for they were losing the fairest of their precious gifts; but to those who had no eye to see the true happiness, they appeared glorious and blessed at the very time when they were full of avarice and unrighteous power.

Zeus, the god of gods, who rules according to law, and is able to see into such things, perceiving that an honourable race was in a woeful plight, and wanting to inflict punishment on them, that they might be chastened and improve, collected all the gods into their [1] most holy habitation, which, being placed in the centre of the world, beholds all created things. And when he had called them together, he spake as follows:— * * *

THE LAWS

WE have now reached the work which seems to have occupied the last years of Plato's long life, the 'swan song' with which he takes his leave of the world (Phaedo 84 E). The Laws may be called either a remodelling of the Republic, or a companion treatise on a slightly altered theme. The question, in Aristotle's language, is no longer, 'What State is best in the abstract?' but 'What State is the best relatively to circumstances?' (Pol. iv. 1.) In every respect the two Dialogues form a striking contrast.

The Republic is written with the greatest literary skill, and with the utmost grace and refinement: the Laws are ill composed, and put together without order or purpose; the dialogue is halting and badly sustained; the language is harsh and obscure. Yet the later work has also some merits such as are hardly possessed in an equal degree by any other composition of Plato, and which render it one of the most remarkable remains of Classical Antiquity.

There is a singular power of insight in many passages, and an exalted moral tone pervades the whole. It is marked, too, by an earnestness and intensity of feeling which rather remind us of a Jewish prophet than of an Hellenic philosopher. The veil of irony

---

[1] Reading αὐτῶν.

and humour behind which Plato has hitherto concealed his deepest reflections is cast aside, and he preaches, as it were, to us so eagerly and sincerely that the utterance of his thoughts is impeded, and he can no longer clothe them with an artistic dress.

These peculiarities of the Laws have been made a reason for throwing a doubt upon the genuineness of the Dialogue, though without any real ground. The deficiency of arrangement, the faults of language, the contradictions and obscurities, which are unquestionably to be discovered in the Laws, become intelligible when we consider that it was written by Plato in the decline of his life, and most probably never received its final shape from him. And on the other hand, the extraordinary genius which is everywhere manifested in the work, forbids us to suppose that the author could have been any other than Plato. The reader, if he will not allow himself to be deterred by the uncouth exterior, but will persist in his perusal until the dialogue has grown thoroughly familiar to him, will find a rich reward; the irregularities and difficulties will gradually disappear from view, and he will recognize 'as familiar friends' the spirit of enquiry and the love of truth, which are no less characteristic of the Laws than of all the other writings of Plato.

The persons of the dialogue are three old men, an Athenian, to whom no name is given, Megillus a Spartan, Cleinias a Cretan. They are walking together from Cnosus to the cave and Temple of Zeus, and spend the time, as becomes the citizens of such famous states, in discoursing on laws and government. After the conversation has proceeded to a considerable length, Cleinias announces that he is one of the commissioners appointed by the Cnosians to establish a new colony in Crete, and begs his companions to assist him in drawing up a constitution. This they consent to do, and the Athenian, (for he is the only speaker of importance), accordingly details the institutions which he thinks suitable for the proposed State.

BOOK I.

THE First Book opens with a criticism of the Lacedaemonian and Cretan institutions.

Both have a single object in view,—to inspire courage in war. But the lawgiver should have regard to all the virtues, and not to one only. Better is he who has temperance and courage than he who has courage alone; and better also is he who is faithful in civil strife than he who is merely a good soldier. Peace, again, is better than war; reconciliation than conquest. Moreover, there are two kinds of courage: a courage which arms a man against fear, and teaches him to endure hardships ; and a courage which inspires him to resist the insidious assaults of pleasure and desire. Neither quality ought to be wanting in him who aims at being perfect in virtue.

How can this nobler spirit be implanted in the citizens of a state? Clearly, they must be educated from the first to fight against the temptations of pleasure, just as children are taught in their earliest years to play at the occupations which they will one day follow in earnest. There must be festive gatherings, presided over by sober ' rulers of the feast,' at which there will be a free use of wine under proper regulations. For wine is a test of character,—'*in vino veritas*,' says the proverb, and the older citizens especially will only show their real natures under its stimulating influence.

1. The true nature of Education.

We have already seen how deep an interest Plato, like many other of the great Greek philosophers, took in the subject of education. It may indeed be doubted whether the most advanced of modern nations have established systems of education which would wholly satisfy the aspirations of Plato and Aristotle.

In this passage Plato gives expression to the important principle that children should be trained from the first with an eye to the callings which they will pursue in after-life. And we have ourselves begun to realize that education does not begin and end merely with a knowledge of books ; but that the eye and the hand require training no less than the ear and the mind. Nor is the advantage of such studies by any means confined to those who will find them of practical service hereafter ; for there is no child who will not receive benefit from a knowledge of drawing or an acquaintance with the simpler mechanical arts, even though he may never need to use them in order to gain a livelihood.

Steph.
643
A
Athenian Stranger. You seem to be quite ready to listen ; and I am also ready to perform as much as I can of an almost impossible task, which I will nevertheless attempt. At the outset of the discussion, let me define the nature and power of education ; for this is the way by which our argument must travel onwards to the God Dionysus.

Cleinias. Let us proceed, if you please.

Ath. Well, then, if I tell you what are my notions of education, will you consider whether they satisfy you ?

Cle. Let us hear.

Ath. According to my view, any one who would be good at anything must practise that thing from his youth upwards, both in sport and earnest, in its several branches: for example, he who is to be a good builder, should play at building children's houses; he who is to be a good husbandman, at tilling the ground; and those who have the care of their education should provide them when young with mimic tools. They should learn beforehand the knowledge which they will afterwards require for their art. For example, the future carpenter should learn to measure or apply the line in play; and the future warrior should learn riding, or some other exercise, for amusement, and the teacher should endeavour to direct the children's inclinations and pleasures, by the help of amusements, to their final aim in life. The most important part of education is right training in the nursery. The soul of the child in his play should be guided to the love of that sort of excellence in which when he grows up to manhood he will have to be perfected. Do you agree with me thus far?

Cle. Certainly.

Ath. Then let us not leave the meaning of education ambiguous or ill-defined. At present, when we speak in terms of praise or blame about the bringing-up of each person, we call one man educated and another uneducated, although the uneducated man may be sometimes very well educated for the calling of a retail trader, or of a captain of a ship, and the like. For we are not speaking of education in this narrower sense, but of that other education in virtue from youth upwards, which makes a man eagerly pursue the ideal perfection of citizenship, and teaches him how rightly to rule and how to obey.

644   This is the only education which, upon our view, deserves the name; that other sort of training, which aims at the acquisition of wealth or bodily strength, or mere cleverness apart from intelligence and justice, is mean and illiberal, and is not worthy to be called education at all. But let us not quarrel with one another about a word, provided that the proposition which has just been granted hold good : to wit, that those who are rightly educated generally become good men. Neither must we cast a slight upon education, which is the first and fairest thing that the best of men can ever have, and which, though liable to take a wrong direction, is capable of reformation. And this work of reformation is the great business of every man while he lives.

Cle. Very true; and we entirely agree with you.

2. Man the puppet of the Gods.

The Laws, as we have previously had occasion to observe, are pervaded by a tone of pessimism and bitterness, which appears to have grown upon Plato during his later years. The world is a stage on which men and women play their several parts in the tragi-comedy of life : human affairs are hardly worthy of serious consideration : the incurable wickedness of man makes the work of the legislator a sad necessity; for even in the best-governed states evil natures which are proof against instruction and admonition will spring up like weeds in a fair garden.

Plato himself was not unconscious that this feeling sometimes carried him too far : ' You have a low opinion of mankind, stranger,' says Megillus to the Athenian on one occasion (vii. 804 B). It may have been due partly to the chilling effect of age, which, while it sharpened the mental vision (iv. 715 E), diminished enthusiasm and hope in a proportionate degree. In the earlier dialogues, at least, there is a brighter and serener atmosphere; but in the Republic and the Theaetetus Plato begins to moralize upon the pettiness and insignificance of mortal things (Rep. vi. 486 A ; x. 604 B ; Theaet. 173); and in the Statesman he speaks of men and governments in the same depreciatory manner which is so marked in the Laws.

Steph.   *Athenian Stranger.* Let us look at the matter thus: May
644
D   we not conceive each of us living beings to be a puppet

of the gods, either their plaything only, or created with a purpose—which of the two we cannot certainly know? But we do know, that these affections in us are like cords and strings, which pull us different and opposite ways, and to opposite actions; and herein lies the difference between virtue and vice. According to the argument there is one among these cords which every man ought to grasp and never let go, but to pull with it against all the rest; and this is the sacred and golden cord of reason, called by us the common law of the State; there are others which are hard and of iron, but this one is soft because golden; and there are several other kinds. Now we ought always to co-operate with the lead of the best, which is law. For inasmuch as reason is beautiful and gentle, and not violent, her rule must needs have ministers in order to help the golden principle in vanquishing the other principles.

645

And thus the moral of the tale about our being puppets will not have been lost, and the meaning of the expression 'superior or inferior to a man's self' will become clearer; and the individual, attaining to right reason in this matter of pulling the strings of the puppet, should live according to its rule; while the city, receiving the same from some god or from one who has knowledge of these things, should embody it in a law, to be her guide in her dealings with herself and with other states. In this way virtue and vice will be more clearly distinguished by us.

BOOK II.

IN the Second Book Plato continues the subject of education.

During the early years of life children are educated by perceptions of pleasure and pain, and the pleasure is chiefly conferred by means of dance and song. These, which are the gifts of our 'kind playfellows the gods,' should not be left unregulated, as is now the case;

they should be fixed and established by law after the manner of the Egyptians. The criterion of excellence in music should be pleasure, yet not the pleasure of the base or the foolish; the pleasant, the just, and the noble will be declared by the law to be identical. There will be three choruses at our festivals, one of children, another of youth, a third of elder men from thirty to sixty; and all will utter the same strain,—' that virtue and happiness are inseparable.' The aged, too, who cannot sing, will tell stories to the like effect, as with the voice of an oracle. The elder men may be permitted some indulgence in wine, which will warm their hearts and overcome their diffidence; to children and the young in general it will be forbidden. Our fifty-year old choristers must be true judges of music, well grounded in the principles of harmony and rhythm.

But how can they receive the necessary training? If they are allowed to drink without regulation at their festivals, they will be disorderly and mutinous; and therefore, as we have before said, they must have sober rulers of the feast, men of ripe age and experience, who will enforce discipline among them, and teach them to choose good and fitting melodies and reject those which are unsuitable.

A final word may be added about the use of wine :—Drinking must be kept under strict control, and only tolerated at all in a few cases which will be determined by the legislator.

The habit of drinking not to be encouraged in the State.

With the concluding words of the Second Book Plato completes the discussion of the question :—Whether his future citizens may be permitted to drink wine? The enquiry has a modern sound; and we perhaps wonder that Plato should raise it. For intoxication was not a national vice among the Greeks, but rather a mark of barbarism. The ' paradise of drunkenness,' which Musaeus sang (Rep. ii. 363 D), was, we may suppose, an idea derived with the Orphic mysteries from Thrace. We know, indeed, that drinking was fashionable among certain circles at Athens, (cp. Symp. 176 A, 212 D), yet this may have been a custom borrowed from the Persians or Macedonians, or the Sicilian tyrants. And when Plato tells us that he had seen ' all Tarentum drunk at the Dionysia,' (Laws i. 637 B), we must remember that he is speaking of a religious festival; and that the intoxication was hardly more than the gaiety and infectious light-heartedness of a Southern race enjoying a holiday. The Hellenic temperament was in general averse to excess: even in matters of food and drink the Greek was abstemious, and conscious of a limit which should not be passed.

It is probable that Plato's prohibition of wine is due to Spartan influence. The sentiment grew partly out of the ascetic dislike of pleasure which the institutions of Lycurgus had impressed on the Spartans, and partly out of the feeling that a habit which might 'deprive a man of his wits' at some critical moment was a dangerous vice for the citizens of a Greek state who personally took part in war and in government cp. Shakespeare, Othello A. ii, sc. 3:—'O that men should put an enemy in their mouths to steal away their brains!').

Plato, therefore, will only allow a limited use of wine in his new colony. He has already strictly forbidden it to the young [1], while permitting, perhaps as much in jest as earnest, some indulgence to the aged (666 A). And now he seriously declares his conviction that men and women engaged in the various pursuits of life, whether in war or peace, ought entirely to refrain from the perilous habit. We have had a wider experience than Plato, and our motives of action are not entirely the same; but we, too, seem inclined more and more to return to the old Hellenic ideals, and to insist that our youth shall be educated in an atmosphere of sobriety and temperance.

Athenian Stranger. ONE part of this subject has already been discussed by us, and there still remains another to be discussed.

Cleinias. Exactly.

Ath. I have first a final word to add to my discourse about drink, if you will allow me to do so.

Cle. What more have you to say?

Ath. I should say that if a city seriously means to adopt the practice of drinking under due regulation and with a view to the enforcement of temperance, and in like manner, and on the same principle, will allow of other pleasures, designing to gain the victory over them—in this way all of them may be used. But if the

Steph.
673
D

---

[1] The reader may compare a passage from the Politics of Aristotle, (vii. 17, § 1), where, speaking of the rearing of children, he says:—'It would appear from the example of animals, and of those nations who desire to create the military habit, that the food which has most milk in it is best suited to human beings; but the less wine the better, if they would escape diseases.'

State makes drinking an amusement only, and whoever likes may drink whenever he likes, and with whom he likes, and add to this any other indulgences, I shall never agree or allow that this city or this man should practise drinking. I would go farther than the Cretans and Lacedaemonians, and am disposed rather to the law of the Carthaginians, that no one while he is on a campaign should be allowed to taste wine at all, but that he should drink water during all that time, and that in the city no slave, male or female, should ever drink wine; and that no magistrates should drink during their year of office, nor should pilots of vessels or judges while on duty taste wine at all, nor any one who is going to hold a consultation about any matter of importance; nor in the daytime at all, unless in consequence of exercise or as medicine; nor again at night.

There are numberless other cases also in which those who have good sense and good laws ought not to drink wine, so that if what I say is true, no city will need many vineyards. Their husbandry and their way of life in general will follow an appointed order, and their cultivation of the vine will be the most limited and the least common of their employments. And this, Stranger, shall be the crown of my discourse about wine. if you agree.

Cle. Excellent, we agree.

BOOK III.

PLATO now diverges abruptly to another part of his theme:—the origin of the various forms of government.

There have been many destructions of mankind by deluges and other catastrophes in past ages. And after each calamity society has grown up again in the same way:—First, the isolated families live under the rule of the eldest; next, several families live under one chief; thirdly, cities are built, small, originally, and on high ground; fourthly, the cities become larger and are built in the plains; and lastly, confederations or nations are formed by the union of a number of cities.

Such a confederation was the mighty Dorian league of Sparta, Argos, and Messenè, and its history will furnish us with an important lesson. Why did this union fail? Because the balance of power was not observed in two out of the three states, Argos and Messenè. Sparta, by a happier fate, obtained a better regulated constitution ; and she only has retained her original greatness. . . . A similar lesson is taught by the history of Persia and Athens ; unbridled tyranny has ruined the one, and excessive freedom the other.

At this point Cleinias mentions the new Cretan colony, and requests the aid of his companions.

The Origin of Government.

The growth and development of human society was a subject of keen interest to the Greek philosophers. They knew very little of the history of the past ; but their scanty information merely served to stimulate and intensify their curiosity. The long-recorded antiquity of the East offered a striking contrast to the brief and imperfect annals of Hellas. And it seemed natural to resort for an explanation to the ancient traditions which told how parts of the earth had often been destroyed, sometimes by fire and sometimes by water , cp. Tim. 22 C ; *supra* p. 112). There had been many civilizations in the progress of time : man had not proceeded so far along the road to perfection as he would have done, because the fruit of his labours was perpetually liable to be swept away by some overwhelming catastrophe. And then society had to be reconstructed from the very base : the knowledge of antiquity had perished ; the arts were lost ; and the human race was only represented by a few scattered shepherds and herdsmen. The stages by which mankind advanced from barbarism are related in much the same manner by Aristotle in the First Book of the Politics as by Plato in the Laws, and their account is no doubt true, in the main, at least, to the history of Hellas.

The earliest form of society in which there is no common head, and each family is an independent unit, is, though rare, still to be met with among primitive races, and was once widely prevalent. The family gives place to the tribe or clan, which is little more than a union of families under a single head. But civilization progresses, and the necessities of defence and protection impel men to collect together in settlements. City life begins at this point, and the Hellene, accustomed to the small polities of his own country, could hardly rise beyond the city to the formation of a great nation.

The ancients, we may also remark, fell into the error of supposing that such changes were more uniform than they really were. They did not understand the degree to which men are affected by circumstances; how, for instance, level and fertile plains, such as those of Egypt and Assyria, afford a natural field for the growth of large and highly organized communities, while impenetrable forests and rugged mountains are the appropriate refuge of weak and barbarous races, like the Arcadians or the Epeirots, who are thus enabled to retain their independence at the cost of progress in the arts of civilization.

Steph.
676
A

Athenian Stranger. ENOUGH of this. And what, then, is to be regarded as the origin of government? Will not a man be able to judge of it best from a point of view in which he may behold the progress of states and their transitions to good or evil?

Cleinias. What do you mean?

Ath. I mean that he might watch them from the point of view of time, and observe the changes which take place in them during infinite ages.

Cle. How so?

Ath. Why, do you think that you can reckon the time which has elapsed since cities first existed and men were citizens of them?

Cle. Hardly.

Ath. But you are sure that it must be vast and incalculable?

Cle. Certainly.

Ath. And have not thousands and thousands of cities come into being during this period and as many perished? And has not each of them had every form of government many times over, now growing larger, now smaller, and again improving or declining?

Cle. To be sure.

Ath. Let us endeavour to ascertain the cause of these changes; for that will probably explain the first origin and development of forms of government.

Cle. Very good. You shall endeavour to impart your thoughts to us, and we will make an effort to understand you.

THE SURVIVORS OF THE DELUGE 155

Ath. Do you believe that there is any truth in ancient 677 traditions?

Cle. What traditions?

Ath. The traditions about the many destructions of mankind which have been occasioned by deluges and pestilences, and in many other ways, and of the survival of a remnant?

Cle. Every one is disposed to believe them.

Ath. Let us consider one of them, that which was caused by the famous deluge.

Cle. What are we to observe about it?

Ath. I mean to say that those who then escaped would only be hill shepherds,— small sparks of the human race preserved on the tops of mountains.

Cle. Clearly.

Ath. Such survivors would necessarily be unacquainted with the arts and the various devices which are suggested to the dwellers in cities by interest or ambition, and with all the wrongs which they contrive against one another.

Cle. Very true.

Ath. Let us suppose, then, that the cities in the plain and on the sea-coast were utterly destroyed at that time.

Cle. Very good.

Ath. Would not all implements have then perished and every other excellent invention of political or any other sort of wisdom have utterly disappeared?

Cle. Why, yes, my friend; and if things had always continued as they are at present ordered, how could any discovery have ever been made even in the least particular? For it is evident that the arts were unknown during ten thousand times ten thousand years. And no more than a thousand or two thousand years have elapsed since the discoveries of Daedalus, Orpheus, and Palamedes,— since Marsyas and Olympus invented music, and Amphion the lyre,—not to speak of numberless other inventions which are but of yesterday.

Ath. Have you forgotten, Cleinias, the name of a friend who is really of yesterday?

Cle. I suppose that you mean Epimenides.

Ath. The same, my friend; he does indeed far overleap the heads of all mankind by his invention; for he carried out in practice, as you declare, what of old Hesiod[1] only preached.

Cle. Yes, according to our tradition.

Ath. After the great destruction, may we not suppose that the state of man was something of this sort:—In the beginning of things there was a fearful illimitable desert and a vast expanse of land; a herd or two of oxen would be the only survivors of the animal world; and there might be a few goats, these too hardly enough to maintain the shepherds who tended them?

Cle. True.

Ath. And of cities or governments or legislation, about which we are now talking, do you suppose that they could have any recollection at all?

Cle. None whatever.

Ath. And out of this state of things has there not sprung all that we now are and have: cities and governments, and arts and laws, and a great deal of vice and a great deal of virtue?

---

[1] Works and Days, ll. 40, 41. [The famous lines of Hesiod:—

'Foolish men, who know not how much more the half is than the whole,
Nor how great the refreshment which mallow and asphodel give,'—

which are really a recommendation of a simple diet, were supposed by the ancients to allude to certain herbs which would prevent men from feeling hunger and thirst. And Epimenides, the Cretans believed, actually invented a compound of this nature. The subject is amusingly treated in Plutarch (Goodwin's Plutarch's Morals, vol. ii. p. 27).]

THE AGE BEFORE THE USE OF METALS

Cle. What do you mean?

Ath. Why, my good friend, how can we possibly suppose that those who knew nothing of all the good and evil of cities could have attained their full development, whether of virtue or of vice?

Cle. I understand your meaning, and you are quite right.

Ath. But, as time advanced and the race multiplied, the world came to be what the world is.

Cle. Very true.

Ath. Doubtless the change was not made all in a moment, but little by little, during a very long period of time.

Cle. A highly probable supposition.

Ath. At first, they would have a natural fear ringing in their ears which would prevent their descending from the heights into the plain.

Cle. Of course.

Ath. The fewness of the survivors at that time would have made them all the more desirous of seeing one another; but then the means of travelling either by land or sea had been almost entirely lost, as I may say, with the loss of the arts, and there was great difficulty in getting at one another; for iron and brass and all metals were jumbled together and had disappeared in the chaos; nor was there any possibility of extracting ore from them; and they had scarcely any means of felling timber. Even if you suppose that some implements might have been preserved in the mountains, they must quickly have worn out and vanished, and there would be no more of them until the art of metallurgy had again revived.

Cle. There could not have been.

Ath. In how many generations would this be attained?

Cle. Clearly, not for many generations.

Ath. During this period, and for some time afterwards, all the arts which require iron and brass and the like would disappear.

Cle. Certainly.

Ath. Faction and war would also have died out in those days, and for many reasons.

Cle. How would that be?

Ath. In the first place, the desolation of these primitive men would create in them a feeling of affection and goodwill towards one another; and, secondly, they would have no occasion to quarrel about their subsistence, for they would have pasture in abundance, except just at first, and in some particular cases; and from their pasture-land they would obtain the greater part of their food in a primitive age, having plenty of milk and flesh; moreover they would procure other food by the chase, not to be despised either in quantity or quality. They would also have abundance of clothing, and bedding, and dwellings, and utensils either capable of standing on the fire or not; for the plastic and weaving arts do not require any use of iron: and God has given these two arts to man in order to provide him with all such things, that, when reduced to the last extremity, the human race may still grow and increase.

Hence in those days mankind were not very poor; nor was poverty a cause of difference among them; and rich they could not have been, having neither gold nor silver:—such at that time was their condition. And the community which has neither poverty nor riches will always have the noblest principles; in it there is no insolence or injustice, nor, again, are there any contentions or envyings. And therefore they were good, and also because they were what is called simple-minded; and when they were told about good and evil, they in their simplicity believed what they heard to be very truth and practised it. No one had the wit to suspect another of a falsehood, as men do now; but what they heard about gods and men they believed to be true, and lived accordingly; and therefore they were in all respects such as we have described them.

Cle. That quite accords with my views, and with those of my friend here.

Ath. Would not many generations living on in a simple manner, although ruder, perhaps, and more ignorant of the arts generally, and in particular of those of land or naval warfare, and likewise of other arts, termed in cities legal practices and party conflicts, and including all conceivable ways of hurting one another in word and deed;—although inferior to those who lived before the deluge, or to the men of our day in these respects, would they not, I say, be simpler and more manly, and also more temperate and altogether more just? The reason has been already explained.

Cle. Very true.

BOOK IV.

In the Fourth Book the new colony is further discussed, and some first principles of government are laid down.

The site proposed for the city is at a considerable distance from the sea, and this is an advantage : for maritime states are unstable and given to the pursuit of gain. The colonists are to be Hellenes, and Peloponnesians will have the preference.

The legislator, like other artists, requires favourable conditions for the exercise of his art ; and the greatest good fortune which can befall him is that he should be aided in his work by a young tyrant, who possesses both virtue and absolute power. But such a conjunction occurs very rarely in the course of ages.

What is to be the constitution? Modern states are governed in the selfish interests of the ruling class; in our commonwealth the law will be supreme, and the rulers will be only the ministers of the law.

The citizens will be exhorted by the legislator to follow virtue, and to pay due honour to Gods and to parents. His words will be a general prelude to legislation; and the laws, which should be clearly and precisely stated, should each likewise have a preamble, intended to explain the law and make men more inclined to obey it.

1. The virtuous Tyrant.

The idea of the 'virtuous tyrant' who supplies the force necessary to set the new machinery of government in motion, is a somewhat paradoxical expression of a thought which has arisen in the minds of many philosophers and political writers. It is not, perhaps, an impossible task to frame an imaginary polity which would be an improvement upon any constitution known to exist in the world. But how can the legislator induce or compel mankind to obey his commands? The answer seems obvious :—Let him for a short time enjoy absolute power, or let his efforts be seconded by some 'benevolent despot' or 'saviour of society,' and the rest will be easy; —to use the language of Plato in the familiar passage of the Republic, 'the evils of the world will only cease when philosophers are kings or kings are philosophers.'

To the Greek especially such a conception was natural. He was inclined to exaggerate the power of the legislator to alter the entire character of a nation, as Lycurgus was supposed to have done at Sparta; and the rapid rise of Hellenic civilization prevented him from clearly seeing that states grow rather than are made, and are, like men, 'conditioned by their circumstances.' The uncertain equilibrium of the small Greek commonwealths and the violent changes which they underwent,—from aristocracy or oligarchy to tyranny, from tyranny to democracy, from democracy to oligarchy again,—also contributed to strengthen this feeling. In the larger and more solidly based communities of modern Europe, on the other hand, the continuity of history is generally better maintained, and the reform of existing institutions, which, in the words of Aristotle, 'is no less difficult a task than the establishment of new ones,' (Pol. iv. 1, § 7), is the principal object of the statesman's efforts.

Steph. 709 C

Athenian Stranger. And does not a like principle apply to legislation as well as to other things: even supposing all the conditions to be favourable which are needed for the happiness of the state, yet the true legislator must from time to time appear on the scene?

Cleinias. Most true.

Ath. In each case the artist would be able to pray

rightly for certain conditions, and if these were granted by fortune, he would then only require to exercise his art?

Cle. Certainly.

Ath. And all the other artists just now mentioned, if they were bidden to offer up each their special prayer, would do so?

Cle. Of course.

Ath. And the legislator would do likewise?

Cle. I believe that he would.

Ath. 'Come, legislator,' we will say to him; 'what are the conditions which you require in a state before you can organize it?' How ought he to answer this question? Shall I give his answer?

Cle. Yes.

Ath. He will say—'Give me a state which is governed by a tyrant, and let the tyrant be young and have a good memory; let him be quick at learning, and of a courageous and noble nature; let him have that quality which, as I said before, is the inseparable companion of all the other parts of virtue, if there is to 710 be any good in them.'

Cle. I suppose, Megillus, that this companion virtue of which the Stranger speaks, must be temperance?

Ath. Yes, Cleinias, temperance in the vulgar sense; not that which in the forced and exaggerated language of some philosophers is called prudence, but that which is the natural gift of children and animals, of whom some live continently and others incontinently, but when isolated, was, as we said, hardly worth reckoning in the catalogue of goods[1]. I think that you must understand my meaning.

Cle. Certainly.

Ath. Then our tyrant must have this as well as the

[1] Cp. *supra*, iii. 696 D.

other qualities, if the state is to acquire in the best manner and in the shortest time the form of government which is most conducive to happiness; for there neither is nor ever will be a better or speedier way of establishing a polity than by a tyranny.

Cle. By what possible arguments, Stranger, can any man persuade himself of such a monstrous doctrine?

Ath. There is surely no difficulty in seeing, Cleinias, what is in accordance with the order of nature?

Cle. You would assume, as you say, a tyrant who was young, temperate, quick at learning, having a good memory, courageous, of a noble nature?

Ath. Yes; and you must add fortunate; and his good fortune must be that he is the contemporary of a great legislator, and that some happy chance brings them together. When this has been accomplished, God has done all that He ever does for a state which He desires to be eminently prosperous; He has done second best for a state in which there are two such rulers, and third best for a state in which there are three. The difficulty increases with the increase, and diminishes with the diminution of the number.

Cle. You mean to say, I suppose, that the best government is produced from a tyranny, and originates in a good lawgiver and an orderly tyrant, and that the change from such a tyranny into a perfect form of government takes place most easily; less easily when from an oligarchy; and, in the third degree, from a democracy: is not that your meaning?

Ath. Not so; I mean rather to say that the change is best made out of a tyranny; and secondly, out of a monarchy; and thirdly, out of some sort of democracy: fourth, in the capacity for improvement, comes oligarchy, which has the greatest difficulty in admitting of such a change, because the government is in the hands of a number of potentates. I am supposing that the legislator is by nature of the true sort, and that his strength is united with that of the chief men of the state; and when the ruling element is numerically small, and at the same time very strong, as in a tyranny, there the 711 change is likely to be easiest and most rapid.

Cle. How? I do not understand.

Ath. And yet I have repeated what I am saying a good many times; but I suppose that you have never seen a city which is under a tyranny?

Cle. No, and I cannot say that I have any great desire to see one.

Ath. And yet, where there is a tyranny, you might certainly see that of which I am now speaking.

Cle. What do you mean?

Ath. I mean that you might see how, without trouble and in no very long period of time, the tyrant, if he wishes, can change the manners of a state: he has only to go in the direction of virtue or of vice, whichever he prefers, he himself indicating by his example the lines of conduct, praising and rewarding some actions and reproving others, and degrading those who disobey.

Cle. But how can we imagine that the citizens in general will at once follow the example set to them; and how can he have this power both of persuading and of compelling them?

Ath. Let no one, my friends, persuade us that there is any quicker and easier way in which states change their laws than when the rulers lead: such changes never have, nor ever will, come to pass in any other way. The real impossibility or difficulty is of another sort, and is rarely surmounted in the course of ages; but when once it is surmounted, ten thousand or rather all blessings follow.

Cle. Of what are you speaking?

Ath. The difficulty is to find the divine love of temperate and just institutions existing in any powerful forms of government, whether in a monarchy or oligarchy of wealth or of birth. You might as well hope to reproduce the character of Nestor, who is said to have excelled all men in the power of speech, and yet more in his temperance. This, however, according to the tradition, was in the times of Troy; in our own days there is nothing of the sort; but if such an one either has or ever shall come into being, or is now among us, blessed is he and blessed are they who hear the wise words that flow from his lips.

And this may be said of power in general: When the supreme power in man coincides with the greatest wisdom and temperance, then the best laws and the best constitution come into being; but in no other way. And let what I have been saying be regarded as a kind of sacred legend or oracle, and let this be our proof that, in one point of view, there may be a difficulty for a city to have good laws, but that there is another point of view in which nothing can be easier or sooner effected, granting our supposition.

2. The Life of Virtue.

The Laws, among other singular features, are remarkable for the number of addresses and exhortations which they contain, and which take the place of the dialectical arguments of the earlier dialogues. The following passage is one of these discourses, supposed to be addressed to the newly-arrived colonists, and intended to inform them of the moral and religious principles by which their life would have to be guided. There appears to us something strange in a legislator giving such admonitions to a band of settlers: the Greek philosopher saw no boundary fixed between ethics and politics, between the legal and the moral code.

The ideal State which Plato has outlined in the Laws exemplifies this tendency in the highest degree. The ἦθος of the community may be compared in Platonic phraseology to the soul which pervades and animates the whole body. The citizens are to have a certain mould impressed upon them from their first entrance into the world to the time when they take leave of it. The children are to be educated in a uniform manner, and no allowance is made for individual fancies and peculiarities. A round of duties is prescribed for the citizens, and the women are, as far as possible, to share the training and occupations of the men.

Plato is not unaware that many of his minute regulations cannot be enforced by law : but he thinks that the approbation of the legislator and the force of public opinion will ensure their acceptance vii. 788, 807 E). He does not sufficiently realize the feeble and unprogressive character which such a community would assume. There would be no spring of life or energy among the young: no career for promising talent : no expansion of mind or thought. If Plato could have seen his dreams carried into effect, he would have found that he had purchased uniformity by the loss of much that is most valuable in the existence of nations and individuals.

Athenian Stranger. And now, what is to be the next step ? May we not suppose the colonists to have arrived, and proceed to make our speech to them ? Steph. 715 E.

Cleinias. Certainly.

Ath. 'Friends,' we say to them,— 'God, as the old tradition declares, holding in His hand the beginning, middle, and end of all that is, travels according to His nature in a straight line towards the accomplishment of His end. Justice always accompanies Him, and is the punisher of those who fall short of the divine law. To justice, he who would be happy holds fast, and follows in her company with all humility and order ; but he who is lifted up with pride, or elated by wealth or rank, or beauty, who is young and foolish, and has a soul hot with insolence, and thinks that he has no need of any guide or ruler, but is able himself to be the guide of others, he, I say, is left deserted of God ; and being thus deserted, he takes to him others who are like himself, and dances about, throwing all things into confusion, and many think that he is a great man, but in a short time he pays a penalty which justice cannot but approve, and is utterly destroyed, and his family 716 and city with him. Wherefore, seeing that human things are thus ordered, what should a wise man do or think, or not do or think?'

Cle. Every man ought to make up his mind that he will be one of the followers of God; there can be no doubt of that.

Ath. Then what life is agreeable to God, and becoming in His followers? One only, expressed once for all in the old saying that 'like agrees with like, with measure measure,' but things which have no measure agree neither with themselves nor with the things which have. Now God ought to be to us the measure of all things, and not man[1], as men commonly say (Protagoras): the words are far more true of Him. And he who would be dear to God must, as far as is possible, be like Him and such as He is. Wherefore the temperate man is the friend of God, for he is like Him; and the intemperate man is unlike Him, and different from Him, and unjust. And the same applies to other things; and this is the conclusion, which is also the noblest and truest of all sayings,—that for the good man to offer sacrifice to the Gods, and hold converse with them by means of prayers and offerings and every kind of service, is the noblest and best of all things, and also the most conducive to a happy life, and very fit and meet. But with the bad man, the opposite of this is true: for the bad man has an impure soul, whereas the good is pure; and from one who is polluted, neither a good man nor God can without impropriety receive gifts. Wherefore the unholy do only waste their much service upon the Gods, but when offered by any holy man, such service is most acceptable to them.

This is the mark at which we ought to aim. But what weapons shall we use, and how shall we direct

[1] Cp. Crat. 386 A foll.; Theaet. 152 A.

them ? In the first place, we affirm that next after the Olympian Gods and the Gods of the State, honour should be given to the Gods below ; they should receive everything in even numbers, and of the second choice, and ill omen, while the odd numbers, and the first choice, and the things of lucky omen, are given to the Gods above, by him who would rightly hit the mark of piety. Next to these Gods, a wise man will do service to the demons or spirits, and then to the heroes, and after them will follow the private and ancestral Gods, who are worshipped as the law prescribes in the places which are sacred to them.

Next comes the honour of living parents, to whom, as is meet, we have to pay the first and greatest and oldest of all debts, considering that all which a man has belongs to those who gave him birth and brought him up, and that he must do all that he can to minister to them, first, in his property, secondly, in his person, and thirdly, in his soul, in return for the endless care and travail which they bestowed upon him of old, in the days of his infancy, and which he is now to pay back to them when they are old and in the extremity of their need. And all his life long he ought never to utter, or to have uttered, an unbecoming word to them ; for of light and fleeting words the penalty is most severe ; Nemesis, the messenger of justice, is appointed to watch over all such matters. When they are angry and want to satisfy their feelings in word or deed, he should give way to them; for a father who thinks that he has been wronged by his son may be reasonably expected to be very angry.

At their death, the most moderate funeral is best, neither exceeding the customary expense, nor yet falling short of the honour which has been usually shown by the former generation to their parents. And let a man not forget to pay the yearly tribute of respect to the dead, honouring them chiefly by omitting nothing that conduces to a perpetual remembrance of them, and giving a reasonable portion of his fortune to the dead. Doing this, and living after this manner, we shall receive our reward from the Gods and those who are above us [i.e. the demons]; and we shall spend our days for the most part in good hope.

BOOK V.

The Fifth Book of the Laws falls naturally into two divisions:—

(1) The first part is a long monologue of the Athenian, in which the citizens are further instructed in ethical and moral principles. . . . The soul is to be duly honoured as the divinest element of man's nature. A mean state of the bodily habits is to be desired, and excess must also be shunned in the acquisition of property. . . . Reverence should be paid to the elder; and our duties towards kindred, strangers, and suppliants, are to be scrupulously fulfilled. . . . In the relations of life a man should be just, faithful, sincere, unenvious. Injustice is involuntary; the unjust are to be pitied, and only the incurable punished. . . . Selfishness should be avoided. . . . Men should have a true taste for pleasure, and the highest pleasures are those of a temperate life.

(2) The preamble thus finished, we turn to the construction of the state. . . . The citizens are to be 5040 in number, and each of them will receive an equal allotment of land. The constitution will be, not the best, but the second best: communism must be abandoned, being unsuited for citizens reared as ours will have been. Population must be regulated by various devices, and no addition or diminution permitted. . . . The accumulation of wealth will be discouraged. A little money may be coined, of a kind, however, which will not pass current elsewhere. Dowries may not be given, and usury will be disallowed. The state is to be virtuous, not wealthy; both at once it cannot be. A good education is far above riches. . . . The citizens will be divided into four classes according to a property qualification; and there will be twelve tribes, with a presiding deity assigned to each. . . . The legislator must pay great attention to numerical proportions and ratios in the arrangement of his state; and he must also encourage the citizens to study Arithmetic, which is an invaluable mental training.

1. The honour of the Soul. Precepts for a virtuous life.

The opening of the Fifth Book of the Laws is one of the most noble and striking passages in all the writings of Plato. In solemn and earnest language he lays down the principles which are to guide the soul on her 'voyage through life' (Laws vii. 803 A; 2 Alcib. 146 E). He wishes his citizens to have true notions respecting the objects of human existence; they are not to regard the accumulation of wealth as the end to which they are to 'devote their most serious endeavours,' or to degrade themselves by self-indulgence and luxury. They will be the citizens of a State which will have few rivals on earth (Laws xii. 950 D), and they must strive to be worthy of her.

Plato perceives clearly that, without this ethical foundation, the best laws and institutions will be of little avail; and, although he is aware that even 'in a State which is perfectly adapted for virtue' (Laws ix. 853) the evil passions of men will bear their inevitable fruit, he is not disposed to relax his efforts for the improvement of the human race. He remains to the end an idealist, though his estimate of mankind has sunk lower and lower with advancing years. He is filled with disappointment and despair; his spirit is more bitter and pessimistic than in earlier and brighter days; yet he cannot bring himself to think that the repeated admonitions and exhortations of the legislator will fall unheeded on the ears of the citizens.

Like Socrates in the Phaedo, he feels that he is soon about to go to 'other Gods who are wise and good' (Phaedo 63); and he would fain stay one brief moment before he takes the final journey, and address a few last words of encouragement and advice to all who will listen to him. The pathos and impressiveness of this parting discourse are greatly heightened by a dignified and lofty tone which was justified by age and the consciousness of a life spent in the service of virtue.

Athenian Stranger. LISTEN, all ye who have just now heard the laws about Gods, and about our dear forefathers:—Of all the things which a man has, next to the Gods, his soul is the most divine and most truly his own. Now in every man there are two parts: the better and superior, which rules, and the worse and inferior, which serves; and the ruling part of him is always to be preferred to the subject. Wherefore I am

Steph. 726

727

right in bidding every one next to the Gods, who are our masters, and those who in order follow them [i. e. the demons], to honour his own soul, which every one seems to honour, but no one honours as he ought; for honour is a divine good, and no evil thing is honourable; and he who thinks that he can honour the soul by word or gift, or any sort of compliance, without making her in any way better, seems to honour her, but honours her not at all. For example, every man, from his very boyhood, fancies that he is able to know everything, and thinks that he honours his soul by praising her, and he is very ready to let her do whatever she may like. But I mean to say that in acting thus he injures his soul, and is far from honouring her; whereas, in our opinion, he ought to honour her as second only to the Gods.

Again, when a man thinks that others are to be blamed, and not himself, for the errors which he has committed from time to time, and the many and great evils which befell him in consequence, and is always fancying himself to be exempt and innocent, he is under the idea that he is honouring his soul; whereas the very reverse is the fact, for he is really injuring her. And when, disregarding the word and approval of the legislator, he indulges in pleasure, then again he is far from honouring her; he only dishonours her, and fills her full of evil and remorse; or when he does not endure to the end the labours and fears and sorrows and pains which the legislator approves, but gives way before them, then, by yielding, he does not honour the soul, but by all such conduct he makes her to be dishonourable; nor when he thinks that life at any price is a good, does he honour her, but yet once more he dishonours her; for the soul having a notion that the world below is all evil, he yields to her, and does not resist and teach or convince her that, for aught she knows, the world of the Gods below, instead of being evil, may be the greatest of all goods.

Again, when any one prefers beauty to virtue, what is this but the real and utter dishonour of the soul? For such a preference implies that the body is more honourable than the soul; and this is false, for there is nothing of earthly birth which is more honourable than the heavenly, and he who thinks otherwise of the soul has no idea how greatly he undervalues this wonderful possession; nor, again, when a person is willing, or 728 not unwilling, to acquire dishonest gains, does he then honour his soul with gifts—far otherwise; he sells her glory and honour for a small piece of gold; but all the gold which is under or upon the earth is not enough to give in exchange for virtue.

In a word, I may say that he who does not estimate the base and evil, the good and noble, according to the standard of the legislator, and abstain in every possible way from the one and practise the other to the utmost of his power, does not know that in all these respects he is most foully and disgracefully abusing his soul, which is the divinest part of man; for no one, as I may say, ever considers that which is declared to be the greatest penalty of evil-doing—namely, to grow into the likeness of bad men, and growing like them to fly from the conversation of the good, and be cut off from them, and cleave to and follow after the company of the bad. And he who is joined to them must do and suffer what such men by nature do and say to one another,—a suffering which is not justice but retribution; for justice and the just are noble, whereas retribution is the suffering which waits upon injustice; and whether a man escape or endure this, he is miserable,—in the former case, because he is not cured; while in the latter, he perishes in order that the rest of mankind may be saved.

Speaking generally, our glory is to follow the better and improve the inferior, which is susceptible of improvement, as far as this is possible. And of all human possessions, the soul is by nature most inclined to avoid the evil, and track out and find the chief good; which when a man has found, he should take up his abode with it during the remainder of his life. Wherefore the soul also is second [or next to God] in honour; and third, as every one will perceive, comes the honour of the body in natural order.

Having determined this, we have next to consider that there is a natural honour of the body, and that of honours some are true and some are counterfeit. To decide which are which is the business of the legislator; and he, I suspect, would intimate that they are as follows:—Honour is not to be given to the fair body, or to the strong or the swift or the tall, or to the healthy body (although many may think otherwise), any more than to their opposites; but the mean states of all these habits are by far the safest and most moderate; for the one extreme makes the soul braggart and insolent, and the other, illiberal and base; and money, and property, and distinction all go to the same tune. The excess of any of these things is apt to be a source of hatreds and divisions among states and individuals; and the defect of them is commonly a cause of slavery.

And, therefore, I would not have any one fond of heaping up riches for the sake of his children, in order that he may leave them as rich as possible. For the possession of great wealth is of no use, either to them or to the state. The condition of youth which is free from flattery, and at the same time not in need of the necessaries of life, is the best and most harmonious of all, being in accord and agreement with our nature, and making life to be most entirely free from sorrow. Let parents, then, bequeath to their children not a heap of riches, but the spirit of reverence. We, indeed, fancy that they will inherit reverence from us, if we rebuke them when they show a want of reverence. But this quality is not really imparted to them by the present style of admonition, which only tells them that the young ought always to be reverential. A sensible legislator will rather exhort the elders to reverence the younger, and above all to take heed that no young man sees or hears one of themselves doing or saying anything disgraceful; for where old men have no shame, there young men will most certainly be devoid of reverence. The best way of training the young is to train yourself at the same time ; not to admonish them, but to be always carrying out your own admonitions in practice.

He who honours his kindred, and reveres those who share in the same Gods and are of the same blood and family, may fairly expect that the Gods who preside over generation will be propitious to him, and will quicken his seed. And he who deems the services which his friends and acquaintances do for him, greater and more important than they themselves deem them, and his own favours to them less than theirs to him, will have their good-will in the intercourse of life. And surely in his relations to the state and his fellow-citizens, he is by far the best, who rather than the Olympic or any other victory of peace or war, desires to win the palm of obedience to the laws of his country, and who, of all mankind, is the person reputed to have obeyed them best through life.

In his relations to strangers, a man should consider that a contract is a most holy thing, and that all concerns and wrongs of strangers are more directly dependent on the protection of God, than wrongs done to citizens; for the stranger, having no kindred and friends, is more to be pitied by Gods and men. Wherefore, also, he who is most able to avenge him is most zealous in his cause; and he who is most able is the Genius and the God of the stranger, who follow in the train of Zeus, the God of strangers. And for this reason, he who has a spark of caution in him, will do his best to pass through life without sinning against the stranger. And of offences committed, whether against strangers or fellow-countrymen, that against suppliants is the greatest. For the God who witnessed to the agreement made with the suppliant, becomes in a special manner the guardian of the sufferer; and he will certainly not suffer unavenged.

Thus we have fairly described the manner in which a man is to act about his parents, and himself, and his own affairs; and in relation to the state, and his friends, and kindred, both in what concerns his own countrymen, and in what concerns the stranger. We will now consider what manner of man he must be who would best pass through life in respect of those other things which are not matters of law, but of praise and blame only; in which praise and blame educate a man, and make him more tractable and amenable to the laws which are about to be imposed.

Truth is the beginning of every good thing, both to Gods and men; and he who would be blessed and happy, should be from the first a partaker of the truth, that he may live a true man as long as possible, for then he can be trusted; but he is not to be trusted who loves voluntary falsehood, and he who loves involuntary falsehood is a fool. Neither condition is enviable, for the untrustworthy and ignorant has no friend, and as time advances he becomes known, and lays up in store for himself isolation in crabbed age when life is on the wane : so that, whether his children or friends are alive or not, he is equally solitary.

Worthy of honour is he who does no injustice, and of more than twofold honour, if he not only does no injustice himself, but hinders others from doing any; the first may count as one man, the second is worth many men, because he informs the rulers of the injustice of others. And yet more highly to be esteemed is he who co-operates with the rulers in correcting the citizens as far as he can—he shall be proclaimed the great and perfect citizen, and bear away the palm of virtue. The same praise may be given about temperance and wisdom, and all other goods which may be imparted to others, as well as acquired by a man for himself; he who imparts them shall be honoured as the man of men, and he who is willing, yet is not able, may be allowed the second place ; but he who is jealous and will not, if he can help, allow others to partake in a friendly way of any good, is deserving of blame : the good, however, which he has, is not to be undervalued by us because it is possessed by him, but must be acquired by us also to the utmost of our power. Let every man, then, freely strive for the prize of virtue, and let there be no envy. For the unenvious nature increases the greatness of states— he himself contends in the race, blasting the fair fame of no man ; but the envious, who thinks that he ought to get the better by defaming others, is less energetic himself in the pursuit of true virtue, and reduces his rivals to despair by his unjust slanders of them. And so he makes the whole city to enter the arena untrained in the practice of virtue, and diminishes her glory as far as in him lies.

Now every man should be valiant, but he should

also be gentle. From the cruel, or hardly curable, or altogether incurable acts of injustice done to him by others, a man can only escape by fighting and defending himself and conquering, and by never ceasing to punish them; and no man who is not of a noble spirit is able to accomplish this. As to the actions of those who do evil, but whose evil is curable, in the first place, let us remember that the unjust man is not unjust of his own free will. For no man of his own free will would choose to possess the greatest of evils, and least of all in the most honourable part of himself. And the soul, as we said, is of a truth deemed by all men the most honourable. In the soul, then, which is the most honourable part of him, no one, if he could help, would admit, or allow to continue the greatest of evils[1]. The unrighteous and vicious are always to be pitied in any case; and one can afford to forgive as well as pity him who is curable, and refrain and calm one's anger, not getting into a passion, like a woman, and nursing ill-feeling. But upon him who is incapable of reformation and wholly evil, the vials of our wrath should be poured out; wherefore I say that good men ought, when occasion demands, to be both gentle and passionate.

Of all evils the greatest is one which in the souls of most men is innate, and which a man is always excusing in himself and never correcting; I mean, what is expressed in the saying that 'Every man by nature is and ought to be his own friend.' Whereas the excessive love of self is in reality the source to each man of all offences; for the lover is blinded about the beloved, so that he judges wrongly of the just, the good, and the honourable, and thinks that he ought always to prefer himself to the truth. But he who would be a great man ought to regard, not himself or

---

[1] Cp. Rep. ii. 382.

his interests, but what is just, whether the just act be his own or that of another. Through a similar error men are induced to fancy that their own ignorance is wisdom, and thus we who may be truly said to know nothing, think that we know all things; and because we will not let others act for us in what we do not know, we are compelled to act amiss ourselves. Wherefore let every man avoid excess of self-love, and condescend to follow a better man than himself, not allowing any false shame to stand in the way.

There are also minor precepts which are often repeated, and are quite as useful; a man should recollect them and remind himself of them. For when a stream is flowing out, there should be water flowing in too; and recollection flows in while wisdom is departing. Therefore I say that a man should refrain from excess either of laughter or tears, and should exhort his neighbour to do the same; he should veil his immoderate sorrow or joy, and seek to behave with propriety, whether the genius of his good fortune remains with him, or whether at the crisis of his fate, when he seems to be mounting high and steep places, the gods oppose him in some of his enterprises. Still he may ever hope, in the case of good men, that whatever afflictions are to befall them in the future God will lessen, and that present evils He will change for the better; and as to the goods which are the opposite of these evils, he will not doubt that they will be added to them, and that they will be fortunate. Such should be men's hopes, and such should be the exhortations with which they admonish one another, never losing an opportunity, but on every occasion distinctly reminding themselves and others of all these things, both in jest and earnest.

2. The best and the second-best State.

In the passage which follows, Plato explains the relation between the perfect state of the Republic and the commonwealth described in the Laws. He holds to the opinion that the government of philosophers and the community of women, children, and property are necessary to the highest and best form of the state, although he now concedes that men as they exist in the world are unfitted to live under such institutions. In the Laws, therefore, communism is abandoned, and the rulers are only magistrates whose training has been chiefly of a practical kind. The place of communism is, however, supplied to some extent by the limits imposed upon the accumulation of wealth, by the common education which is given to men and women, and also by the extension of the common meals to women.

The constitution of the new or 'second-best' state can hardly be said with propriety to be 'next to the perfect form.' It has no ideal character, but is an aristocratic government of an ordinary Greek type. The citizens are divided into four classes according to a property qualification; the more important magistracies, though nominally open to all, are practically confined to men of wealth and position by means of complicated methods of election (cp. Arist. Pol. iv. 12, § 6 foll.); the Assembly is reduced to a mere shadow, having no functions of importance, and subject to the control of the Senate.

The distrust of the popular element which Plato shows throughout these arrangements is somewhat remarkable when we consider that he is proposing to construct a state in which there would be no proletariate; for the citizens are to be in a middle condition, equally removed from the extremes of wealth and poverty, and are forbidden to trade or to engage in husbandry. Evidently he is still influenced by his dislike to the city populace of Athens; he forgets that he is legislating for a community of an entirely different nature. This is one of several inconsistencies which are found in the Laws, and may be compared with the manner in which Plato praises the life of peace and yet gives his whole commonwealth a military cast resembling that of Sparta, or in which, while denouncing the evils caused by riches, he makes the distinction of classes and the right to office rest upon the possession of property.

Steph
739
A

Athenian Stranger. The next move in our pastime of legislation, like the withdrawal of the stone from the holy line in the game of draughts[1], being an unusual

[1] [The allusion is obscure. It is thus explained by the Scholiast:—The draught-board in its ancient form (which was attributed to

one, will probably excite wonder when mentioned for the first time. And yet, if a man will only reflect and weigh the matter with care, he will see that our city is ordered in a manner which, if not the best, is the second best. Perhaps also some one may not approve this form, because he thinks that such a constitution is ill adapted to a legislator who has not despotic power. The truth is, that there are three forms of government, the best, the second and the third best, which we may just mention, and then leave the selection to the ruler of the settlement. Following this method in the present instance, let us speak of the states which are respectively first, second, and third in excellence, and then we will leave the choice to Cleinias now, or to any one else who may hereafter have to make a similar choice among constitutions, and may desire to give to his state some feature which is congenial to him and which he approves in his own country.

The first and highest form of the state and of the government and of the law is that in which there prevails most widely the ancient saying, that 'Friends have all things in common.' Whether there is anywhere now, or will ever be, this communion of women and children and of property, in which the private and individual is altogether banished from life, and things which are by nature private, such as eyes and ears and hands, have become common, and in some way see and hear and act in common, and all men express praise and blame and feel joy and sorrow on the same occasions,

---

Palamedes) was divided by five lines of which the middle was called the 'holy line.' From this the stone was only moved in case of urgent need. The phrase 'to move from the holy line' was therefore applied to those who in desperate circumstances made great efforts to save themselves. Here, however, it appears to have a modified sense, = 'to take an unusual step.']

and whatever laws there are unite the city to the utmost,—whether all this is possible or not, I say that no man, acting upon any other principle, will ever constitute a state which will be truer or better or more exalted in virtue. Whether such a state is governed by Gods or sons of Gods, one, or more than one, happy are the men who, living after this manner, dwell there; and therefore to this we are to look for the pattern of the state, and to cling to this, and to seek with all our might for one which is like this. The state which we have now in hand, when created, will be nearest to immortality and the only one which takes the second place; and after that, by the grace of God, we will complete the third one. And we will begin by speaking of the nature and origin of the second.

Let the citizens at once distribute their land and
740 houses, and not till the land in common, since a community of goods goes beyond their proposed origin, and nurture, and education. But in making the distribution, let the several possessors feel that their particular lots also belong to the whole city; and seeing that the earth is their parent, let them tend her more carefully than children do their mother. For she is a goddess and their queen, and they are her mortal subjects. Such also are the feelings which they ought to entertain to the Gods and demi-gods of the country. And in order that the distribution may always remain, they ought to consider further that the present number of families should be always retained, and neither increased nor diminished.

This may be secured for the whole city in the following manner:—Let the possessor of a lot leave the one of his children who is his best beloved, and one only to be the heir of his dwelling, and his successor in the duty of ministering to the Gods, the state, and the family, as well the living members of it as those who are departed when he comes into the inheritance ; but of his other children, if he have more than one, he shall give the females in marriage according to the law to be hereafter enacted [1], and the males he shall distribute as sons to those citizens who have no children, and are disposed to receive them ; or if there should be none such, and particular individuals have too many children, male or female, or too few, as in the case of barrenness —in all these cases let the highest and most honourable magistracy created by us judge and determine what is to be done with the redundant or deficient, and devise a means that the number of 5040 houses shall always remain the same. There are many ways of regulating numbers ; for they in whom generation is affluent may be made to refrain [2], and, on the other hand, special care may be taken to increase the number of births by rewards and stigmas, or we may meet the evil by the elder men giving advice and administering rebuke to the younger—in this way the object may be attained.

And if after all there be very great difficulty about the equal preservation of the 5040 houses, and there be an excess of citizens, owing to the too great love of those who live together, and we are at our wits' end, there is still the old device often mentioned by us of sending out a colony, which will part friends with us, and be composed of suitable persons. If, on the other hand, there come a wave bearing a deluge of disease, or a plague of war, and the inhabitants become much fewer than the appointed number by reason of bereavement, we ought not to introduce citizens of spurious birth and education, if this can be avoided ; but even God is said not to be able to fight against necessity.

[1] Cp. *infra*, xi. 923-926.
[2] Cp. Arist. Pol. vii. 16, § 15.

3. Riches and Godliness.

There is hardly any subject in the Laws on which Plato speaks with greater emphasis and frequency than on his determination to banish from his state the ills which arise out of excessive wealth and the pursuit of gain: 'no gold or silver Plutus,' as he says in one passage, 'shall dwell in our city' (vii. 801 B). To effect this object he proposes:—(1) to make the lot inalienable; (2) to abolish dowries; (3) to debar the citizens from money-making, and from receiving usury; (4) to forbid the acquisition of property beyond a certain limit; (5) to restrict the power of bequest in various ways (xi. 922). He is aware that the worst evils owe their origin to the accumulation of wealth in a few hands, and he may have had in mind the decadent condition of Sparta, which, according to Aristotle, was largely due to a similar cause (Arist. Pol. ii. 9, §§ 13-16).

The only impracticable part of his plan is, probably, the enactment which fixes a limit to the acquisition of wealth. In modern times we should be more inclined to suggest the imposition of a graduated property tax on the owners of large incomes, the resumption of the 'unearned increment' by the state, or the exaction of heavy 'death duties.' The other proposals of Plato seem to be derived from the actual practice of Hellenic states, or at least to have been put forward by previous writers and thinkers. For the inequalities of property had been from the earliest times the 'very spring and fountain of revolutions' (Arist. Pol. v. 1, § 8) in the cities of Hellas, which were, as Plato and Aristotle agree in telling us, rent asunder by the endless quarrel of rich and poor.

But although Plato hopes by wise legislation to diminish, if not entirely to destroy, this great social danger, he is not ignorant of the truth on which Aristotle afterwards enlarges, that 'it is more important to equalize the desires than the possessions of men' (Pol. ii. 7, § 8). Here is the province of education, which is the basis and foundation of the whole state. By its aid he expects to render his citizens 'receptive of virtue,' while the Spartan severity and simplicity of their training will raise them above the lower instincts of their nature, and make them docile and obedient to the guiding hand of the legislator.

Steph.
742
D

Athenian Stranger. The intention, as we affirm, of a reasonable statesman, is not what the many declare to be the object of a good legislator, namely, that the state for the true interests of which he is advising should be as great and as rich as possible, and should possess gold and silver, and have the greatest empire by sea and land;—this they imagine to be the real object of legislation, at the same time adding, inconsistently, that the true legislator desires to have the city the best and happiest possible. But they do not see that some of these things are possible, and some of them are impossible; and he who orders the state will desire what is possible, and will not indulge in vain wishes or attempts to accomplish that which is impossible.

The citizen must indeed be happy and good, and the legislator will seek to make him so; but very rich and very good at the same time he cannot be, not, at least, in the sense in which the many speak of riches. For they mean by 'the rich' the few who have the most valuable possessions, although the owner of them may quite well be a rogue. And if this is true, I can never assent to the doctrine that the rich man will be happy—he must be good as well as rich. And good in a high degree, and rich in a high degree at the same time, he cannot be.

Some one will ask, why not? And we shall answer,— Because acquisitions which come from sources which are just and unjust indifferently, are more than double those which come from just sources only; and the sums which are expended neither honourably nor disgracefully, are only half as great as those which are expended honourably and on honourable purposes. Thus, if the one acquires double and spends half, the other who is in the opposite case and is a good man cannot possibly be wealthier than he. The first—I am speaking of the saver and not of the spender—is not always bad; he may indeed in some cases be utterly bad, but, as I was saying, a good man he never is. For he who receives money unjustly as well as justly, and spends neither justly nor unjustly, will be a rich man if he be also thrifty. On the other hand, the utterly bad is in general profligate, and therefore very poor; while he who spends on noble objects, and acquires wealth by just means only, can hardly be remarkable for riches, any more than he can be very poor. Our statement, then, is true, that the very rich are not good, and, if they are not good, they are not happy.

But the intention of our laws was, that the citizens should be as happy as may be, and as friendly as possible to one another. And men who are always at law with one another, and amongst whom there are many wrongs done, can never be friends to one another, but only those among whom crimes and lawsuits are few and slight. Therefore we say that gold and silver ought not to be allowed in the city, nor much of the vulgar sort of trade which is carried on by lending money, or rearing the meaner kinds of live stock; but only the produce of agriculture, and only so much of this as will not compel us in pursuing it to neglect that for the sake of which riches exist,—I mean, soul and body, which without gymnastics, and without education, will never be worth anything; and therefore, as we have said not once but many times, the care of riches should have the last place in our thoughts.

For there are in all three things about which every man has an interest; and the interest about money, when rightly regarded, is the third and lowest of them: midway comes the interest of the body; and, first of all, that of the soul; and the state which we are describing will have been rightly constituted if it ordains honours according to this scale. But if, in any of the laws which have been ordained, health has been preferred to temperance, or wealth to health and temperate habits, that law must clearly be wrong. Wherefore, also, the legislator ought often to impress upon himself the question—'What do I want?' and 'Do I attain my aim, or do I miss the mark?' In this way, and in this way only, he may acquit himself and free others from the work of legislation.

BOOK VI.

THE Sixth Book, like the Fifth, may be divided into two parts. (1) The mode of appointing the chief magistrates and officials of the new state is described. These include Guardians of the Law, Military Officers, a Council or Senate, Priests, Interpreters of Sacred Matters, Temple Treasurers, Wardens of the City, of the Agora, and of the Country, Rural Police, Directors of Music and Gymnastic, a Minister of Education, Judges of Public and Private Causes. (2) A commencement is made with legislation; and laws concerning Marriage, Slaves, Common Meals, Registration of Births, Age for Military and Political Service, are enacted.

BOOK VII.

IN the Seventh Book the subject of education is resumed and completed.

During the first three years of life children will chiefly require attention to their bodily growth and development. They must not be allowed to walk, lest their tender limbs should become distorted by too early exercise; but, since motion is highly beneficial to them, they must be constantly carried about by their nurses. And motion is no less good for the soul: it quiets fear and promotes courage and cheerfulness. The children should be kept free from pain, yet not be spoiled by too much pleasure.

From three to six they may pass their time in sports and games.... At the age of six, boys, and girls, too, if they like, should commence to learn military exercises and the use of weapons: they must be taught to employ both hands with equal skill.

Education has two branches:—gymnastic, or the training of the body, and music, or the cultivation of the soul. All gymnastic must be practised with a view to war. Music should be simple, and conform to fixed types; for even in amusement innovation is dangerous. The law will prescribe certain principles, from which the composers are not to depart. But with what object are our citizens to learn music? We reply:—In order that they may be better fitted to live the life of peace, propitiating the Gods by dance and song, which is a nobler occupation than the pursuits of war.

Education is to be common to all. Both gymnastic and music must be taught to boys and girls alike. Women should be a help to the state in the hour of peril, and not a useless burden, as they are in most cities. . . . The citizens must lead an active life, rising early and taking little rest.

At daybreak boys must go to school, where they will spend three years in learning to read and write, and three more in the study of music. The compositions which the children commit to memory must be carefully selected. The music must be such as can be readily acquired by every one. Dancing is of two kinds; there is the dance of peace and the dance of war; both must be of a serious and dignified character. Comedy may be performed only by slaves and hirelings. The tragic poets must submit their plays to the censor, before they can be allowed to exhibit.

Three subjects of education remain :—Arithmetic, Geometry, Astronomy. (1) Arithmetic is an invaluable aid to knowledge, and every freeman should strive to gain skill in it. (2) Geometry is too much neglected by the Hellenes: it will be an easy and innocent study for our scholars. (3) Astronomy is useful in many ways, and teaches us correct notions about the Sun and Moon and the other Gods in Heaven.

A word may be added about hunting. Lazy sports, such as angling and fowling, are objectionable. Let our youth confine themselves to the chase of land animals by day with dogs and horses, which will be a test of their endurance and courage.

1. **The good citizen must not lead an inactive life.**

The life of strenuous activity which Plato imposes on his citizens, both in the Republic and in the Laws, is probably a reflection of the restless energy of the Athenians in the days of their greatness, when, in the familiar words of Thucydides, 'they knew no holiday except to do their duty, and deemed the quiet of inaction to be as tedious as the most tiresome business' (Thucyd. i. 170). We may also, perhaps, see in it a trace of Plato's own character and habits; for he shows in several passages of his writings a certain impatience or dislike of sickness and weakness which suggests that he himself had never felt the restraint of 'Theages' bridle,' (cp. the remarks on the passage quoted from the Timaeus, *supra* p. 118).

He was well aware, too, that idleness was a fertile source of evil both to the individual and to the state, and he would have agreed with the modern moralist that ' it is only in some corner of the brain which we leave empty that Vice can obtain a lodging.' His citizens,

THE DUTIES OF CIVIC LIFE 187

therefore, are subjected to a discipline which is almost monastic in
its severity, although the austere spirit of the cloister is far removed
from the cheerfulness and gaiety of Hellenic life. And if, like
Adeimantus in the Republic, we were to object that such an existence
would be no better than that of a soldier who is compelled to be ever
on duty (Rep. iv. 419), Plato's reply would still be the same :—That
his aim in founding the state was not the disproportionate happiness
of a privileged class, but the greatest happiness of the whole.

Athenian Stranger. WHAT will be the manner of Steph.
life among men who may be supposed to have their $\overset{806}{D}$
food and clothing provided for them in moderation,
and who have entrusted the practice of the arts to
others, and whose husbandry committed to slaves paying
a part of the produce brings them a return sufficient for
men living temperately; who, moreover, have common
tables in which the men are placed apart, and near them
are the common tables of their families, of their daughters
and mothers, which day by day, the officers, male and
female, are to inspect—they shall see to the behaviour
of the company, and so dismiss them; after which the
presiding magistrate and his attendants shall honour
with libations those Gods to whom that day and night
are dedicated, and then go home? To men whose lives 807
are thus ordered, is there no work remaining to be
done which is necessary and fitting, but shall each one
of them live fattening like a beast? Such a life is
neither just nor honourable, nor can he who lives it fail
of meeting his due; and the due reward of the idle
fatted beast is that he should be torn in pieces by some
other valiant beast whose fatness is worn down by
brave deeds and toil. These regulations, if we duly
consider them, will never be exactly carried into execution under present circumstances, nor as long as women
and children and houses and all other things are the
private property of individuals; but if we can attain
the second-best form of polity, we shall be very well off.

And to men living under this second polity there remains a work to be accomplished which is far from being small or insignificant, but is the greatest of all works, and ordained by the appointment of righteous law. For the life which may be truly said to be concerned with the virtue of body and soul is twice, or more than twice, as full of toil and trouble as the pursuit after Pythian and Olympic victories[1], which debars a man from every employment of life. For there ought to be no byework interfering with the greater work of providing the necessary exercise and nourishment for the body, and instruction and education for the soul. Night and day are not long enough for the accomplishment of their perfection and consummation; and therefore to this end all freemen ought to arrange the way in which they will spend their time during the whole course of the day, from morning till evening and from evening till the morning of the next sunrise.

There may seem to be some impropriety in the legislator determining minutely the numberless details of the management of the house, including such particulars as the duty of wakefulness in those who are to be perpetual watchmen of the whole city; for that any citizen should continue during the whole of any night in sleep, instead of being seen by all his servants, always the first to awake and get up—this, whether the regulation is to be called a law or only a practice, should be deemed base and unworthy of a freeman; also that the mistress of the house should be awakened by her handmaidens instead of herself first awakening them, is what the slaves, male and female, and the serving-boys, and, if that were possible, everybody and everything in the house should regard as base. If

[1] Cp. Rep. v. 465 D, 466 A.

they rise early, they may all of them do much of their public and of their household business, as magistrates in the city, and masters and mistresses in their private houses, before the sun is up. Much sleep is not required by nature, either for our souls or bodies, or for the actions which they perform. For no one who is asleep is good for anything, any more than if he were dead; but he of us who has the most regard for life and reason keeps awake as long as he can, reserving only so much time for sleep as is expedient for health; and much sleep is not required, if the habit of moderation be once rightly formed. Magistrates in states who keep awake at night are terrible to the bad, whether enemies or citizens, and are honoured and reverenced by the just and temperate, and are useful to themselves and to the whole state.

2. The Education of the Young.

The scheme of education which is laid down in the Laws is thoroughly Hellenic in character, and seems to agree in the main with the course of instruction which was actually followed in Greek schools (cp. Protag. 325 D; *supra* i. 19).

Plato expects the children to acquire their 'rudiments' in the comparatively short space of three years; for when he speaks of 'learning to read and write' it is natural to suppose that he includes under the term elementary arithmetic, and, probably, drawing (cp. Arist. Pol. viii. 3, § 1). We must remember, however, that the curriculum of a Greek school in his time was necessarily simple; there were no lessons in history or geography or grammar, and no religious teaching: all that the child learned of these subjects was derived from the innumerable verses of Homer and other poets which he committed to memory.

Music is deferred to a rather late age, thirteen, and is also only to be studied for three years. Plato regards music as a means towards the attainment of virtue, and as an 'innocent pleasure' for the citizens. They are not to pursue the art beyond a certain point, or to aim at complete proficiency. Here Plato follows the common Greek sentiment, which considered the skill of the professional artist a 'vulgar thing' (βάναυσόν τι), beneath the dignity of the freeman.

It is not easy to gather from Plato's language, either in the Republic or in the Laws, in what way he intended that women should be educated. In both dialogues he tells us that the two sexes are to learn music and gymnastic on an equal footing (Rep. v. 451, 466; Laws vii. 804 E). But in the present passage he appears to have the boys only in view; nothing whatever is said about the girls. If he meant that they should be left to receive instruction at home, according to the general custom, when and as much as the parents pleased, this is hardly in agreement with the high position which he assigns to women in the state. It may perhaps be a concession to popular prejudice, like the abandonment of communism (v. 739). (It should be remarked, however, that in a previous passage (vi. 764 C), he speaks of 'school buildings for boys and girls.')

His ideal of education is in many ways rather Spartan than Athenian, although in an earlier part of the work he is disposed to criticize the Lacedaemonian institutions (Laws ii. 666 E). He admires, and desires to imitate, the manner in which the Spartans made 'education the business of the State, and took the greatest pains about their children' (Arist. Pol. viii. 1, § 4). He has failed to remember how feeble and stunted the intellectual life of Sparta became under the discipline of Lycurgus; nor does he reflect that the 'city of the Magnetes' would have offered little or no scope for the growth and development of mental powers such as his own.

Steph.
808
D

Athenian Stranger. When the day breaks, the time has arrived for youth to go to their schoolmasters. Now neither sheep nor any other animals can live without a shepherd, nor can children be left without tutors, or slaves without masters. And of all animals the boy is the most unmanageable, inasmuch as he has the fountain of reason in him not yet regulated[1]; he is the most insidious, sharp-witted, and insubordinate of animals. Wherefore he must be bound with many bridles; in the first place, when he gets away from mothers and nurses, he must be under the management of tutors on account of his childishness and foolishness; then, again, being a freeman, he must be controlled by teachers, no matter what they teach, and by studies; but he is also a slave, and in that regard any freeman who

[1] Cp. *supra,* vi. 766 A.

comes in his way may punish him and his tutor and his instructor, if any of them does anything wrong; and he who comes across him and does not inflict upon him the punishment which he deserves, shall incur the greatest disgrace; and let the guardian of the law, who is the director of education, see to him who coming in the way of the offences which we have mentioned, does not chastise them when he ought, or chastises them in a way which he ought not; let him keep a sharp look-out, and take especial care of the training of our children, directing their natures, and always turning them to good according to the law. . . . 809

A fair time for a boy of ten years old to spend in letters is three years; the age of thirteen is the proper time for him to begin to handle the lyre, and he may continue at this for another three years, neither more nor less, and whether his father or himself like or dislike the study, he is not to be allowed to spend more or less time in learning music than the law allows. And let him who disobeys the law be deprived of those youthful honours of which we shall hereafter speak[1]. Hear, however, first of all, what the young ought to learn in the early years of life, and what their instructors ought to teach them. 810

They ought to be occupied with their letters until they are able to read and write; but the acquisition of perfect beauty or quickness in writing, if nature has not stimulated them to acquire these accomplishments in the given number of years, they should let alone. And as to the learning of compositions committed to writing which are not set to the lyre, whether metrical or without rhythmical divisions, compositions in prose, as they are termed, having no rhythm or harmony —

[1] Cp. *infra*, viii. 829 C.

seeing how dangerous are the writings handed down to us by many writers of this class—what will you do with them, O most excellent guardians of the law? or how can the lawgiver rightly direct you about them? I believe that he will be in great difficulty.

Cleinias. What troubles you, Stranger? and why are you so perplexed in your mind?

Ath. You naturally ask, Cleinias, and to you and Megillus, who are my partners in the work of legislation, I must state the more difficult as well as the easier parts of the task.

Cle. To what do you refer in this instance?

Ath. I will tell you. There is a difficulty in opposing many myriads of mouths.

Cle. Well, and have we not already opposed the popular voice in many important enactments?

Ath. That is quite true; and you mean to imply that the road which we are taking may be disagreeable to some but is agreeable to as many others, or if not to as many, at any rate to persons not inferior to the others, and in company with them you bid me, at whatever risk, to proceed along the path of legislation which has opened out of our present discourse, and to be of good cheer, and not to faint.

Cle. Certainly.

Ath. And I do not faint; I say, indeed, that we have a great many poets writing in hexameter, trimeter, and all sorts of measures—some who are serious, others who aim only at raising a laugh—and all mankind declare that the youth who are rightly educated should be brought up in them and saturated with them; some insist that they should be constantly hearing them read aloud, and always learning them, so as to get by heart entire poets; while others select choice passages and long speeches, and make compendiums of them, saying that these ought to be committed to memory, if a man is to be made good and wise by experience and learning of many things. And you want me now to tell them plainly in what they are right and in what they are wrong.

Cle. Yes, I do.

Ath. But how can I in one word rightly comprehend all of them? I am of opinion, and, if I am not mistaken, there is a general agreement, that every one of these poets has said many things well and many things the reverse of well; and if this be true, then I do affirm that much learning is dangerous to youth.

Cle. How would you advise the guardian of the law to act?

Ath. In what respect?

Cle. I mean to what pattern should he look as his guide in permitting the young to learn some things and forbidding them to learn others. Do not shrink from answering.

Ath. My good Cleinias, I rather think that I am fortunate.

Cle. How so?

Ath. I think that I am not wholly in want of a pattern, for when I consider the words which we have spoken from early dawn until now, and which, as I believe, have been inspired by Heaven, they appear to me to be quite like a poem. When I reflected upon all these words of ours, I naturally felt pleasure, for of all the discourses which I have ever learnt or heard, either in poetry or prose, this seemed to me to be the justest, and most suitable for young men to hear; I cannot imagine any better pattern than this which the guardian of the law who is also the director of education can have. He cannot do better than advise the teachers to teach the young these words and any which are of a like nature, if he should happen to find them, either in poetry or prose, or if he come across unwritten discourses akin to ours, he should certainly preserve them, and commit them to writing. And, first of all, he shall constrain the teachers themselves to learn and approve them, and any of them who will not, shall not be employed by him, but those whom he finds agreeing in his judgment, he shall make use of and shall commit to them the instruction and education of youth. And here and on this wise let my fanciful tale about letters and teachers of letters come to an end.

BOOK VIII.

The Eighth Book treats of a variety of subjects which are more or less loosely connected.

(1) There are to be daily sacrifices, monthly feasts dedicated to the Twelve Gods, and festivals for men and for women.

(2) Military pastimes and tournaments shall be regularly held, in order that the citizens may be better prepared for war. This is an excellent practice, which is commonly neglected, first, because men are absorbed by the pursuit of gain, and, secondly, because existing states are ruled by selfish partisans who have no regard to the common weal. Also there must be races for armed runners, conflicts in armour, and horse races, three kinds of each, one of boys, another of youths, and a third of men: and similar competitions must be arranged for girls and women, in which they will take part according to their age.

(3) The mention of these various contests and festivals in which men and women meet together serves to introduce a difficult and vexed topic,—the relation of the sexes. Licentiousness is utterly abominable. Men should live in moderation, as nature enjoins, and not fall below the level of the beasts. If the law cannot ensure this, at least we must insist upon some observance of decency.

(4) There must be laws relating to (*a*) husbandmen and the cultivation of the soil, (*b*) artisans, (*c*) imports and exports, (*d*) division of produce, (*e*) the arrangement of hamlets and country dwellings, (*f*) market regulations, (*g*) resident aliens.

BOOK IX.

WITH the Ninth Book the criminal code of the new State commences.

Laws are enacted against Temple robbing, Treason, Theft. . . . Capital causes are to go before the Guardians of the Law and a Court of Select Judges.

A distinction is drawn between voluntary and involuntary crimes; or, as it would be better to say, between 'injustice' and 'hurt.' There are many causes of crime and motives of action, but all may be brought under these two heads.

Homicide is divided into various classes :—(1) the killing of another by accident or misadventure : (2) homicide committed in anger, whether with or without premeditation : (3) killing in self-defence : (4) deliberate murder, a crime which is due to three causes,—avarice, ambition, fear : (5) suicide : (6) slaying a thief or burglar or other persons engaged in unlawful acts. An animal which kills a man is to be slain and cast beyond the border.

In cases of wounding, with or without intent to kill, much may be left to the law courts, if they are well constituted. The degree of premeditation has to be borne in mind when fixing the punishment.

Lastly, there is the kindred crime of assault, and in this also the different cases must be distinguished, and appropriate penalties laid down for each.

BOOK X.

IN the Tenth Book Plato deals with the offences of those who disbelieve in the Gods or have erroneous notions concerning them. They are divided into three classes :—(1) Atheists : (2) men who, although they acknowledge the existence of the Gods, think that they take no care of us; or, (3), imagine that they may be propitiated by gifts. Each class is solemnly reasoned with before the law is declared, in the hope that the offenders may be brought to a better frame of mind.

(1) The existence of the Gods is proved by the order of the Universe and by the general belief of mankind. Nowadays there are many who assert that chance rules the world, and that law and religion are mere conventions designed to protect the weak against the strong. They falsely suppose that the four elements came into being before the soul, whereas the soul is really prior to all that is material. She alone is self-moved and the origin of motion in other things. But there are two souls, a good and an evil, and it is the

good soul which moves the sun, the moon, and the other heavenly bodies and carries them round in their orbits. And as this soul of good is certainly a Divine Principle, we may truly say that 'the Universe is full of Gods.'

(2) The opinion that the Gods exist, yet take no heed of human affairs, grows up when men see the unrighteous prospering in the land. They forget that the Gods, who are all-wise and all-good, cannot fitly be compared to unworthy artists, attending only to the great and neglecting the small. Man is made for the Universe, the part for the whole, not the whole for the part. Providence designs that good shall triumph over evil, but there is an element of free will and choice in the soul, and we must each in some degree work out our own destiny. The good soul at every change of existence goes to a better place; the soul which has done evil sinks lower and lower into the abyss. This is the justice of Heaven which none may escape.

(3) The third and wickedest class of unbelievers cannot be addressed with patience :—they who say that the Gods can be propitiated by gifts and sacrifices, must conceive them to resemble the vilest of men who will betray their trust to gain a paltry bribe.

After the prelude comes the law. The more innocent unbelievers shall be punished with five years' imprisonment, and, in case of a second offence, with death. The worse sort, mendicant priests and the like, who offer 'for a consideration' to win the favour of Heaven and to bring up the dead from Hades, shall be imprisoned during life, and never again hold intercourse with their fellows, and when they die, their bodies shall be cast beyond the borders.... There shall be no religious rites in private houses : all public worship must take place in the Temples of the State, under the direction of duly appointed priests and priestesses.

The three classes of Unbelievers.

The Tenth Book of the Laws is a peculiarly interesting instance of the manner in which that work is related to the Republic (cp. *supra* p. 144). The main ideas are the same; the difference is chiefly one of tone and emphasis. We have already made acquaintance in the Republic with the threefold errors of men respecting the Gods; and now Plato returns to the attack with renewed vigour and zeal.

He first undertakes to prove the existence of the Gods, a subject upon which in his previous writings he had only lightly touched. His arguments, like those which he employs in the Phaedo to demonstrate the immortality of the soul (cp. *supra* i. 162), are not satisfactory or convincing to us; but we, too, feel the force of the appeal which he makes to the better mind of the world in all ages, and acknowledge, as we contemplate the order of the Universe, that God is everywhere. These thoughts move us, as no metaphysical arguments can, and,—slightly to change Plato's own metaphor,—we cling fast to the instinctive belief in the existence of God, as our support in passing through the flood of doubt and discussion (892 D .

When, however, Plato proceeds to speak with passionate sincerity of the Goodness of God and His care for His creatures, he is on firmer ground, and we are still more at one with him. He is perplexed to understand how evil can find a place in the scheme of Providence, and discovers the solution in the idea that all things work together to a common end,—the victory of good. His language is vague, but he appears to speak of evil as a principle which is inherent in matter, and cannot be eliminated even by the Creator (cp. Statesm. 273 B, and the striking passage in the Theaetetus, 176 A :—'There must always remain something which is antagonistic to good'). On the other hand, he supposes that there is in man a real, though limited, freedom of the will, which is assisted in the struggle against evil by the general tendency of the Universe. Life is thus at once the school of character, and the preparation for the world to come.

On the third class of offenders,—those who believe that the Gods favour the wicked in return for their gifts,—Plato does not waste much argument. In his eyes they are moral outlaws, and their opinions must be stamped out of the State like a pestilence. Yet in the law which he proceeds to enact, he distinguishes, as in other cases of unbelief, between a greater and a lesser degree of guilt. The more serious offenders, in his opinion, are they who make a gain out of the fears and terrors of mankind, and lead the weak and foolish into the extravagancies of superstition. We can scarcely say that we know of grave social evils which had arisen from such a cause in his day ; but he is speaking almost in 'a prophetic strain,' and his words are in a measure justified by the corruptions of religion in the Roman Empire and in Mediaeval and Modern Europe.

The somewhat intolerant temper which Plato exhibits is remarkable in a Greek philosopher of the Fourth Century B. C. We may observe, however, that his zeal is directed against what he considers an injury to the moral well-being of the State. His feeling is different to the ordinary Greek sentiment, which only objected to 'new Gods' as an innovation on the established order of things, and had little or nothing to do with ethical principles ; and it is equally removed from the fanaticism with which we are more familiar, and which endeavours to force upon all by any or every means the adoption of a series of dogmatic propositions.

1. **The universal belief of mankind in the existence of God is not hastily to be set aside.**

Athenian Stranger. WE have already said in general terms what shall be the punishment of sacrilege, whether fraudulent or violent, and now we have to determine what is to be the punishment of those who speak or act insolently toward the Gods. But first we must give them an admonition which may be in the following terms: —No one who in obedience to the laws believed that there were Gods, ever intentionally did any unholy act, or uttered any unlawful word; but he who did must have supposed one of three things,—either that they did not exist,—which is the first possibility, or secondly, that, if they did, they took no care of man, or thirdly, that they were easily appeased and turned aside from their purpose by sacrifices and prayers.

Cleinias. What shall we say or do to these persons?

Ath. My good friend, let us first hear the jests which I suspect that they in their superiority will utter against us.

Cle. What jests?

Ath. They will make some irreverent speech of this sort :—' O inhabitants of Athens, and Sparta, and Cnosus,' they will reply, ' in that you speak truly ; for some of us deny the very existence of the Gods, while others, as you say, are of opinion that they do not care about us; and others that they are turned from their course by gifts. Now we have a right to claim, as you yourself allowed, in the matter of laws, that before you are hard upon us and threaten us, you should argue with us and convince us [1]—you should first attempt to teach and persuade us that there are Gods by reasonable evidences, and also that they are too good to be

---

[1] Cp. *supra*, iv. 718 foll.

unrighteous, or to be propitiated, or turned from their course by gifts. For when we hear such things said of them by those who are esteemed to be the best of poets, and orators, and prophets, and priests, and by innumerable others, the thoughts of most of us are not set upon abstaining from unrighteous acts, but upon doing them and atoning for them [1]. When lawgivers profess that they are gentle and not stern, we think that they should first of all use persuasion to us, and show us the existence of Gods, if not in a better manner than other men, at any rate in a truer; and who knows but that we shall hearken to you? If then our request is a fair one, please to accept our challenge.'

Cle. But is there any difficulty in proving the existence of the Gods? 886

Ath. How would you prove it?

Cle. How? In the first place, the earth and the sun, and the stars and the universe, and the fair order of the seasons, and the division of them into years and months, furnish proofs of their existence; and also there is the fact that all Hellenes and barbarians believe in them.

Ath. I fear, my sweet friend, though I will not say that I much regard, the contempt with which the profane will be likely to assail us. For you do not understand the nature of their complaint, and you fancy that they rush into impiety only from a love of sensual pleasure.

Cle. Why, Stranger, what other reason is there?

Ath. One which you who live in a different atmosphere would never guess.

Cle. What is it?

Ath. A very grievous sort of ignorance which is imagined to be the greatest wisdom.

Cle. What do you mean?

Ath. At Athens there are tales preserved in writing

[1] Cp. Rep. ii. 364.

which the virtue of your state, as I am informed, refuses to admit. They speak of the Gods in prose as well as verse, and the oldest of them tell of the origin of the heavens and of the world, and not far from the beginning of their story they proceed to narrate the birth of the Gods, and how after they were born they behaved to one another. Whether these stories have in other ways a good or a bad influence, I should not like to be severe upon them, because they are ancient; but, looking at them with reference to the duties of children to their parents, I cannot praise them, or think that they are useful, or at all true[1].

Of the words of the ancients I have nothing more to say; and I should wish to say of them only what is pleasing to the Gods. But as to our younger generation and their wisdom, I cannot let them off when they do mischief. For do but mark the effect of their words: when you and I argue for the existence of the Gods, and produce the sun, moon, stars, and earth, claiming for them a divine being, if we would listen to the aforesaid philosophers we should say[2] that they are earth and stones only[3], which can have no care at all of human affairs, and that all religion is a cooking up of words and a make-believe.

Cle. One such teacher, O Stranger, would be bad enough, and you imply that there are many of them, which is worse.

Ath. Well, then; what shall we say or do?—Shall we assume that some one is accusing us among unholy men, who are trying to escape from the effect of our legislation; and that they say of us—How dreadful that you should legislate on the supposition that there are Gods! Shall we make a defence of ourselves? or shall we leave them and return to our laws, lest the prelude

[1] Cp. Rep. ii. 378 foll. [2] Reading λέγοιμεν. [3] Cp. Apol., 26 foll.

should become longer than the law? For the discourse will certainly extend to great length, if we are to treat the impiously disposed as they desire, partly demonstrating to them at some length the things of which they demand an explanation, partly making them afraid or dissatisfied, and then proceed to the requisite enactments.

Cle. Yes, Stranger; but then how often have we repeated already that on the present occasion there is no reason why brevity should be preferred to length[1]; for who is 'at our heels'?—as the saying goes, and it would be paltry and ridiculous to prefer the shorter to the better. It is a matter of no small consequence, in some way or other to prove that there are Gods, and that they are good, and regard justice more than men do. The demonstration of this would be the best and noblest prelude of all our laws. And therefore, without impatience, and without hurry, let us unreservedly consider the whole matter, summoning up all the power of persuasion which we possess.

Ath. Seeing you thus in earnest, I would fain offer up a prayer that I may succeed :—but I must proceed at once. Who can be calm when he is called upon to prove the existence of the Gods? Who can avoid hating and abhorring the men who are and have been the cause of this argument; I speak of those who will not believe the tales which they have heard as babes and sucklings from their mothers and nurses, repeated by them both in jest and earnest, like charms, who have also heard them in the sacrificial prayers, and seen sights accompanying them,—sights and sounds delightful to children,—and their parents during the sacrifices showing an intense earnestness on behalf of their children and of themselves, and with eager interest

[1] Cp. *supra*, iv. 719 E foll.; ix. 857, 858.

talking to the Gods, and beseeching them, as though they were firmly convinced of their existence; who likewise see and hear the prostrations and invocations which are made by Hellenes and barbarians at the rising and setting of the sun and moon, in all the vicissitudes of life, not as if they thought that there were no Gods, but as if there could be no doubt of their existence, and no suspicion of their non-existence; when men, knowing all these things, despise them on no real grounds, as would be admitted by all who have any particle of intelligence, and when they force us to say what we are now saying, how can any one in gentle terms remonstrate with the like of them, when he has to begin by proving to them the very existence of the Gods? Yet the attempt must be made; for it would be unseemly that one half of mankind should go mad in their lust of pleasure, and the other half in their indignation at such persons.

Our address to these lost and perverted natures should not be spoken in passion; let us suppose ourselves to select some one of them, and gently reason with him, smothering our anger:—O my son, we will say to him, you are young, and the advance of time will make you reverse many of the opinions which you now hold. Wait awhile, and do not attempt to judge at present of the highest things; and that is the highest of which you now think nothing—to know the Gods rightly and to live accordingly.

And in the first place let me indicate to you one point which is of great importance, and about which I cannot be deceived:—You and your friends are not the first who have held this opinion about the Gods. There have always been persons more or less numerous who have had the same disorder. I have known many of them, and can tell you, that no one who had taken up in youth this opinion, that the Gods do not exist, ever continued in the same until he was old; the two other notions certainly do continue in some cases, but not in many; the notion, I mean, that the Gods exist, but take no heed of human things, and the other notion that they do take heed of them, but are easily propitiated with sacrifices and prayers. As to the opinion about the Gods which may some day become clear to you, I advise you to wait and consider if it be true or not; ask of others, and above all of the legislator. In the meantime take care that you do not offend against the Gods. For the duty of the legislator is and always will be to teach you the truth of these matters.

Cle. Our address, Stranger, thus far, is excellent.

2. God is not an idle Ruler of the Universe; but orders all, even the smallest things, for our good.

Athenian Stranger. And now we are to address him who, believing that there are Gods, believes also that they take no heed of human affairs: To him we say,—O thou best of men, in believing that there are Gods you are led by some affinity to them, which attracts you towards your kindred and makes you honour and believe in them. But the fortunes of evil and unrighteous men in private as well as public life, which, though not really happy, are wrongly counted happy in the judgment of men, and are celebrated both by poets and prose writers [1]—these draw you aside from your natural piety. Perhaps you have seen impious men growing old and leaving their children's children in high offices, and their prosperity shakes your faith—you have known or heard or been yourself an eye-witness of many monstrous impieties, and have beheld men by such criminal means from small beginnings attaining to sovereignty

[1] Cp. Rep. ii. 364 A.

and the pinnacle of greatness; and considering all these things you do not like to accuse the Gods of them, because they are your relatives; and so from some want of reasoning power, and also from an unwillingness to find fault with them, you have come to believe that they exist indeed, but have no thought or care of human things.

Now, that your present evil opinion may not grow to still greater impiety, and that we may if possible use arguments which may conjure away the evil before it arrives, we will add another argument to that originally addressed to him who utterly denied the existence of the Gods. And do you, Megillus and Cleinias, answer for the young man as you did before; and if any impediment comes in our way, I will take the word out of your mouths, and carry you over the river as I did just now.

Cleinias. Very good; do as you say, and we will help you as well as we can.

Ath. There will probably be no difficulty in proving to him that the Gods care about the small as well as about the great. For he was present and heard what was said, that they are perfectly good, and that the care of all things is most entirely natural to them[1].

Cle. No doubt he heard that.

Ath. Let us consider together in the next place what we mean by this virtue which we ascribe to them. Surely we should say that to be temperate and to possess mind belongs to virtue, and the contrary to vice?

Cle. Certainly.

Ath. Yes; and courage is a part of virtue, and cowardice of vice?

Cle. True.

Ath. And the one is honourable, and the other dishonourable?

[1] Cp. *supra*, 899 B.

Cle. To be sure.

Ath. And the one, like other meaner things, is a human quality, but the Gods have no part in anything of the sort?

Cle. That again is what everybody will admit.

Ath. But do we imagine carelessness and idleness and luxury to be virtues? What do you think?

Cle. Decidedly not.

Ath. They rank under the opposite class?

Cle. Yes.

Ath. And their opposites, therefore, would fall under the opposite class?

Cle. Yes.

Ath. But are we to suppose that one who possesses all these good qualities will be luxurious and heedless and idle, like those whom the poet compares to stingless drones[1]?

Cle. And the comparison is a most just one.

Ath. Surely God must not be supposed to have a nature which He Himself hates?—he who dares to say this sort of thing must not be tolerated for a moment.

Cle. Of course not. How could He have?

Ath. Should we not on any principle be entirely mistaken in praising any one who has some special business entrusted to him, if he have a mind which takes care of great matters and no care of small ones? Reflect; he who acts in this way, whether he be God or man, must act from one of two principles.

Cle. What are they?

Ath. Either he must think that the neglect of the small matters is of no consequence to the whole, or if he knows that they are of consequence, and he neglects them, his neglect must be attributed to carelessness and indolence. Is there any other way in which his neglect

---
[1] Hesiod, Works and Days, 307.

can be explained? For surely, when it is impossible for him to take care of all, he is not negligent if he fails to attend to these things great or small, which a God or some inferior being might be wanting in strength or capacity to manage?

Cle. Certainly not.

Ath. Now, then, let us examine the offenders, who both alike confess that there are Gods, but with a difference,—the one saying that they may be appeased, and the other that they have no care of small matters: there are three of us and two of them, and we will say to them,—In the first place, you both acknowledge that the Gods hear and see and know all things, and that nothing can escape them which is matter of sense and knowledge:—do you admit this?

Cle. Yes.

Ath. And do you admit also that they have all power which mortals and immortals can have?

Cle. They will, of course, admit this also.

Ath. And surely we three and they two—five in all—have acknowledged that they are good and perfect?

Cle. Assuredly.

Ath. But, if they are such as we conceive them to be, can we possibly suppose that they ever act in the spirit of carelessness and indolence? For in us inactivity is the child of cowardice, and carelessness of inactivity and indolence.

Cle. Most true.

Ath. Then not from inactivity and carelessness is any God ever negligent; for there is no cowardice in them.

Cle. That is very true.

Ath. Then the alternative which remains is, that if the Gods neglect the lighter and lesser concerns of the universe, they neglect them because they know that they ought not to care about such matters—what other alternative is there but the opposite of their knowing?

Cle. There is none.

Ath. And, O most excellent and best of men, do I understand you to mean that they are careless because they are ignorant, and do not know that they ought to take care, or that they know, and yet like the meanest sort of men, knowing the better, choose the worse because they are overcome by pleasures and pains?

Cle. Impossible.

Ath. Do not all human things partake of the nature of soul? And is not man the most religious of all animals [1]?

Cle. That is not to be denied.

Ath. And we acknowledge that all mortal creatures are the property of the Gods, to whom also the whole of heaven belongs [2]?

Cle. Certainly.

Ath. And, therefore, whether a person says that these things are to the Gods great or small—in either case it would not be natural for the Gods who own us, and who are the most careful and the best of owners, to neglect us.—There is also a further consideration.

Cle. What is it?

Ath. Sensation and power are in an inverse ratio to each other in respect to their ease and difficulty.

Cle. What do you mean?

Ath. I mean that there is greater difficulty in seeing and hearing the small than the great, but more facility in moving and controlling and taking care of small and unimportant things than of their opposites.

Cle. Far more.

Ath. Suppose the case of a physician who is willing and able to cure some living thing as a whole,—how

[1] Cp. Tim. 42 A.   [2] Cp. Phaedo 62.

will the whole fare at his hands if he takes care only of the greater and neglects the parts which are lesser?

Cle. Decidedly not well.

Ath. No better would be the result with pilots or generals, or householders or statesmen, or any other such class, if they neglected the small and regarded only the great;—as the builders say, the larger stones do not lie well without the lesser.

Cle. Of course not.

Ath. Let us not, then, deem God inferior to human workmen, who, in proportion to their skill, finish and perfect their works, small as well as great, by one and the same art; or that God, the wisest of beings, who is both willing and able to take care, is like a lazy good-for-nothing, or a coward, who turns his back upon labour and gives no thought to smaller and easier matters, but to the greater only.

Cle. Never, Stranger, let us admit a supposition about the Gods which is both impious and false.

Ath. I think that we have now argued enough with him who delights to accuse the Gods of neglect.

Cle. Yes.

Ath. He has been forced to acknowledge that he is in error, but he still seems to me to need some words of consolation.

Cle. What consolation will you offer him?

Ath. Let us say to the youth:—The ruler of the universe has ordered all things with a view to the excellence and preservation of the whole, and each part, as far as may be, has an action and passion appropriate to it. Over these, down to the least fraction of them, ministers have been appointed to preside, who have wrought out their perfection with infinitesimal exactness. And one of these portions of the universe is thine own, unhappy man, which, however little, contributes to the whole ; and you do not seem to be aware that this and every other creation is for the sake of the whole, and in order that the life of the whole may be blessed ; and that you are created for the sake of the whole, and not the whole for the sake of you. For every physician and every skilled artist does all things for the sake of the whole, directing his effort towards the common good, executing the part for the sake of the whole, and not the whole for the sake of the part. And you are annoyed because you are ignorant how what is best for you happens to you and to the universe, as far as the laws of the common creation admit. Now, as the soul combining first with one body and then with another undergoes all sorts of changes, either of herself, or through the influence of another soul, all that remains to the player of the game is that he should shift the pieces; sending the better nature to the better place, and the worse to the worse, and so assigning to them their proper portion.

Cle. In what way do you mean ?

Ath. In a way which may be supposed to make the care of all things easy to the Gods. If any one were to form or fashion all things without any regard to the whole [1],—if, for example, he formed a living element of water out of fire, instead of forming many things out of one or one out of many in regular order attaining to a first or second or third birth [2], the transmutation would have been infinite ; but now the ruler of the world has a wonderfully easy task.

. *Cle.* How so ?

Ath. I will explain :—When the king saw that our actions had life, and that there was much virtue in them and much vice, and that the soul and body, although not, like the Gods of popular opinion, eternal, yet

---

[1] Reading μὴ πρὸς τὸ ὅλον.   [2] Cp. Timaeus 42 B, C.

having once come into existence, were indestructible (for if either of them had been destroyed, there would have been no generation of living beings); and when he observed that the good of the soul was ever by nature designed to profit men, and the evil to harm them—he, seeing all this, contrived so to place each of the parts that their position might in the easiest and best manner procure the victory of good and the defeat of evil in the whole. And he contrived a general plan by which a thing of a certain nature found a certain seat and room. But the formation of qualities[1] he left to the wills of individuals. For every one of us is made pretty much what he is by the bent of his desires and the nature of his soul.

Cle. Yes, that is probably true.

Ath. Then all things which have a soul change, and possess in themselves a principle of change, and in changing move according to law and to the order of destiny: natures which have undergone a lesser change move less and on the earth's surface, but those which have suffered more change and have become more criminal sink into the abyss, that is to say, into Hades and other places in the world below, of which the very names terrify men, and which they picture to themselves as in a dream, both while alive and when released from the body. And whenever the soul receives more of good or evil from her own energy and the strong influence of others—when she has communion with divine virtue and becomes divine, she is carried into another and better place, which is perfect in holiness; but when she has communion with evil, then she also changes the place of her life.

'This is the justice of the Gods who inhabit Olympus[2].'

O youth or young man, who fancy that you are

[1] Reading τοῦ ποίου.   [2] Hom. Odyss. xix. 43.

neglected by the Gods, know that if you become worse you shall go to the worse souls, or if better to the better, and in every succession of life and death you will do and suffer what like may fitly suffer at the hands of like. This is the justice of heaven, which neither you nor any other unfortunate will ever glory in escaping, and which the ordaining powers have specially ordained; take good heed thereof, for it will be sure to take heed of you.

If you say :—I am small and will creep into the depths of the earth, or I am high and will fly up to heaven, you are not so small or so high but that you shall pay the fitting penalty, either here or in the world below or in some still more savage place whither you shall be conveyed. This is also the explanation of the fate of those whom you saw, who had done unholy and evil deeds, and from small beginnings had grown great, and you fancied that from being miserable they had become happy; and in their actions, as in a mirror, you seemed to see the universal neglect of the Gods, not knowing how they make all things work together and contribute to the great whole. And thinkest thou, bold man, that thou needest not to know this?—he who knows it not can never form any true idea of the happiness or unhappiness of life or hold any rational discourse respecting either. If Cleinias and this our reverend company succeed in proving to you that you know not what you say of the Gods, then will God help you; but should you desire to hear more, listen to what we say to the third opponent, if you have any understanding whatsoever.

3. God cannot be propitiated by the gifts of the wicked.

Athenian Stranger. I think that we have sufficiently proved the existence of the Gods, and that they care for men :—The other notion that they are appeased by the wicked, and take gifts, is what we must not concede to any one, and what every man should disprove to the utmost of his power.

Cleinias. Very good ; let us do as you say.

Ath. Well, then, by the Gods themselves I conjure you to tell me,—if they are to be propitiated, how are they to be propitiated ? Who are they, and what is their nature ? Must they not be at least rulers who have to order unceasingly the whole heaven ?

Cle. True.

Ath. And to what earthly rulers can they be compared, or who to them ? How in the less can we find an image of the greater ? Are they charioteers of contending pairs of steeds, or pilots of vessels ? Perhaps they might be compared to the generals of armies, or they might be likened to physicians providing against the diseases which make war upon the body, or to husbandmen observing anxiously the effects of the seasons on the growth of plants ; or perhaps to shepherds of flocks. For as we acknowledge the world to be full of many goods and also of evils, and of more evils than goods, there is, as we affirm, an immortal conflict going on among us, which requires marvellous watchfulness ; and in that conflict the Gods and demigods are our allies, and we are their property.

Injustice and insolence and folly are the destruction of us, and justice and temperance and wisdom are our salvation ; and the place of these latter is in the life of the Gods, although some vestige of them may occasionally be discerned among mankind. But upon this earth we know that there dwell souls possessing an unjust spirit[1], who may be compared to brute animals, which fawn upon their keepers, whether dogs or shep-

---
[1] Reading λῆμα.

herds, or the best and most perfect masters; for they in like manner, as the voices of the wicked declare, prevail by flattery and prayers and incantations, and are allowed to make their gains with impunity. And this sin, which is termed dishonesty, is an evil of the same kind as what is termed disease in living bodies or pestilence in years or seasons of the year, and in cities and governments has another name, which is injustice.

Cle. Quite true.

Ath. What else can he say who declares that the Gods are always lenient to the doers of unjust acts, if they divide the spoil with them? As if wolves were to toss a portion of their prey to the dogs, and they, mollified by the gift, suffered them to tear the flocks [1]. Must not he who maintains that the Gods can be propitiated argue thus?

Cle. Precisely so.

Ath. And to which of the above-mentioned classes of guardians would any man compare the Gods without absurdity? Will he say that they are like pilots, who are themselves turned away from their duty by 'libations of wine and the savour of fat,' and at last overturn both ship and sailors?

Cle. Assuredly not.

Ath. And surely they are not like charioteers who are bribed to give up the victory to other chariots?

Cle. That would be a fearful image of the Gods.

Ath. Nor are they like generals, or physicians, or husbandmen, or shepherds; and no one would compare them to dogs who have been silenced by wolves.

Cle. A thing not to be spoken of.

Ath. And are not all the Gods the chiefest of all guardians, and do they not guard our highest interests?

907

[1] Cp. Rep. ii. 365 E.

Cle. Yes; the chiefest.

Ath. And shall we say that those who guard our noblest interests, and are the best of guardians, are inferior in virtue to dogs, and to men even of moderate excellence, who would never betray justice for the sake of gifts which unjust men impiously offer them?

Cle. Certainly not; nor is such a notion to be endured, and he who holds this opinion may be fairly singled out and characterized as of all impious men the wickedest and most impious.

Ath. Then are the three assertions—that the Gods exist, and that they take care of men, and that they can never be persuaded to do injustice, now sufficiently demonstrated? May we say that they are?

Cle. You have our entire assent to your words.

Ath. I have spoken with vehemence because I am zealous against evil men; and I will tell you, dear Cleinias, why I am so. I would not have the wicked think that, having the superiority in argument, they may do as they please and act according to their various imaginations about the Gods; and this zeal has led me to speak too vehemently; but if we have at all succeeded in persuading the men to hate themselves and love their opposites, the prelude of our laws about impiety will not have been spoken in vain.

Cle. So let us hope; and even if we have failed, the style of our argument will not discredit the lawgiver.

BOOK XI.

In the Eleventh Book Plato takes up another part of legislation,—that which regulates dealings between man and man.

Laws are enacted concerning Treasure Trove, Deposited Property, Runaway Slaves, Freedmen, Sale of Goods, Fraudulent Sale of Slaves, Adulteration, Retail Trade, Contracts, Wills and Testamentary Bequests, Intestacy, Orphans, Family Disputes and Quarrels, Divorce,

Neglect of Parents, Poisoning and Witchcraft, Lunatics, Abuse and Ridicule, Beggars, Witnesses and False Witness, Dishonesty of Advocates.

1. **The evils of retail trade, and the cure of them.**

There was probably no feeling more deeply implanted in the Greek mind than that which taught the essentially 'vulgar' character of retail trade. And this is worthy of peculiar remark because the Greeks were themselves the keenest of traders and merchants. They expelled the Phoenicians from their trading stations in the Mediterranean; they went to Tartessus for silver and other metals,— to the shores of the Baltic for amber,—to the steppes of Scythia for grain; they travelled, like Pytheas, to Britain and 'farthest Thule' in search of new openings for commerce. No doubt, in Greece, not less than in England, the scale of the operations made a difference to the manner in which they were regarded. The wealthy aristocrat might employ his slaves in a workshop, or let them out for hire as artisans and mechanics: he could not without social degradation, to use Plato's humorous language, 'open a shop or keep a tavern.' Moreover, and this sentiment also is by no means unknown among ourselves, there appears to have been a distinction drawn between the trader retired with a fortune and the man who was actually engaged in trade. At least, Aristotle asserts that it was not uncommon in oligarchies to allow only those to hold office who had left business for a period of ten years or more (Arist. Pol. iii. 5, § 6).

In most of his previous writings Plato has shown that he shared in the general prejudice; and in the Republic, even while he acknowledges that retail trade is one of the primary necessities of life in the social community, he adds that 'in well-ordered states the retailers are commonly those who are the weakest in bodily strength, and therefore of little use for any other purpose' (Rep. ii. 371 C). In the Laws, however, he takes a step further. He has told us in the Fourth Book that a city of merchants and shopkeepers will be 'unfriendly and unfaithful, both to her own citizens and to other nations' (705 A); but now he begins to reflect that it would be much to the good of the state, if the better class of men and women would follow the pursuits of trade, and turn away the reproach which at present clings to them.

The wish, he admits, is futile; the insatiable desire for riches will always throw an insurmountable obstacle in the way. Here he exhibits the characteristic tone which runs through the Laws:— He has still, in this latest hour of his life, a consuming zeal for the improvement of mankind. Yet the 'creeping touch' of age has saddened his temper, and lowered his estimate of the world, and he cannot persuade himself that the human race will ever 'make it their first and last and constant and all-absorbing aim to exceed in virtue' (Menex. 246 E).

Athenian Stranger. AFTER the practices of adulteration naturally follow the practices of retail trade. Concerning these, we will first of all give a word of counsel and reason, and the law shall come afterwards. Retail trade in a city is not by nature intended to do any harm, but quite the contrary; for is not he a benefactor who reduces the inequalities and incommensurabilities of goods to equality and common measure? And this is what the power of money accomplishes, and the merchant may be said to be appointed for this purpose. The hireling and the tavern-keeper, and many other occupations, some of them more and others less seemly —all alike have this object;—they seek to satisfy our needs and equalize our possessions[1]. Let us then endeavour to see what has brought retail trade into ill-odour, and wherein lies the dishonour and unseemliness of it, in order that if not entirely, we may yet partially, cure the evil by legislation. To effect this is no easy matter, and requires a great deal of virtue.

Cleinias. What do you mean?

Ath. Dear Cleinias, the class of men is small—they must have been rarely gifted by nature, and trained by education,—who, when assailed by wants and desires, are able to hold out and observe moderation, and when they might make a great deal of money are sober in their wishes, and prefer a moderate to a large gain. But the mass of mankind are the very opposite: their desires are unbounded, and when they might gain in moderation they prefer gains without limit; wherefore all that relates to retail trade, and merchandise, and

---

[1] Cp. Arist. Pol. i. 9, §§ 1-11.

the keeping of taverns, is denounced and numbered among dishonourable things. For if what I trust may never be and will not be, we were to compel, if I may venture to say a ridiculous thing, the best men everywhere to keep taverns for a time, or carry on retail trade, or do anything of that sort; or if, in consequence of some fate or necessity, the best women were compelled to follow similar callings, then we should know how agreeable and pleasant all these things are; and if all such occupations were managed on incorrupt principles, they would be honoured as we honour a mother or a nurse. But now that a man goes to desert places and builds houses which can only be reached by long journeys, for the sake of retail trade, and receives strangers who are in need at the welcome resting-place, and gives them peace and calm when they are tossed by the storm, or cool shade in the heat; and then instead of behaving to them as friends, and showing the duties of hospitality to his guests, treats them as enemies and captives who are at his mercy, and will not release them until they have paid the most unjust, abominable, and extortionate ransom,—these are the sort of practices, and foul evils they are, which cast a reproach upon the succour of adversity. And the legislator ought always to be devising a remedy for evils of this nature.

There is an ancient saying, which is also a true one—'To fight against two opponents is a difficult thing,' as is seen in diseases and in many other cases. And in this case also the war is against two enemies—wealth and poverty; one of whom corrupts the soul of man with luxury, while the other drives him by pain into utter shamelessness. What remedy can a city of sense find against this disease? In the first place, they must have as few retail traders as possible; and in the second place, they must assign the occupation to that class of men whose corruption will be the least injury to the state; and in the third place, they must devise some way whereby the followers of these occupations themselves will not readily fall into habits of unbridled shamelessness and meanness.

2. The honour of Parents.

The respect for age which is everywhere apparent in the Laws may be partly explained by the natural feeling of Plato, writing in the decline of life; but it is also, we cannot doubt, due to the influence which Spartan customs and institutions exercised over his mind. The sentiment had a strong hold in a community which preserved so many traces of the patriarchal age of society wherein the eldest bore rule, 'because with them government originated in the authority of a father and mother' (iii. 680 E). In the busy city life of Athens, the elder was apt to be pushed aside by his younger and stronger rival; and we observe a similar tendency in the democratic nations of modern times.

At Athens, however, the worship of ancestors still underlay the whole fabric of social and domestic existence, and, probably, as in some Eastern countries, may have retained vitality when other parts of the national religion were in more or less complete decay; and this primitive belief must have helped to maintain a degree of consideration in the young towards their parents and elders. Such a disposition was most welcome to Plato, both for its own sake, and because it would encourage the mildness of temper and subordination to authority which he desired to see incorporated in the citizens of his new State.

And therefore he indicts a brief prelude to the law concerning the right treatment of parents, in which his ancient power of language once again seems to return to him, and in words of singular beauty and pathos he urges upon the young the duty of paying reverence and veneration to the aged, who are far more potent for good and ill than the lifeless statues of the Gods.

Steph.
930
E

Athenian Stranger. Neither God, nor a man who has understanding, will ever advise any one to neglect his parents. To a discourse concerning the honour and dishonour of parents, a prelude such as the following, about the service of the Gods, will be a suitable introduction :—There are ancient customs about the Gods which are universal, and they are of two kinds: some of the Gods we see with our eyes and we honour them, of others we honour the images, raising statues of them which we adore ; and though they are lifeless, yet we imagine that the living Gods have a good will and gratitude to us on this account. Now, if a man has a father or mother, or their fathers or mothers treasured up in his house stricken in years, let him consider that no statue can be more potent to grant his requests than they are, who are sitting at his hearth, if only he knows how to show true service to them.

931

Cleinias. And what do you call the true mode of service?

Ath. I will tell you, O my friend, for such things are worth listening to.

Cle. Proceed.

Ath. Oedipus, as tradition says, when dishonoured by his sons, invoked on them curses which every one declares to have been heard and ratified by the Gods, and Amyntor in his wrath invoked curses on his son Phoenix, and Theseus upon Hippolytus, and innumerable others have also called down wrath upon their children, whence it is clear that the Gods listen to the imprecations of parents ; for the curses of parents are, as they ought to be, mighty against their children as no others are. And shall we suppose that the prayers of a father or mother who is specially dishonoured by his or her children, are heard by the Gods in accordance with nature; and that if a parent is honoured by them, and in the gladness of his heart earnestly entreats the Gods in his prayers to do them good, he is not equally heard, and that they do not minister to his request ? If not, they would be very unjust ministers of good, and that we affirm to be contrary to their nature.

Cle. Certainly.

Ath. May we not think, as I was saying just now, that we can possess no image which is more honoured by the Gods, than that of a father or grandfather, or of a mother stricken in years? whom when a man honours, the heart of the God rejoices, and he is ready to answer their prayers. And, truly, the figure of an ancestor is a wonderful thing, far higher than that of a lifeless image. For the living, when they are honoured by us, join in our prayers, and when they are dishonoured, they utter imprecations against us; but lifeless objects do neither. And therefore, if a man makes a right use of his father and grandfather and other aged relations, he will have images which above all others will win him the favour of the Gods.

Cle. Excellent.

Ath. Every man of any understanding fears and respects the prayers of parents, knowing well that many times and to many persons they have been accomplished. Now these things being thus ordered by nature, good men think it a blessing from heaven if their parents live to old age and reach the utmost limit of human life, or if taken away before their time they are deeply regretted by them; but to bad men parents are always a cause of terror. Wherefore let every man honour with every sort of lawful honour his own parents, agreeably to what has now been said.

BOOK XII.

THE Twelfth Book continues the subject of legislation.—It contains laws respecting Heralds, Theft, Failure of Service, Desertion, Throwing away of Arms and Cowardice in War, Examiners and Censors of Magistrates and the Burial Rites of those who die holding this office, Oaths in Courts of Justice, Neglect of Public Duties, Foreign Travel and the Reception of Strangers, Surety, Right of Search, Limitation of Time in Disputes about Property,

Intimidation of Witnesses or Competitors, Receiving Exiles, Making private War or Peace, Taking Bribes, Registration and Assessment of Property, Offerings to the Gods, Suits at Law and their Execution.

Thus the regulations for the round of civil life are concluded; and Plato proceeds to add a few words upon the disposal of the dead. Interment must take place in ground which is unfit for cultivation; the mounds must be low and the stones small. Funerals are to be simple; the amount spent upon them will be fixed by law. Public lamentations and processions through the streets will not be permitted.

Finally, Plato deals with the question,—How can the permanence of his institutions be assured? He proposes to establish an assembly called the 'Nocturnal Council,' composed of the ten oldest guardians, of all those who have gained the prize of virtue, of the Director and the ex-Director of Education, and of those who have travelled to see the institutions of other countries, besides an equal number of younger colleagues between thirty and forty, appointed one by each of the seniors. The Council will be 'the mind of the State,' and its members will know the true object of laws, which is not power or wealth or freedom, but virtue. Now virtue is one, although we distinguish four virtues,—courage, temperance, wisdom, justice; and the guardians of the State ought to understand the nature of virtue, and be far better teachers of it than any chance poet or wandering sophist. They will require a special training for this purpose; and they must also have a right knowledge of the Gods, and be firmly grounded in the belief that the soul is prior to the body, and that soul and mind rule the Universe.

The Nocturnal Council, of which the members are men who have been educated in such ideas, will be the salvation of the whole State. If it can be duly established and set up, then will our City become a waking reality and not the mere imagination of a dream.

I. The good state in its intercourse with the world.

The following passage treats of a subject in respect to which the customs of ancient states were singularly unlike those of modern communities. The Hellenic cities were divided by barriers of race, of dialect, of manners, of civil and social institutions, and within their walls the rich were at constant feud with the poor, the oligarch with the democrat:—'all men,' says Cleinias at the very beginning of the long discourse, 'are always at war with one another' (i. 625 E). The traditions of past ages lingered, especially in the more backward states, and 'stranger' and 'enemy' continued to be almost synonymous terms.

In this regard, as in every other, Sparta and Athens represented the opposite poles of Hellenic sentiment. Sparta remained the rude warrior state with the virtues and vices and prejudices of primaeval days. The stranger was an object of suspicion and dread; and the 'harsh and morose' practice of expelling foreigners from the land,—the so-called 'Xenelasia,'—was often enforced, while the young men were forbidden to go out into other countries (cp. Protag. 342 D). But at Athens the prevailing conditions were of another kind: the democratic government was less haughty and exclusive: the habits of daily life were free and unconstrained: commercial interests were strong: and in culture and intelligence the city was the 'school of Hellas,' and the resort of strangers from the whole Hellenic world (cp. Thucyd. ii. 41; vii. 69).

We are not surprised, therefore, to observe that Plato when he comes to speak of travel and the reception of foreigners, endeavours, in his usual fashion, to combine Athenian and Spartan ideas. He is true to his native origin, and is unwilling to exchange Attic grace and freedom for the blunt and unsociable manners of the Lacedaemonians, 'whose existence was modelled after that of a camp' (ii. 666 E). Moreover he is aware that the criticism of the world is by no means to be despised. Yet he is afraid that the distasteful spirit of innovation will find new entrance into the commonwealth, if the love of wandering is too much encouraged. And so he draws up an ingenious scheme, which will, he hopes, secure a due amount of intercourse with other lands, and at the same time keep the desire of change in subordination. The modern reader, however, will hardly be able to sympathize with him, or to refrain from the remark that a wider experience of the course of history would most probably have led him to a different conclusion.

Steph. 949 E.
Athenian Stranger. Now a state which makes money from the cultivation of the soil only, and has no foreign trade, must consider what it will do about the emigration of its own people to other countries, and the reception of strangers from elsewhere. About these matters the legislator has to consider, and he will begin by trying to persuade men as far as he can.

The intercourse of cities with one another is apt to create a confusion of manners; strangers are always 950 suggesting novelties to strangers[1]. When states are

[1] Cp. *supra*, iv. 704 E.

well governed by good laws the mixture causes the greatest possible injury; but seeing that most cities are the reverse of well-ordered, the confusion which arises in them from the reception of strangers, and from the citizens themselves rushing off into other cities, when any one either young or old desires to travel anywhere abroad at whatever time, is of no consequence. On the other hand, the refusal of states to receive others, and for their own citizens never to go to other places, is an utter impossibility, and to the rest of the world is likely to appear ruthless and uncivilized; it is a practice adopted by people who use harsh words, such as xenelasia or banishment of strangers, and who have harsh and morose ways, as men think. And to be thought or not to be thought well of by the rest of the world is no light matter; for the many are not so far wrong in their judgment of who are bad and who are good, as they are removed from the nature of virtue in themselves. Even bad men have a divine instinct which guesses rightly, and very many who are utterly depraved form correct notions and judgments of the differences between the good and bad. And the generality of cities are quite right in exhorting us to value a good reputation in the world, for there is no truth greater and more important than this—that he who is really good (I am speaking of the man who would be perfect) seeks for reputation with, but not without, the reality of goodness. And our Cretan colony ought also to acquire the fairest and noblest reputation for virtue from other men; and there is every reason to expect that, if the reality answers to the idea, she will be one of the few well-ordered cities which the sun and the other Gods behold.

Wherefore, in the matter of journeys to other countries and the reception of strangers, we enact as follows:—In the first place, let no one be allowed to go anywhere at all into a foreign country who is less than forty years of age; and no one shall go in a private capacity, but only in some public one, as a herald, or on an embassy, or on a sacred mission. Going abroad on an expedition or in war is not to be included among travels of the class authorized by the state. To Apollo at Delphi and to Zeus at Olympia and to Nemea and to the Isthmus, citizens should be sent to take part in the sacrifices and games there dedicated to the Gods; and they should send as many as possible, and the best and fairest that can be found, and they will make the city renowned at holy meetings in time of peace, procuring a glory which shall be the converse of that which is gained in war; and when they come home they shall teach the young that the institutions of other states are inferior to their own. And they shall send spectators of another sort, if they have the consent of the guardians, being such citizens as desire to look a little more at leisure at the doings of other men; and these no law shall hinder. For a city which has no experience of good and bad men or intercourse with them, can never be thoroughly and perfectly civilized, nor, again, can the citizens of a city properly observe the laws by habit only, and without an intelligent understanding of them[1]. And there always are in the world a few inspired men whose acquaintance is beyond price, and who spring up quite as much in ill-ordered as in well-ordered cities. These are they whom the citizens of a well-ordered city should be ever seeking out, going forth over sea and over land to find him who is incorruptible—that he may establish more firmly institutions in his own state which are good already, and amend what is deficient;

[1] Cp. Rep. x. 619.

for without this examination and enquiry a city will never continue perfect any more than if the examination is ill-conducted.

2. The Burial of the Dead.

Few subjects, as Plato has discovered, occasion more trouble to the legislator, than the disposal of the dead. The deepest feelings and the most unreasonable prejudices of mankind unite to increase the difficulty; and religion is so intimately bound up everywhere with the sentiment of veneration and respect for the departed, that it becomes almost impossible to alter the prevailing practices except by a slow and gradual process of enlightenment.

The regulations which Plato desires to introduce are admirable, and contain much which is worthy of our serious consideration. He expressly enjoins that the dead are to be interred in remote and barren spots; and this was easy to effect in a rugged and mountainous country, like Greece, where there are extensive districts which can never be brought under cultivation. He would certainly have censured the customs of European nations, which long permitted the dead to be placed in sacred buildings and in churchyards amid the crowded populations of cities, and which still allow large tracts of soil to be diverted from their natural purpose 'of affording sustenance to the living.'

Cremation, we observe with some surprise, is not mentioned by him, either here or in a previous passage relating to the burial of the Censors (xii. 947). The rite was probably more common in the heroic ages of Greece than in the historic period; but it is alluded to by Herodotus in the story of King Darius and the Callatians (iii. 38), and also by Thucydides in his description of the Plague at Athens (ii. 52). Plato may have thought that it would not be required in a state such as the Cnosian colony, chiefly composed of husbandmen spread over a wide area of territory. In our own day it appears to be the best solution of a very difficult question.

The preference of Plato for short epitaphs and simple monuments will meet with general approval in modern times. He shared in full measure the moderation and restraint which marked the Hellenic character; the bad taste and adulation by which our memorials of the dead are too often disfigured would have been revolting to him. And we, when we look with regret upon the 'heavy load' which by-gone generations have left to us, may well wish that Plato's rules could have been put in force four or five centuries ago.

The same good sense appears in his law against extravagant expenditure upon funerals. This has been in every age a source of mischief, and has contributed much to the impoverishment of the people. It is one of the evils which are universally deplored, but which no efforts seem able to exterminate. And even Plato, the boldest and most undaunted of reformers, acknowledges that great concessions must be made in these matters to the weakness of human nature. The legislator must have resort to 'persuasion rather than to force'; and we may be allowed to borrow Plato's own language, and to say that 'men will listen with more gentleness and good-will to the precepts of the lawgiver, if their souls are prepared to receive his words; even a little done in the way of conciliation gains their ear, and is always worth having' (iv. 718 C).

Steph.
958
C

Athenian Stranger. THUS a man is born and brought up, and after this manner he begets and brings up his own children, and has his share of dealings with other men, and suffers if he has done wrong to any one, and receives satisfaction if he has been wronged, and so at length in due time he grows old under the protection of the laws, and his end comes in the order of nature. Concerning the dead of either sex, the religious ceremonies which may fittingly be performed, whether appertaining to the Gods of the under-world or of this, shall be decided by the interpreters with absolute authority. Their sepulchres are not to be in places which are fit for cultivation, and there shall be no monuments in such spots, either large or small, but they shall occupy that part of the country which is naturally adapted for receiving and concealing the bodies of the dead with as little hurt as possible to the living. No man, living or dead, shall deprive the living of the sustenance which the earth, their foster-parent, is naturally inclined to provide for them. And let not the mound be piled higher than would be the work of five men completed in five days; nor shall the stone which is placed over the spot be larger than would be sufficient to receive the praises of the dead included in four heroic lines. Nor shall the laying out 959 of the dead in the house continue for a longer time than is sufficient to distinguish between him who is in a trance only and him who is really dead, and speaking generally, the third day after death will be a fair time for carrying out the body to the sepulchre.

Now we must believe the legislator when he tells us that the soul is in all respects superior to the body, and that even in life what makes each one of us to be what we are is only the soul; and that the body follows us about in the likeness of each of us, and therefore, when we are dead, the bodies of the dead are quite rightly said to be our shades or images; for the true and immortal being of each one of us which is called the soul goes on her way to other Gods, before them to give an account—which is an inspiring hope to the good, but very terrible to the bad, as the laws of our fathers tell us; and they also say that not much can be done in the way of helping a man after he is dead. But the living—he should be helped by all his kindred, that while in life he may be the holiest and justest of men, and after death may have no great sins to be punished in the world below. If this be true, a man ought not to waste his substance under the idea that all this lifeless mass of flesh which is in process of burial is connected with him; he should consider that the son, or brother, or the beloved one, whoever he may be, whom he thinks he is laying in the earth, has gone away to complete and fulfil his own destiny, and that his duty is rightly to order the present, and to spend moderately on the lifeless altar of the Gods below.

But the legislator does not intend moderation to be taken in the sense of meanness. Let the law, then, be as follows:—The expenditure on the entire funeral of him who is of the highest class, shall not exceed five minae; and for him who is of the second class, three minae, and for him who is of the third class, two minae, and for him who is of the fourth class, one mina, will be a fair limit of expense. The guardians of the law ought to take especial care of the different ages of life, whether childhood, or manhood, or any other age. And at the end of all, let there be some one guardian of the law presiding, who shall be chosen by the friends of the deceased to superintend, and let it be glory to him to manage with fairness and moderation what relates to the dead, and a discredit to him if they are not well managed. Let the laying out and other ceremonies be in accordance with custom, but to the statesman who adopts custom as his law we must give way in certain particulars. It would be monstrous for example that he should command any man to weep or abstain from weeping over the dead; but he may forbid cries of lamentation, and not allow the voice of the mourner to be heard outside the house; also, he may forbid the bringing of the dead body into the open streets, or the processions of mourners in the streets, and may require that before daybreak they should be outside the city. Let these, then, be our laws relating to such matters, and let him who obeys be free from penalty; but he who disobeys even a single guardian of the law shall be punished by them all with a fitting penalty.

INDEX

A.

Absolute, the, unknown, vol. i. p 202;—absolute beauty, i. 41, 47; ii. 59; absolute equality, i. 200; absolute essence, i. 144, 205; absolute existence, i. 38; absolute greatness and smallness, i. 200, 201; absolute ideas, i. 144, 202; absolute justice, ii. 71; absolute knowledge, i. 37, 38; possessed by God, i. 204, 205; absolute like and unlike, i. 196; absolute unity, i. 226; absolute virtue, i. 37.
Achaemenes, i. 181.
Acheron, i. 158.
Acherusian lake, i. 159.
Achilles, i. 95.
Acropolis, the, of ancient Athens, ii. 131.
Adeimantus, (1) son of Cepis, i. 16; (2) son of Leucolophides, i. 16; (3) brother of Plato, i. 102, 193; ii. 5.
Adonis, the gardens of, i. 58.
Aeacus, i. 181; a judge among the dead, i. 111, 173.
Acantodorus, i. 102.
Aeschines, i. 102, 134.
Aesop, i. 136, 183.
Agathon, i. 68.
Ajax, soul of, chooses a lion's life, ii. 106.

Alcibiades, i. 78; praises Socrates, i. 70; with Socrates at Delium, i. 74; at Potidaea, i. 72, 74; a descendant of Eurysaces, i. 181.
Amasis, king of Egypt, ii. 111.
Ambassadors to the public games, ii. 224.
Amestris, wife of Xerxes, i. 184.
Ammon, the Egyptian God, i. 56, 187.
Amphion, inventor of the lyre, ii. 156.
Amphipolis, Socrates at, i. 95.
Amphitryon, i. 216.
Amusement, to be made a means of education, ii. 146.
Amyntor, ii. 219.
Anaxagoras, his doctrine of Mind, i. 52; his books and opinions, i. 92; ii. 200.
Animals, the, conversed with men in the days of Cronos, i. 236; choose their destiny in the next world, ii. 107 (cp. i. 40); —blemished animals offered to the Gods by the Lacedaemonians, i. 187.
Antiochis, the tribe of Socrates, i. 100.
Antiphon, (1) of Cephisus, i. 102; (2) half-brother of Adeimantus, i. 193.
Antiquity, reasons for our ignorance of, ii. 128.

Antisthenes, i. 134.
Anytus, one of the accusers of Socrates, i. 80.
Apaturia, the, ii. 110.
Aphroditè, = the principle of love which unites the Universe, i. 223.
Apodyterium, the, i. 3.
Apollodorus, i. 102, 108, 133, 166.
Appetitive element of the soul, i. 34, 46.
Ardiaeus the Great, his punishment in Hades, ii. 100.
Arginusae, battle of, i. 67, 100.
Aristeides, the Just, i. 176.
Aristippus, of Cyrenè, not present at the death of Socrates, i. 134.
Aristodemus, i. 68.
Ariston, father of Adeimantus and Glaucon, i. 102; ii. 4.
Aristoteles, i. 194, 206.
Armour, fighting in, i. 9.
Art, moderation and reserve of Greek, i. 32, 113 :—Arts, the, stolen from Athenè and Hephaestus by Prometheus, i. 17, 239; unequally distributed among men, i. 18; unknown for many centuries, ii. 155, 159 (cp. i. 239; ii. 113, 128) ;—the arts which preserve life, i. 169 ; —the plastic and weaving arts do not require the use of iron, ii. 158.
Artist, the, requires certain conditions for his art, ii. 160.
Asclepius, 'we owe a cock to,' i. 166.
Asia, prince of, i. 8, 182.
Atalanta, the soul of, chooses the life of an athlete, ii. 106.
Atheism, charged against Socrates, i. 91 ; refuted, ii. 199.
Atheists, ii. 198, 200 ; advice to, ii. 202. Cp. God.
Athenè, the art of, stolen by Prometheus, i. 17 ; the goddess of arts, i. 239 ; = Neith, ii. 111. 114 ; foundress of Athens and Sais, ii. 114; Goddess of Attica, ii. 127, 131 ; why represented in full armour, ii. 128.
Athens, the ancient city of, ii. 110, 111, 114; founded by the Goddess Athenè, ii. 114; its war with Atlantis, ii 115, 126; destruction of, ii. 116 ; described, ii. 131 :—
Athenians, the, considered the best judges of tragedy, i. 10 ; their embassy to the Oracle of Ammon, i. 186.
Atlantic, supposed not to be navigable, ii. 115, 116, 127 ; origin of the name, ii. 134.
Atlantis, legend of, ii. 109 ; related by Critias, ii. 110, 126 ; destruction of, ii. 116, 127 ; named after Atlas, son of Poseidon, ii. 134 ; productions of, ii. 134, 135 : arrangement of the country, ii. 135 ; temples, buildings, and harbours, ii. 136-139 ; mountains and plain in. ii. 139; population, army, and government, ii. 140 ; degeneracy and corruption of, ii. 143.
Atlas, ii. 134, 143.
Atreus, the legend of, i. 231.
Atropos, ii. 103, 107.
Attica, ancient, description of, ii. 129.

B.

Bacchic women, i. 63.
Barbarians, the natural enemies of the Hellenes, ii. 47.
Beast, the many-headed, ii. 90, 91.
Being and the many, i. 194 ; being in early Greek philosophy, i. 223 ;—true being beheld by the soul which follows God, i. 40, 41 ; the object of the philosopher's desire, i. 144, 214; ii. 74.
Bendis, the festival of, ii. 4.
Birth, pride of, i. 170, 215.
Blindness, the two kinds of, ii. 71.
Body and soul, connexion of, i. 1; ii. 118;—the body, the prison of the soul, i. 42 ; a source of

evil, i. 144; motions of the body, ii 121; inferior to the soul, ii 169, 170, 184, 227; how to be honoured, ii. 171; not eternal, but indestructible, ii. 209;—bodies and shades, ii. 227.
Boreas, legend of, and Orithyia, i. 30.
Boys, the education of, i. 20; ii. 191, 192; the most unmanageable of animals, ii. 190. Cp. Education.
Brasidas, i. 75.
Bulls with gilded horns offered to the Gods, i. 188; sacrifice of bulls in Atlantis, ii. 141.
Burials, see Funerals.

C.

Callias, i. 14, 82.
Callicles, i. 168.
Carthaginians, use leather money, i. 190.
Caste, in ancient Attica and in Egypt, ii. 114, 129.
Cave, allegory of the, ii. 66.
Cebes, i. 116, 131, 134.
Censorship of fiction, ii. 19;—of the arts, ii. 32.
Cephalus, the father of Lysias and Polemarchus, ii. 6.
Chaerophon, i. 84, 168.
Charmantides, ii. 6.
Charmides, i. 1; one of the Thirty Tyrants, i. 78.
Children, must not hear improper stories, ii. 20; must be reared amid fair sights and sounds, ii. 32; must receive education even in their games, ii. 146, 147; must honour and reverence their parents, ii. 167, 219; are happiest when only possessed of a moderate fortune, ii. 172.
City, the, of which the pattern is laid up in heaven, ii. 95.
Clazomenae, i. 193.
Cleito, the nymph, ii. 133, 137.
Cleombrotus, not present at the death of Socrates, i. 134.
Cleverness, the true kind of, i. 218;

no match for honesty, ii. 35; needs an ideal direction, ii. 72.
Clotho, ii. 103. 107.
Cocytus, i. 159.
Column, the, of light, ii. 101.
Comic poets, the enemies of Socrates, i. 80, 81.
Communism, the advantages of, ii. 179, 187.
Contracts, sometimes not protected by law, ii. 78.
Conversion of the soul, ii. 71.
Corybantes, i. 63, 66, 71.
Courage, a special virtue of the philosopher, i. 148; ii. 59.
Cratylus, i. 27.
Crete, praised for its good government, i.128; Theseus' voyage to, i. 132.
Criminals, great, chiefly come from the class of kings and tyrants, i. 175; ii. 100; are usually men of strong character spoiled by bad education, ii. 61.
Critias, the elder, son of Dropidas, ii. 110, 111.
Critias, the younger, son of Callaeschrus, ii. 132; one of the Thirty Tyrants, i. 1, 78; relates the legend of Atlantis, ii. 110, 126.
Criticism, impossible without knowledge, ii. 125.
Crito. i. 22, 102; offers to be one of Socrates' sureties, i. 108, 163; comes to Socrates in prison, i. 113; urges Socrates to escape, i 116; present at the death of Socrates, i. 134; receives the last commands of Socrates, i. 162, 167.
Critobulus, i. 25, 102, 108, 134.
Cronos, judgment of men under, i. 172; the reign of, i. 232; legend of, ii. 21.
Ctesippus, i. 4, 134.
Cycles, recurrence of, in nature, i. 234.

D.

Daedalus, Socrates descended from, i. 181; his date, ii. 155.

Dead, the, judgment of, i. 111, 152, 171, 172; ii. 99 foll.; the dead in battle not to be stripped, ii. 46; respect to be paid to the dead, ii. 167; disposal of the dead, ii. 226.

Death, is not feared by the wise man, i. 96, 103, 139-149, 171; its approach brings prophetic power to men, i. 109; either a sleep or a migration. i. 111; philosophic desire of, i. 138, 142, 147; the nature of. i. 142, 173; not the end of all, i. 152; the fear of, increases in old age, ii. 9.

Delium, battle of, i. 13, 74, 95.

Delos, the mission-ship to, i. 114, 132, 134.

Delphi, inscriptions in the Temple at, i. 31, 185.

Deluge, the, of Deucalion, ii. 112, 131;—traditions of deluges, ii. 128, 129, 131, 155, 156.

Demigods, i. 93; assist in the government of the world, i. 235; honour to be paid to, ii. 167, 180; are our allies against evil, ii. 212.

Democracy, the origin of, ii. 77; the magistrates in, elected by lot, ii. 80; freedom of, ii. 80; —the democratical man, ii. 82.

Demons, *see* Demigods.

Desires, the, of men, unlimited, ii. 216.

Destiny, the, of man in his own power, ii. 103; the order of destiny, ii. 210.

Destructions of mankind in past ages, i. 234; ii. 112, 128, 155.

Deucalion, ii. 112. 131.

Dialectic, i. 240; divides things into their classes, i. 59; the method of, practised by Zeno, i. 206; 'the first taste of,' i. 240; a gift of heaven, i. 241.

Dialectician, the, sows the seed of knowledge in the soul, i. 59.

Dinomachè, mother of Alcibiades, i. 184.

Dionysodorus, i. 21.

Director of Education, the, (in the Model City), ii. 191.

Disease, the physician must have experience of, ii. 34; the nature of, ii. 121;—disease and vice compared, ii. 42, 213.

Draughts, comparison of an argument to a game of, ii. 55; the 'holy line' in the draught board, ii. 178.

Drones, the, ii. 78, 84 (cp. ii. 205).

Dropides, ii. 110, 132.

E.

Earth, the, true nature of, i. 154; the first men sprung from, i. 232, 234; a goddess, ii. 180.

Echecrates of Phlius, i. 131.

Education, subjects of, in Greek schools, i. 20; ii. 191; of the Persian Princes, i. 182, 183; should be a training for the work of after-life, ii. 146; in the higher and lower sense, ii. 147; the value of, ii. 184.

Egypt, antiquity of, ii. 112; caste in, ii. 114.

Eleatic philosophers, the, i. 222.

Elephants in Atlantis, ii. 135.

Enemies, the treatment of, ii. 45.

Envy, an enemy of virtue, ii. 175.

Epeus, soul of, takes the form of a woman, ii. 106.

Ephors, the, watch over the queens of Sparta, i. 181.

Epigenes, i. 102, 134.

Epimenides, ii. 156.

Epimetheus, ii. 16, 17.

Epitaphs, ii. 226.

Er, myth of, ii. 98.

Eriphylè, ii. 92.

Eryximachus, i. 15, 70.

Essence, perceived by the mind, i. 38; in early Greek philosophy, i. 228;—absolute essence, i. 144, 205.

Ethiopians, use stones for money, i. 190, 191.

INDEX

Euclid of Megara, i. 134.
Eumolpus, the son of Musaeus, ii. 12.
Euripides, inventor of the name magnet, i. 63.
Eurysaces, i. 181.
Euthydemus, i. 21.
Euthydemus, brother of Lysias, ii. 6.
Evenus of Paros, i. 82, 137.
Evil, not to be rendered for evil, i. 123; can never wholly pass away, i. 217; origin of, i. 237; God not the author of, ii. 23, 24; involuntary, ii. 176; ultimate defeat of, designed by the Creator, ii. 210; more evil than good in the world, ii. 212 :— Evil-doing, the penalty of, to become like the evil, i. 218; ii. 171 :—Evil men cannot enjoy friendship, i. 48; cannot injure the good, i. 98, 112; more numerous than the good, ii. 35; their gifts not received by God, i. 188; ii. 166 (cp. ii. 15); their prosperity, ii. 203, 211 (cp. ii. 13); have a correct judgment about good and bad, ii. 223. Cp. Wicked.
Excess, in grief and joy, to be avoided, ii. 177.

F.

Family life, cares of, i. 26; in the state, ii. 180, 181;—family pride, i. 170, 216;—family worship, ii. 201.
Fate and Free Will, i. 34.
Fates, the, ii. 102, 107.
Finite and infinite, i. 242
Forgetfulness, the Plain of, ii. 107.
Freedom, characteristic of democracy, ii. 80. 87;—of action acquired by knowledge, i. 7 :— of the will, i. 34; ii. 210 (cp. ii. 103).
Friendship, unknown to the bad, i. 48.
Funerals, expenditure on, to be moderate, ii. 167; regulations respecting, ii. 227.
Future life, i. 40, 111, 112, 141, 146, 148, 150, 152. 159, 172, 178, 218; ii. 12, 210, 227. Cp. World below.

G.

Gadfly, Socrates compared to a, i. 98.
Games [the Olympic &c.], training for, ii. 188; ambassadors sent to, ii. 224.
Gifts of nature, may be perverted, ii. 60, 72
Glaucon, son of Ariston, i. 193; ii. 4.
Glaucus, 'the art of,' i. 153.
God, alone is wise, i. 61, 86; alone has absolute knowledge, i. 205; is perfect righteousness, i. 218; the Creator, i. 232; the Shepherd, i. 235; not the author of evil, i. 237; ii. 23, 24; never changes, ii. 25; will not lie, ii. 27; moves in a straight line towards His end, ii. 165; the measure of all things, ii. 166; will not receive the gifts of the wicked, ii. 166; watches over the stranger and the suppliant, ii. 174; cannot fight against necessity, ii. 181; has no cowardice or weakness, ii. 205, 206; takes thought for all, ii. 207.
Gods, the, procession of, i. 37; the guardians of mankind, i. 140; not to be appeased by gifts, i. 188; ii. 15, 166, 198, 203, 212; human ignorance of, i. 205; ii. 15. 124; supposed to take no heed of human affairs, i. 205; ii. 15, 198; disbelief in, ii. 15, 198, 199, 201; common stories about, not to be received, ii. 21, 127, 200; their wars, ii. 22, 24; honour to be paid to, ii. 167. 170; are our masters, ii. 170, 212; existence of, proved, ii. 199; not careless or ignorant,

ii. 204; eternal, but the soul and body indestructible, ii. 209; the aged bear their likeness, ii. 220.

Good, intended to triumph in the Universe, ii. 210.

Good man, the, no harm can happen to, i. 98, 112; does not cling to life, i. 171; is the friend of God and like Him, i. 217; ii. 166; often appears simple from his inexperience of evil, ii. 34; ought to impart his virtue, ii. 175; should be both gentle and passionate, ii. 176; has the consolations of hope, ii. 177; cannot be very wealthy, ii. 183;—good men exist even in ill-ordered cities, ii. 224.

Goods, the scale of, ii. 184.

Goods, community of, ii. 179, 187; in the days of Cronos, i. 235, 236; in ancient Attica, ii. 129.

Gorgias of Leontium, i. 82, 168.

Government, forms of, have undergone many changes in the course of ages, ii. 154; their order in capacity for improvement, ii. 162;—present forms of government in an evil condition, ii. 62;—the first, second, and third forms of the ideal state, ii. 179, 187.

Grace (εὐσχημοσύνη) in life and art, ii. 31.

Gymnastic, as a part of education, i. 19; really designed for the improvement of the soul, ii. 36 (cp. ii. 184); when carried to excess, enfeebles and brutalizes the mind, ii. 37, 38; ought to be combined with intellectual pursuits, ii. 120;—training for the games, ii. 188.

H.

Habit and virtue, ii. 72, 105.
Hades, *see* World below.
Happiness, not conferred by wealth, ii. 183; denied to the unjust, ii. 203, 211; of Olympic victors, ii. 104.

Harmony, chiefly intended for the improvement of the soul, ii. 36; —of words and deeds, i. 12;—justice a harmony, ii. 41;—harmony of the soul effected by temperance, ii. 95.

Health and justice compared, ii. 42; secondary to virtue, ii. 95.

Hellas, frequent occurrence of deluges and other calamities in, ii. 112, 113; war of Hellas and Atlantis, ii. 115:—Hellenes, not to be enslaved by Hellenes, ii. 45; united by ties of blood, ii. 47; not to devastate Hellas, ii. 48; have no knowledge of antiquity, ii. 112, 113; family worship among, ii 201.

Hephaestus, the arts of, stolen by Prometheus, i. 17; the fellow-worker with Athenè, ii. 239; legends of, ii. 22; the God of Attica, ii. 127.

Heracles, the Lacedaemonian kings descended from, ii. 181; genealogies traced to, i. 216;—the columns of, i. 154; ii. 115, 116, 126, 134.

Herè, legends of, ii. 22, 27.
Hermaea, festival of the, i. 3.
Hermocrates, ii. 125.
Hermogenes, i. 27, 134.
Heroes, to be worshipped, ii. 167.

Hesiod, pleasure of conversing with, in the world below, i. 112; his rewards of justice, ii. 12; his stories improper for youth, ii. 20, 21; Hesiod and Epimenides, ii. 156.

Hippias of Elis, i. 14. 15, 82.
Hippocrates, the Asclepiad, i. 53.
Hippocrates, son of Apollodorus, i. 13.
Hippolytus, ii. 219.
Hippothales, i. 4.
Homer, the principal source of inspiration to the rhapsodes, i. 62, 66; pleasure of conversing

INDEX

with, in the world below, i. 112; his rewards of justice, ii. 12; his stories not approved for youth, ii. 20.
Hope, 'the nurse of age,' ii. 9; the consolation of the righteous in misfortune, ii. 177.
Human grandeur, despised by the philosopher, i. 216;—interests, unimportance of, i. 214; ii. 149;—life, full of evils, ii. 23.
Husbandmen, a caste in ancient Attica, ii. 129, 130.

I.

Ibis, the, sacred to Theuth, i. 56.
Idea of good, a cause, like the sun, ii. 70:—recollection of ideas, i. 40, 77; loveliness of ideas, i. 41; ideas the cause of love, i. 43; absolute ideas, i. 144, 202; ideas of likeness and unlikeness, i. 196; ideas and the things which partake of them, i. 196; ideas and moral qualities, i. 198: one and many in the ideas, i. 200; participation of things in, i. 199-202, 206; infinite, i. 201; exist in the mind, i. 201; are patterns, i. 201; necessary to philosophy, i. 206:—the Doctrine of Ideas criticized by Plato, i. 192.
Ideal State, the, ii. 49-52, 74, 164, 179:—Ideals, value of, ii. 51; use of, in education, ii. 147: —Idealists, i. 228.
Ignorance, about the soul, disgraceful to the rhetorician, i. 60; the misery of, ii. 174.
Ilissus, i. 32; ii. 131.
Imitation in language, i. 27;—in painting, ii. 124.
Immortality of the soul, i. 35, 76, 152; ii. 108, 227.
Individual, the, and the idea, i. 202.
Infinite, the, nature of, i. 242.
Inheritance, laws of, ii. 180.
Initiation in the mysteries, i. 150.
Injustice, an evil to the unjust,
i. 122; eulogists of, ii. 17, 18; only blamed by those who have no power to be unjust, ii. 16; the anarchy of the soul, ii. 42 (cp. ii. 212); brings no profit, ii. 90; the true penalty of, i. 218; ii. 171; involuntary, ii. 176 (cp. i. 91; ii. 16; analogous to disease, ii. 213.
Intellectual pursuits, not to be carried to excess, ii. 120:—intellectual world, the divisions of, ii. 70.
Intermediates, nature of, i. 25.
Intoxication, ii. 150.
Involuntary nature of evil and injustice, ii. 176 (cp. i. 91; ii. 16).
Ion, the rhapsode, i. 62.
'Ionian Muses' (Heracleitus, &c.), i. 220, 222;—Ionian soldiers in Athenian service, i. 73.
Isthmus, the, Socrates once went to, i. 127; games at, ii. 224.

J.

Jealousy, unknown to the Gods, i. 37; hatefulness of, ii. 175.
Judge, the good, ii. 33.
Judgment, final, i. 111, 152, 171; ii. 98, 227.
Justice, praised by men for its consequences, ii. 13; the poets on, ii. 12, 13, 14, 15; ought to be praised for itself, ii. 17; the harmony of human life, ii. 41; compared to health, ii. 42: accompanies God, ii. 165; worthy of honour, ii. 175;—absolute justice, ii. 71;—justice and retribution, ii. 171;—'the justice of the Gods,' ii. 211.

K.

Kindred, the honour of, ii. 173.
Knowledge, creates trust, i. 7, 8; the source of, i. 38; a process of recollection, i. 77; ii. 177; previous to birth, ii. 71; absolute knowledge, i. 38, 39, 204; knowledge of self, the proper

study of mankind, i. 32; the conceit of knowledge, i. 85, 95; ii. 170, 177, 199;—the highest knowledge, the Idea of Good, ii. 70 :—the best knowledge, to discern between good and evil, ii. 104;—knowledge of the Gods, unattainable, i. 205; ii. 15, 124.

'Know thyself,' the inscription at Delphi, i 31, 185.

L.

Labour, division of, 'a shadow of justice,' ii. 41.
Lacedaemon, fencing masters do not visit, i. 10; the constitution of, commonly extolled, i. 128; —Lacedaemonians, take the greatest interest in war of all Hellenes, i. 10; use iron for money, i. 190; the prayer of the Lacedaemonians, i. 186;— greatness and wealth of the Lacedaemonian kings, i. 181.
Laches, i. 9; with Socrates at the battle of Delium, i. 13, 74.
Lachesis, ii. 102, 103, 107.
Lamb, the golden, story of, i. 231.
Lamentation at funerals, ii. 228.
Lampido, mother, daughter, and wife of a king, i. 185.
Land, distribution of (in the Model City), ii. 180.
Language, plastic power of, ii. 90.
Law, the rule of the best, ii. 149: —Laws, a species of written composition i. 61; are teachers of youth, i. 89 (cp. i. 21); are for punishment, not instruction, i. 91; plead their cause against Socrates, i. 124; are powerful in the next world, i. 130; bring help to all in the state, ii. 93; must be enforced by the example of the rulers, ii. 163; obedience to, ii. 173; should be understood by the citizens, ii. 224.
Law, the divine, of justice, ii. 165.

'Laws,' the, contrast of, with the 'Republic,' ii. 144; its genuineness, ii. 145; its hortative character, ii. 164; a model for the Director of Education, ii. 193; the constitution described in, the second best, ii. 179, 187.
Lawsuits, will be almost unknown in the Model City, ii. 184.
Lawyer, the, i. 212, 216.
Legislator, the, like other artists, requires favourable conditions, ii. 160; needs the aid of a virtuous tyrant, ii. 161, 162 (cp. ii. 179); the end at which he should aim, ii. 182: must not be expected to attempt impossibilities, ii. 183; ought to use persuasion as well as force, ii. 198; may concede somewhat to custom, ii. 228.
Leon of Salamis, i. 100.
Letters, significance of the various, i. 27.
Liberty, characteristic of democracy, ii. 80.
Lie, the, in words, and in the soul, ii. 27, 28;—the Gods not to be represented as lying, ii. 28;—lies of poets, ii. 20.
Life,—not always to be preferred to death, i. 94, 109, 121, 168; ii. 170; a combat, i. 177; life under Cronos, i. 235; loses its zest in old age, ii. 7; the life of virtue toilsome, ii. 14, 187; the good life acceptable to God, ii. 166.
Light, the column of, ii. 101.
'Like to like,' ii. 166.
Likeness and unlikeness, i. 194, 196.
Lot, election by, characteristic of democracy, ii. 80.
Love and philosophy, i. 34, 67.
Lycon, i. 22, 88, 105.
Lysanias, 1) father of Aeschines, i. 102; (2 father of Cephalus, ii. 8.
Lysias, the speech of, i. 29, 33; message of the Muses to, i. 61; the brother of Polemarchus, ii. 6.

Lysimachus, father of Aristides the younger, i. 210.
Lysis, i. 3.

M.

Magic arts, ii. 13.
Magnet, i. 63.
Man, the creation of, i. 16; primitive man, i. 18;—man needs the knowledge of himself, i. 32; his soul has seen true being, i. 40; a possession of the Gods, i. 140; ii. 170, 207, 212; more intractable than other animals, i. 215; a god to the animals, i. 235; has the power to choose his own destiny, ii. 103, 105; must follow the higher instincts of his nature, ii. 123; the puppet of the Gods, ii. 148; said to be 'the master of himself,' ii. 149: not man, but God, the measure of all things, ii. 166; must honour his own soul, next to the Gods, ii. 170; the most religious of animals, ii. 207; his relation to the Universe, ii. 209; enjoys to some degree a freedom of the will, ii. 210:—the one best man, i. 119:—Men better teachers than nature, i. 33; ignorant about the Gods, i. 205; ii. 15, 124; are not just of their own will, ii. 16; always think others to blame and not themselves, ii. 170 cp. ii. 105); must be moderate in joy and sorrow, ii. 177; the kindred of the Gods, ii. 203 (cp. ii. 122); insatiable in their desires, ii. 216;—periodical destructions of men, i. 234; ii. 112, 113, 128, 155;—the first men born from the earth, i. 232, 234; life of men in the days of Cronos, i. 235; primitive men simpler and better than later generations, ii. 159.
Manners, in education, i. 20.
Many, the, their opinion not to be regarded, i. 116, 118, 121; form a wrong estimate of goods, ii. 182; have correct notions of good and bad, ii. 223.
Many, the, Zeno's argument concerning, i. 194; can co-exist with the one, i. 197, 240.
Marsyas, Socrates like, i. 71; inventor of music, ii. 155.
Materialist philosophers, ancient Greek, i. 228.
Matter, the cause of evil in the Universe, i. 237.
Mean, the, happiness of, ii. 105. 158, 172.
Medicine, must consider the whole, i. 1, 52, 53; ii. 207, 209; inutility of, ii. 121.
Megara, i. 128, 134.
Meletus, i. 81, 87, 105; questioned by Socrates, i. 88-94.
Memory, injured by the invention of writing, i. 56; distinguished from reminiscence, i. 56; most active in childhood, ii. 117; the philosopher should have a good memory, ii. 59.
Mendicant prophets, ii. 13
Menexenus, i. 4, 134.
Meno, i. 76, 78.
Midias, i. 180.
Mind, in the philosophy of Anaxagoras, i. 52; 'mind and virtue,' ii. 204;—'the fair mind in the fair body,' ii. 119.
Minos, a judge among the dead, i. 111, 173.
Moderation, necessity of, ii. 177; disregarded by most men, ii. 216; distinguished from meanness, ii. 227.
Money, nature of, i. 190; the love of, despicable, ii. 92, 93;—money-making, the art of, in Cephalus' family, ii. 8; forbidden in the Model City, ii. 183: why thought dishonourable, ii. 216.
Monuments, ii. 226.
Moon, the, a goddess, i. 92; ii. 199, 202; reputed mother of Orpheus, ii. 14.
Motion, expressed by the letter ρ, i. 28;—of the universe, i. 232,

233; motion of the stars, ii. 102; motion in the soul, i. 35 :— motions of the soul and of the body, ii. 120, 122.
Multitude, *see* Many.
Musaeus, i. 66, 112; ii. 12, 14.
Muses, the, inspire madness in the poet, i. 63 ; Musaeus and Orpheus, their children, ii. 14.
Music, in education, i. 20 ; ii. 32 ; meaning of, in Greek writers, ii. 35 ; the true use of, ii. 36; effect of excessive, ii. 37 ; time to be spent in the study of, ii. 191.
Mysteries, the, i. 42, 130, 150; ii. 14, 16, 21, 86.
Myth, the, of Prometheus and Epimetheus, i. 16; of the Other World, i. 152 ; of the Judgment of Souls, i. 172; of Atreus and Thyestes, i. 231 ; of Er, the son of Armenius, ii. 98 :—myths of the ancient philosophers, i. 222.
Mythology, Socrates' treatment of, i. 31 ; misrepresentations of the Gods in, ii. 199 (cp. ii. 127); only studied when men have leisure, ii. 128.

N.

Names, natural truth of, i. 27.
Natural gifts, i. 52 ; ii. 60, 72 ;— natural philosophers, ii. 200 (cp. i. 92).
Nature, recurrent cycles in, i. 232.
Naucratis, i. 56.
Necessity, the mother of the Fates, ii. 101, 102, 103, 107.
Necessity, God said not to be able to fight against, ii. 181.
Neith, = Athenè, ii. 111, 114.
Nemea, games at, ii. 224.
Nemesis, ii. 167.
Nestor, ii. 164; like Pericles, i. 75.
Niceratus, ii. 5.
Nicias, the Athenian general, i. 9.
Nicostratus, i. 102.
Nile, ii. 111, 113.
Niobè, ii. 24, 112.

Not-being, i. 221.
'Nothing too much,' the inscription at Delphi, i. 185.
Nymphs, i. 33, 45, 61.

O.

Oceanus, i. 158.
Odysseus, i. 112; the soul of, chooses the life of a private man, ii. 107.
Oedipus, ii. 219.
Office, not desired by the good ruler, ii. 74.
Old age, Cephalus' opinion of, ii. 7:—Old men must reverence the young, ii. 173.
Olympic games, ii. 188, 224 ;— Olympic victors, i. 106; ii. 173, 188;—Olympic victories, the three heavenly, i. 50.
Olympus, the musician, i. 71 ; ii. 155.
Omniscience, the conceit of, i. 85, 95; ii. 170, 177, 199.
One, the, Parmenides' doctrine of, i. 195;—one and many, i. 197, 240.
Opinion and knowledge, i. 38, 39 : —the opinion of the many of no value, ii. 116, 118, 121.
Opposites, participation in, i. 196.
Oratory, the true principles of, i. 52, 59.
Orichalcum, ii. 135, 137, 141.
Orithyia, the legend of, i. 31.
Orpheus, i. 66 ; ii. 14, 155 ; soul of, chooses a swan's life, ii. 106.

P.

Pain, cessation of, causes pleasure, i. 135.
Painting, like writing, apt to be unintelligible, i. 57; criticism of, ii. 124.
Palamedes, i. 112 ; ii. 155.
Pandarus, ii. 24.
Paralus, (1) son of Pericles, i. 14 ; (2) son of Demodocus, i. 102.
Parents, anxieties of, i. 25 ; honour to be paid to, ii. 167, 173, 220 ;

ought not to heap up riches for their children, ii. 172; are images of the Gods, ii. 220.
Parmenides, i. 193, 221, 222, 226.
Parts, the, and the whole:—in medicine, i. 2, 53; ii. 207, 209; —in regard to the happiness of the State, ii. 73;—in the Universe, ii. 208, 209.
Passionate element of the Soul, *see* Spirit.
Patroclus, i. 95.
Pattern, the heavenly, ii. 95 (cp. ii. 180);—the two patterns of life, i. 218.
Pausanias, of Cerameis, i. 15.
Perfect state, *see* Ideal state.
Pericles, the most accomplished of rhetoricians, i. 52; not equal to Socrates as an orator, i. 72; compared to Nestor and Antenor, i. 75;—his sons, i. 14.
Perseus, i. 181.
Persia, kings of, their wealth and power, i. 180.
Phaedo, i. 131.
Phaedondes, i. 134.
Phaedrus, i. 15, 30.
Phaëthon, legend of, ii. 112.
Pharmacia, i. 31.
Phasis, i. 154.
Philippides, i. 14.
Philolaus, i. 138.
Philosopher, the, is inspired, i. 41; willing to die, but not to take his own life, i. 138; despises bodily pleasures, i. 143; his virtues, i. 148; ii. 59; helplessness of the philosopher in the law-courts, i. 177, 212; ii. 70; character of the philosopher, i. 213; corruption of the philosopher, ii. 59; the true philosopher will retire from the storms of the world, ii. 63:— Philosophers to be kings, ii. 52, 95; why they are useless, ii. 55; true philosophers, few in number, ii. 62;—the early Greek philosophers, i. 220; the Eleatic, Ionian, and Sicilian philosophers, i. 222;—the old philosophers did not condescend to explain themselves, i. 223;—natural philosophers, i. 92; ii. 200.
Philosophy and love, i. 34, 67; philosophy defended by Socrates, i. 26; the noblest and best of music, i. 137; impossible without ideas, i. 206; the desolation and dishonour of philosophy, ii. 61; true and false philosophy, ii. 62; why philosophy is useless, ii. 70; aids a man to make a wise choice in the next world, ii. 104.
Phlius, i. 131, 132.
Phoenix, son of Amyntor, ii. 219.
Phoroneus, 'the first man,' ii. 112.
Physician, the, ought to have regard to the whole, i. 1, 53; ii. 207, 209;—the good physician, ii. 33.
Pilot, the parable of the, ii. 56.
Pindar, i. 76; ii. 9, 14.
Plato, mysticism of, i. 34; his doctrine of Free Will, i. 35; ii. 197; regards punishment as remedial, i. 35, 151; present at the trial of Socrates, i. 102; offers to be one of Socrates' sureties, i. 108; was ill at the time of Socrates' death, i. 134; relation of, to the Pythagoreans, i. 136, 150; ii. 1, 109; criticises the Doctrine of Ideas, i. 192; his explanation of not-being, i. 219; his doctrine of the 'one best man,' i. 229; ii. 54; attributes the existence of evil to matter, i. 230; ii. 197; his account of the growth of society, i. 231; pessimistic tone of his later writings, ii. 2, 49, 94, 148, 169, 215; his dislike of superstition, ii. 11, 197; his theory of physical training, ii. 36; transcendentalism of, ii. 65; unfriendly to democracy, ii. 77, 178; his legislation against excessive wealth, ii. 182; prefers

the Spartan ideal in education, ii. 190; takes a liberal view of trade in the Laws, ii. 215.
Pleasure, closely conjoined with pain, i. 135; indulgence in, a dishonour to the soul, ii. 170;—the pleasures of the body despised by the philosopher, i. 143;—necessary and unnecessary pleasures, ii. 83, 86.
Plurality in unity, i. 242.
Poetry in education, i. 20; ii. 191, 192; poetry and inspiration, i. 63, 64, 86;—tragic poetry native to Athens, i. 10.
Poets, the, sing by inspiration, i. 63, 86; bear testimony to the immortality of the soul, i. 76; cannot explain their own writings, i. 86; their representations of the Gods, ii. 13, 14, 20, 199;—'the poets who were the children of the Gods,' ii. 16 (cp. ii. 14);—the comic poets the enemies of Socrates, i. 80;—the lyric poets set to music in schools, i. 20;—tragic poets, all come to Athens, i. 10.
Polemarchus, ii. 4.
Political Economy of the ancients, i. 189.
Poor, the, not despised by the rich in time of danger, ii. 79.
Population, regulation of, ii. 181.
Poseidon, the God of Atlantis, ii. 133; his sons, ii. 133; temple of, ii. 137; grove of, ii. 138; the laws of Poseidon, ii. 141.
Potidaea, Socrates at, i. 72, 74, 95.
Poverty, unknown to primitive mankind, ii. 158; poverty and wealth alike injurious, ii. 217.
Power, inimical to virtue, i. 175; the struggle for power, ii. 74; not often conjoined with temperance and justice, ii. 164.
Priam, i. 65.
Primitive man, i. 18, 232-234, 239; ii. 113, 127, 155.
Prodicus of Ceos, i. 14, 24, 82, 210.
Prometheus, the legend of, i. 16-18, 239, 241; commanded by Zeus to deprive men of the foreknowledge of death, i. 173.
Property, community of, abandoned in the second-best state, ii. 180;—in ancient Attica, ii. 129;—restrictions on the disposition of, ii. 78.
Proportion, importance of, ii. 119.
Protagoras, i. 14; his saying false, 'that man is the measure of all things,' ii. 166.
Protarchus, i. 240.
Proteus, ii. 26.
Punishment, not to be vindictive, but corrective, i. 35, 175; ii. 24, 94, 144; of the wicked in the world below, i. 40, 153, 160, 174, 218; ii 9, 13, 99, 210, 227; the true punishment, =likeness to evil, i. 218; ii. 171.
Purification, the, of the soul, i. 147; in the mysteries, i. 150.
Pyriphlegethon, i. 159, 160.
Pyrrha, ii. 112.
Pythagoreans, the, indebtedness of Plato to, i. 136, 150; ii. 1, 109.
Pythian games, ii. 188, 224.
Pythodorus, i. 193, 194.

Q.

Quarrels, dishonourable, ii. 21, 22; the quarrels of the Gods, a fiction, ii. 21, 22, 127.

R.

Reading in schools, i. 20; ii. 191.
Reason, one of the three elements of the soul, i. 34; the 'sacred and golden cord' of reason, ii. 149.
Recollection, the doctrine of (ἀνάμνησις), i. 41, 76.
Religion, despised by natural philosophers, ii 200; influence of, in childhood, ii. 201.
Reminiscence, see Recollection.
Retail trade, why esteemed dishonourable, ii. 216.

INDEX

Retribution, ii. 171; cannot be escaped, ii. 211; in a future life, *see* Future Life, Punishment.
Reverence, the gift of Zeus, i. 19; in and toward the young. ii. 173.
Revolution, causes of, ii. 80.
Rhadamanthus, a judge among the dead, i. 111, 173.
Rhapsodes, i. 62.
Rhetoric, the Art of, i. 53; rhetoric and psychology, i. 54; the true art of, based on an exact analysis of the soul, i. 59.
Rhythm, ii. 31.
Riches, *see* Wealth.
Ruler, the, must not ask his subjects to submit to him, ii. 57:—number of rulers increases the difficulty of making a reform, ii. 162; power of their example, ii. 163;—[in the best state], must attain to the knowledge of the good, ii. 73; will accept office as a necessity, ii. 74:—[in the Model City], must exercise perpetual watchfulness, ii. 188, 189.

S.

Sais, in Egypt, ii. 111.
Sculpture, must only express the image of the good, ii. 32.
Self-conceit, i. 84, 85, 95; ii. 170, 177, 199;—self-knowledge, i. 32, 185; self-love, ii. 176;—self-made men, ii. 8;—self-motion, i. 35.
Senses, the, inaccurate witnesses, i. 143.
Sepulchres, regulations respecting, ii. 226.
Shades and bodies, ii. 227.
Sicily, rivers of mud in, i. 157:—'Sicilian Muses' (Empedocles &c.), i. 222.
Sight, the keenest of our senses, i. 42; illusions of, i. 143;—the world of sight, ii. 70.
Sign, the, of Socrates, i. 99, 110, 210; ii. 62.

Silenus, Socrates compared to a figure of, i. 71, 75.
Simmias, the Theban, i. 116, 134.
Simplicity, the first principle of education, ii. 31;—the two kinds of, ii. 31;—simplicity of the good man, ii. 34;—simplicity in primitive society, i. 235; ii. 128, 158.
Siren, Socrates compared to a, i. 72;—Sirens, the, ii. 102.
Sisyphus, i. 112, 175.
Sleep, much, not required, ii. 188.
Society, origin of, i. 16, 18, 239; ii. 154.
Socrates, a lover of the town, i. 33, 127; his character, i. 67, 77; his fits of abstraction, i. 69, 73; his appearance, i. 71, 75; his conduct at Delium and Potidaea, i. 73, 74, 95 (cp. i. 13); a stranger in courts of law, i. 79 (cp. i. 177); his accusers, i. 80; declared by the Delphian Oracle to be the wisest of men, i. 83; cross-examines the pretenders to wisdom, i. 84, 101 (cp. i. 209); his example imitated by the young men, i. 87; has no fear of death, i. 95; present at the battle of Amphipolis, i. 95; the 'gadfly' of the Athenian people, i. 98; his sign, i. 99, 110, 210; ii. 62; presides at the trial of the generals after Arginusae, i. 100; would not help to bring Leon from Salamis, i. 100; his disciples, i. 101 (cp. i. 210); his sons, i. 103, 112, 117, 129, 164: his conviction, i. 105; proposes his penalty, i. 106, 108; his view of death, i. 106, 109, 111; his dream in prison, i. 115: delay in carrying out his execution, i. 132; told in a dream that he should compose music, i. 137; his death, i. 164; his last words, i. 166; descended from Daedalus, i. 181; his conversation with Parmenides,

i. 193; a man-midwife, i. 209; not unaccustomed to speak in parables, ii. 56.

Solon, i. 61; the tale of Solon, ii. 110, 126.

Sophocles, a remark of, quoted, ii. 7.

Sorrow, not to be indulged, ii. 177 (cp. ii. 170).

Soul and body, connection of, i. 1; ii. 118; the soul incorporate in the body, i. 36; must see true being before it can take a human form, i. 38, 41; imprisoned or entombed in the body, i. 42; desires to be released from the body, i. 142; her purification from the corporeal element, i. 147; superior to the body, ii. 169, 184, 227;—the three elements of the soul, i. 34; ii. 122;—the soul self-moved, i. 36; knowledge of the soul, the basis of rhetoric, i. 53, 59; ascent of, to the intellectual world, ii. 70; conversion of, ii. 71; harmony of the soul, ii. 95; motions of the soul, ii. 122; the soul akin to the Divine, ii. 122; the due honour of, ii. 169, 184; not eternal, but indestructible, ii. 209;—immortality of the soul, i. 35, 76, 152; ii. 108, 227; her condition after death, i. 39, 152, 153, 159, 160, 172; ii. 98, 210, 227; transmigration of souls, i. 35, 38, 77; ii. 103, 209-211;—the wings of the soul, i. 43;—the 'horses' of the soul, i. 46; —the soul compared to a many-headed monster, ii. 90;—like the eye, ii. 71;—the procession of the souls, i. 37;—soul and universe, ii. 123.

Sparta, *see* Lacedaemon.

Spectators, travelling, (in the Model City), ii. 224.

Spirit, one of the three elements of the soul, i. 34; ii. 122; ought to be combined with gentleness, ii. 37, 176.

State, the, existence of, depends on virtue, i. 19, 21; origin of, ii. 156; ought to be in a mean between poverty and wealth, ii. 158; relation of, to the individual, ii. 179; family life in, ii. 180; is not great by reason of wealth or empire, ii. 182; importance of friendship in, ii. 184; honours in, must be given to merit, ii. 184;—[the best state], will be free from quarrels and lawsuits, ii. 22; the government must have the monopoly of lying, ii. 28; classes in, must be kept distinct, ii. 41; is it possible? ii. 49, 51, 52, 74, 164, 179; the rulers must be philosophers, ii. 52, 74; must be happy as a whole, ii. 73; framed after the heavenly pattern, ii. 95; women, children, and goods to be common, ii. 179, 187;—the best state that in which the rulers least desire office, ii. 74; will be most easily produced out of a tyranny, ii. 162; is that which is most completely one, ii. 179;—the 'second-best' state, ii. 179, 187;—existing states, nearly all corrupt, ii. 62, 73, 74, 95, 223;—even bad states are not without good men, ii. 224.

Stesilaus, i. 11.

Stories, improper, not to be told to children, ii. 20.

Strangers, under the protection of God, ii. 173; regulations for the reception of, ii. 223.

Strife, principle of, in the universe, i. 223.

Styx, i. 159.

Suicide, i. 138.

Sun, the, a god, i. 92; ii. 223; the Idea of Good compared to, ii. 70.

T.

Tantalus, i. 175; = Prodicus, i. 15.

Tartarus, i. 157, 159, 160, 172; = hell, ii. 101.

INDEX

Taste, good, importance of, ii. 31, 32.
Taverns, ii. 217.
Temperance, how to be implanted in the soul, i. 2; one of the virtues of the philosopher, i. 148; fostered in the soul by the simpler kind of music, ii. 36; a harmony of the soul, ii. 41, 42, 95; not a virtue, but a condition of virtue, ii. 161; worthy of praise, ii. 175;—temperance in the tyrant, ii. 162;—the temperate man the friend of God, ii. 166.
Terpsion, of Megara, i. 134.
Thales, i. 214, 217.
Thamus, i. 56.
Thamyras, ii. 106.
Theaetetus, i. 209.
Theages, i. 102; the bridle of, ii. 62.
Thebes, i. 128; the home of Philolaus, i. 139;—Simmias and Cebes, Thebans, i. 116, 134.
Thebes, in Egypt, i. 56.
Themistocles, story of, and the Seriphian, ii. 8.
Theodorus, of Cyrenè, i. 212.
Theodotus, i. 102.
Thersites, the soul of, puts on the form of a monkey, ii. 107.
Theseus, i. 132; ii. 128, 219.
Thessaly, i. 117, 129;—Thessalian enchantresses, i. 171.
Theuth, i. 56.
Thetis, i. 95.
Thirty, the, tyranny of, i. 100, 194.
Thought and the ideas, i. 201, 206.
Thracians, their procession in honour of Bendis, ii. 4;—the Thracian Zamolxis, i. 1;—the Thracian handmaid and Thales, i. 214, 217.
Thrasymachus, the Chalcedonian, ii. 6, 17.
Thyestes, i. 231.
Timaeus, ii. 108, 109, 124.
Tinker, the prosperous, ii. 61.
Tityus, i. 175.
Traditions of ancient times, their truth not certainly known to us, i. 55, 234; ii. 28, 124.
Tragic poets, the, all come to Athens, i. 10.
Transmigration of souls, i. 35. *See* Soul.
Travel, regulations for, ii. 222.
Triptolemus, a judge among the dead, i. 111, 171.
Troy, heroes at, i. 95;—Trojan War, i. 112; ii. 24.
Truth, the aim of the philosopher, i. 40, 144, 214; ii. 74; the basis of good speaking and writing, i. 61; the power of, i. 79; attained by dialectic, i. 207; love of, essential in this world and the next, ii. 105; the beginning of every good, ii. 174;—the vision of truth, i. 39.
Tynnichus, i. 64.
Typho, i. 32.
Tyranny, the readiest way of establishing a polity, ii. 162.
Tyrant, the, compared to a tender of animals, i. 215; influence of, on the manners of the citizens, ii. 163;—the young tyrant, ii. 161;—tyrants punished in the world below, i. 175; ii. 100.

U.

Unity, Sophistical puzzles about, i. 224; unity and plurality, i. 240; absolute unity, i. 226; unity in the state, ii. 179.
Universe, the, relation of man to, ii. 208; good intended to triumph in, ii. 210.
Unjust man, the, not unjust of his own free-will, ii. 176. *See* Evil.
Unmindfulness, the river of, ii. 107, 108.
Uranus, the legend of, ii. 21.

V.

Vice, the disease of the soul, ii. 42, 213;—fine names for the vices, ii. 86. Cp. Injustice.

Virtue, can it be taught? i. 16 (cp. ii 175); not perceived by our bodily senses, i. 42; the source of every good, i. 97; associated with wisdom, i. 149; ii. 35; brings happiness, here and hereafter, i. 178; thought by mankind to be toilsome, ii. 14 (cp. ii. 188); akin to harmony, ii. 32; the health of the soul, ii. 42, 212; may be a matter of habit, ii. 72, 105; not often united to power, ii. 164; far above riches, ii. 171; should be freely imparted, ii. 175; impeded by wealth, ii. 183; the chief business of life, ii. 188; the salvation of men, ii. 212;—absolute virtue seen by the soul, i. 38;—the virtues of the philosopher, i. 148; ii. 59.

Visible world, divisions of, ii. 70; —visible things and ideas, i. 197, 206.

W.

Wakefulness, the duty of, ii. 188.
War, causes of, i. 145; the two kinds of, ii. 47; the guilt of, confined to a few persons, ii. 48; unknown in primitive times, ii. 158; the rich and the poor in war, ii. 79; men, women, and children, to take part in war, ii. 50 (cp. ii. 128, 132).
Waves, the three, ii. 50, 52.
Wealth, must be useful, i. 191; the advantage of, in old age, ii. 7, 8; detrimental to virtue, ii. 158, 183, 217; of no value compared to virtue, ii. 171; not to be amassed for the sake of one's children, ii. 172; does not confer happiness, ii. 183; should hold the last place in our thoughts, ii. 184.
Whole, the, and the parts;—in medicine, i. 2, 53; ii. 207, 209; —in regard to the happiness of the State, ii. 73;—in the Universe, ii. 209, 211.

Wicked, the, punishment of, in the world below, i. 40, 153, 160. 174, 218; ii. 9, 13, 99, 210, 227; their gifts not received by God, i. 188; ii. 15. 166, 198, 203, 212; thought by men to be happy, ii. 13, 203; are deserted by God, ii. 165; to be pitied, and, when curable, forgiven, ii. 176.
Will, freedom of the, i. 34; ii. 210 (cp. ii. 103).
Wisdom, loveliness of, i. 42; to be ascribed to God only, i. 61, 86; the one true coin for which all things ought to be exchanged, i. 149; the only release from evil, i. 152; always associated with virtue, ii. 35; the power of, ii. 71, 72; the only virtue which is innate in us, ii. 72;—true and false wisdom, i. 218.
Wise man, the, does not fear death, i. 95, 103, 139-147; life of, ii. 94;—'the wise to go to the doors of the rich,' ii. 57;—Socrates the wisest of men, i. 84.
Women, in ancient Attica, shared in military pursuits, ii. 128, 132; to take part in war, ii. 50; (and children) ought to be common, ii. 179; to have common meals, ii. 187.
World, the, the natural enemy of good men, i. 94; cannot be a philosopher, ii. 59; its judgment not to be despised, ii. 223; more evil than good in the world, ii. 212.
World above, the, i. 155, 156.
World below, pleasure of discourse in, i. 111; punishment of the wicked in, i. 40, 153, 160, 174, 218; ii. 9, 13, 99, 210, 227; ought not to be feared by us, ii. 170.
Writing, the art of, taught in schools, i. 21; ii. 191; invented by Theuth, i. 56; injurious to the memory, i. 56;—written com-

INDEX

positions apt to be unintelligible, i. 57; require the aid of dialectic, i. 59; ought to have a serious purpose, i. 60; inferior to the thoughts and aspirations of the soul, i. 60.

X.

Xanthippè, wife of Socrates, i. 134.
Xanthippus, son of Pericles, i. 14.
Xenelasia, ii. 223.
Xenophanes, of Elea, i. 222.

Y.

Young, the, how affected by the common praises of injustice, ii. 14; cannot understand allegory, ii. 22; must be surrounded by good influences, ii. 32; must revere the aged, ii. 173;—the young man's enthusiasm for metaphysics, i. 240;—youthful regard for authority, i. 198;— youthful scepticism, not of long continuance, ii. 202.

Z.

Zamolxis, the Thracian, i. 1.
Zeno, the Eleatic, i. 193.
Zeus, the keeper of political wisdom, i. 17; procession of, in heaven, i. 37; attendants of, i. 45; makes his sons judges in the world below, i. 173; ancestor of the Persian and Lacedaemonian kings, i. 181; of Alcibiades and Socrates, i. 181; tales of, not to be received, ii. 21, 22, 24; the God of strangers, ii. 174.
Zoroaster, son of Oromasus, i. 182.

THE END.

Oxford
PRINTED AT THE CLARENDON PRESS
BY HORACE HART, PRINTER TO THE UNIVERSITY

PLATO.

APOLOGY, with a revised Text and English Notes, and a Digest of Platonic Idioms, by JAMES RIDDELL, M.A. 8vo, 8s. 6d.

PHILEBUS, with a revised Text and English Notes, by EDWARD POSTE, M.A. 8vo, 7s. 6d.

REPUBLIC; The Greek Text. Edited, with Notes and Essays, by the late B. JOWETT, M.A., and LEWIS CAMPBELL, M.A., LL.D. In Three Volumes. Medium 8vo, cloth, 2l. 2s.

SOPHISTES and *POLITICUS*, with a revised Text and English Notes, by L. CAMPBELL, M.A. 8vo, 18s.

THEAETETUS, with a revised Text and English Notes, by L. CAMPBELL, M.A. Second Edition. 8vo, 10s. 6d.

THE DIALOGUES, translated into English, with Analyses and Introductions, by B. JOWETT, M.A. Third Edition. 5 vols. medium 8vo, 4l. 4s. In half-morocco, 5l.

THE REPUBLIC, translated into English, with Analysis and Introduction, by B. JOWETT, M.A. Third Edition. Medium 8vo, 12s. 6d.; half-roan, 14s.

A SUBJECT-INDEX TO THE DIALOGUES OF PLATO. By EVELYN ABBOTT, M.A. 8vo, cloth, 2s. 6d.

———

Clarendon Press Series.

EDITED BY ST. GEORGE STOCK, M.A.

APOLOGY. 2s. 6d. *CRITO.* 2s. *MENO.* 2s. 6d.

SELECTIONS. With Introductions and Notes by JOHN PURVES, and Preface by B. JOWETT. Second Edition. 5s.

———

OXFORD: CLARENDON PRESS.

www.ingramcontent.com/pod-product-compliance
Lightning Source LLC
Chambersburg PA
CBHW021403230426
43666CB00006B/623